INTO ALL THE
WORLD

In 1936 the author forsook a promising career in engineering to answer God's call to Mission. This epic story is the result.

We find him on the horrendous wartime trek out of Burma to escape the Japanese. Soon afterwards he is a padre ministering to the British garrison forces in India during the wind-down of British rule there. Here is a vivid glimpse of those days. And surely nothing in his future will compete with the scenery, the majestic Himalayas? Except, perhaps, *the finest view on earth* across the Andes Mountains near where he ministers to the Chilean people?

And then there's his fascinating ten-year ministry in different parts of Australia including the sub-antarctic, petrol-freezing Snowy Mountains.

Everywhere he goes he ministers God's word faithfully, finds out what needs to be done, and ACTS. Hence we find him in Suffolk, years later, with his wife, planting 220 000 Christmas trees to save his Parish Church. And always we find him opposing liberal theology and supporting those who teach, preach boldly and heal in Christ's name.

This book is a mighty demonstration that God blesses actions rather than good intentions.

INTO ALL THE
WORLD

Edgar Pearson C F

First published in Great Britain 1993
by Janus Publishing Company

Reprinted in 2005 by Impressions of Monmouth
Limited for Edgar Pearson

British Library Cataloguing-in-Publication Data.
A catalogue record for this book is available from the British Libra

ISBN 1 905037 04 X

Cover design Ian Wileman

Printed and bound in England by
J H Haynes & Co Ltd

Dedicated to
my Mother
Katherine Beatrice

and my Wife
Dorothy Esther

CONTENTS

ACKNOWLEDGEMENTS

In the preparation of this book I have been deeply indebted to a number of people.

Kathy Kay's thorough examination of, and attention to, the manuscript was invaluable. I incorporated practically all of her suggestions.

Also I am grateful to Gervais Angel for commenting on the Theological Appendices to this book.

The Curator of the Royal Botanic Gardens, Kew, very kindly identified from my photographs the names and classifications of rare wild flowers from the Andes mountains.

I am grateful to The Commissioner, The Snowy Mountains Hydro Electric Authority, Australia, for his kind permission for me to reproduce photographs from the official Authority book.

The passage from the *International Standard Bible Encyclopaedia*, Volume I, is reproduced by permission of Wm B. Eerdmans Publishing Company, Michigan, USA.

The Revd John Perrott, Rector of Elmswell, Bury St. Edmunds, very kindly provided the photograph of his father, Sir A. G. Perrott, Inspector of Police, NWF Province.

The Editor of the *Church Times* kindly gave permission for me to include (as an Appendix) a copy of The Open Letter to the Leadership of the Church of England.

A very special thanks to Pastor T. L. Osborn for his permission for me to describe the fruitfulness of his ministry during the past fifty years.

The Revd Graham Bell, Vicar of Wickham Market, Suffolk, kindly supplied me with the latest and encouraging information regarding the continuing health of Ken Harper who was healed from cancer in Dallinghoo in 1986.

INTRODUCTION

Crash! I had been hit in the darkness and was flat on my back. In the morning, I had been ordained Deacon of the Church of England in Chester Cathedral. It was Lady Day, March 25th 1941.

I was the only one to be ordained on that day. Following a celebration lunch in Chester, provided by my brother Arthur, I returned to Handforth Vicarage, Cheshire, to commence my Deacon's ministry under the guidance of the Vicar of Handforth, the Revd Hugh Thomasson.

That evening, on my ordination day, I thought how fitting it would be to walk two miles to visit my sister Marian and my father whom she was looking after.

It was wartime and enemy bombing was almost a nightly occurrence, but tonight was moonless and cloudy, meaning little bombing, if any. I considered that my two-mile walk would be reasonably safe. Making my way along the middle of the quiet country Stanley Road, I could just see the 'cats' eyes' for guidance. On hearing any oncoming traffic I could quickly move away to the side of the road.

Naturally my mind was whirring with exciting thoughts of achievement so far. Ordination had sealed the end of four years of theological studies. I was scheduled to sail as a pioneer missionary to Upper Burma as soon as a wartime shipping passage could be obtained. However, my joyful thinking was tinged with sorrow because my mother was seriously ill in hospital. I had much to think about.

Then it happened, in a flash – crash, bang; *I was flat on my back.* I had been hit by a bicycle whose Irish cyclist, like me, had been using the centre of the road watching those 'cats' eyes'. His cycle had no lights and the inevitable crash happened. I whipped out my torch and shined it on him and myself. He saw my clerical collar and let out a string of Irish horror phrases:

'Holy Jesus, I have hit a priest; save us, Holy Mary . . .'

He was more justified than I in using the middle of the road and I suffered only a bruise or two. I walked on to spend a pleasant hour with my sister and father in Longsight Lane. As the Irishman continued towards the *Waggon and Horses* on the Wilmslow Road, he would have quite a yarn for his pub companions.

Strangely enough, it was only a short time ago, after some fifty years, that this crash incident on my ordination day struck me as a true symbol of what was to be the pattern of my journey through life. Achievement and crash has been my constant, unusual and dramatic experience. As a result, amongst other things, vigorous thinking has continuously motivated my mind – especially relating to God, His Christ, Jesus, the Holy Spirit and things spiritual – in the amazing world in which we live.

What followed, then, is the story of those achievements and crashes – adventures which I invite my reader to share. You will be taken into many countries, see many kinds of peoples and their circumstances, feel the effects of wars, share in the dramatic changes of modern history, exhilarate in the climbing (and enjoy the grandeur) of great and sometimes almost unknown mountains, swim mighty rivers, enjoy the beauty of rare flowers and hear the nearby sounds of animals on plains and in jungle.

My story will speak of sometimes stark and significant Christian action. I hope and pray that Christians who hold a humble and simple faith in Jesus and His glorious Gospel will be greatly encouraged by their reading of this story.

Edgar Pearson
Midsummer 1992
Maendy House,
Penrhos,
Raglan,
Gwent,
Great Britain NP5 2LQ

CHAPTER 1
GROWING UP

I was born in September 1913 at No. 2 Lacy Green, Wilmslow, Cheshire. I was one of seven children. Before me were Arthur, Richard, Marian, Vian and Annie, and my sister Lilian was born in 1915.

My mother, Katherine Beatrice, was one of five children whose father was the Revd Richard Webb, Wesleyan minister. He ministered sometime in the Outer Isles of Scotland and later in Cornwall and the Scilly Isles. Here my mother was born at St Mary's Manse. In due time she was educated at Queenswood Girls' School, Hatfield, North London. In my mother's time, as today, this was a school of high standing. Mother became a schoolteacher, first at Tredegar in the Rhonda Valley, Wales and then at the Church of England School, Handforth, Cheshire. It was here that she met and married my father, also a teacher at that school.

I was very fond of my mother who was sweet, lovely, talented and gentle. I was close to her, perhaps, because I was a very frail and delicate child and needed the care of a mother so much.

My father, Peter John, was quite another cup of tea. He was masculine, strong, sometimes frightening and wont at times to exercise the law of might is right. At other times he could be charming and kind. His demeanour in some measure could have been the result of the death of his mother when he was only one day old. It would appear, from what I have been able to glean, that his father, Joseph, always held it against Peter John that he was the cause of the death of his wife. This grandfather, Joseph, owned several farms in Heald Green, the area now surrounding the Western approaches to Manchester Airport. He was an atheist or agnostic and governed my father by the law to which I have referred: might is right. This undoubtedly helped to form my father's character. My father became a keen Churchman and this was his splendid salvation.

My father had been an outstandingly excellent pupil at Handforth

School. As soon as he had cleared the top class he was co-opted as a teacher at the same school.

His possessive and hard father soon took Peter John away from teaching and made him manage the farms for a considerable number of years, and for pitiful wages. Farmers could be tyrannical in those years and get away with it. During this time my father decided to make a gift of money in response to the Handforth Church restoration appeal. His father severely threatened his son that, should he do this, he would be cut out of his father's Will and Inheritance. In 1918 my grandfather passed away. His Will revealed that he had carried out his threat and my father was left penniless with only the bequest of a house and smallholding of seven acres of land, Willow Bank, in Cheadle Hulme.

Together, then, our poverty-stricken family of nine in all, moved to Willow Bank in 1918. I was five years old.

In his forties, and with no training other than farming, and with seven growing children to provide for, my father tried several jobs without success until, at last, he succeeded in becoming a Royal London Insurance agent. I knew him in this capacity for the rest of my youth. His Insurance books and registers were perfection.

For the first few years at Willow Bank I spent little time at school because I had, supposedly, an undeveloped heart. What I did know was that suddenly, every so often, a pain like a red-hot needle struck my heart and while it lasted I was speechless, terrified and breathless. It was in these terrible attacks that I cleaved to my mother for help. In due time there followed whooping cough, measles, scarlet fever and now, on my ninth birthday, diphtheria. The visiting Dr Craig gave me a gleaming shilling on that day for a birthday present. I was carried out of the house and taken away to Monsal Fever Hospital in Manchester and remained there for more than three months. Once a week, whatever the weather, my angel mother's face appeared outside my window and she brought me what little delicacies she thought I would be allowed to have. The anti-diphtheria toxin injections terrified me. So did the experience of seeing around me dead patients being carried out.

I was allowed home the day before Christmas and what rejoicing there was in the whole family! The members were greatly amused to hear me singing the witty ditties learnt in hospital. I had grown tall and thin, like a stick of rhubarb. Looking back, I put that down to the anti-toxin injections.

Once more school was not to be for many months. And even then

I was not allowed to take part in any physical exercise or school drill. When I was allowed to attend school the lessons seemed like double Dutch. At first I tried and tried to understand. Strangely enough, knowledge came to me, in due time, in sudden flashes of illumination – sometimes within seconds. I learned algebra just like that.

But during those years something else was happening. The seven acres of Willow Bank were providing me with ever-increasing adventure, pleasure, and enjoyment of life. Not being at school for such a long time, freedom was mine – and freedom has been my craving all my life. There were my father's horses, cows, hens, geese (I was scared of them), goats, dogs, cats, rabbits, and fish in the ponds. In the hedgerows peeped periwinkles, violets and other flowers. There were the birds' nests and their young, the cuckoo and the skylarks. In the summertime, haymaking was exciting, with haymaking lunches as we sat on the warm hay. My father was a keen gardener. From his one acre garden he produced abundant vegetables and fruits. He won many prizes at the Bramhall Annual Shows. I used to watch him grafting fruit trees and budding roses. Especially remarkable were the extra large Jargonelle pears growing on a grafted hawthorn hedge. My heart scares became less severe. Did my sitting up in the pear tree and eating pears help in the healing? My father saw me one day sitting in this tree, as I thought, out of sight. He was a crack shot with his catapult and, wang! – his shot of clay caught me squarely on the buttocks. I was not amused. Pear-eating stomach ache was violent and sometimes I thought I would die. Did like cure like? Sometimes I went pond fishing with my brothers to catch either carp, roach, or dace. I roamed around the fields with my sister, Lilian, gathering wild flowers and shimmering grasses and periodically getting up to all kinds of mischief. One day, at the faraway field boundary, I crossed a boundary ditch into the next door neighbour's garden and was surrounded by four huge bulldogs. I was petrified and frozen to the spot.

My father was shotgun happy. From time to time he brought home bags of hare, rabbit, wild pigeon and pheasant. Jugged hare with wine was delicious, especially when eaten with my mother's home-baked bread.

Indoors I found great enjoyment from Meccano sets. In fact, whenever I was treated to a new set, as after returning from Monsal Hospital, I literally trembled with excitement while opening and examining this wonderful mechanism. Later I made a DIY crystal radio and oh the magic of listening to Manchester voices and sounds from Manchester 2LO! After some time I made my first valve-motivated loudspeaker radio set. Again, it was magic! Undoubtedly there was a growing trend in my mind towards engineering.

When I was old enough, the bicycle took me around and in due time to North Wales for a holiday. Later, when I started my first job in Cheadle Hulme, it was the cycle which took me to and from my place of work.

And in the house what a wonderful mother, as most mothers are! The daily cooking and caring for a family of nine. And all this with only a very old-fashioned house fire and grate and oven and a cold old-fashioned kitchen with stone basin. There was neither electricity nor gas. Neither was there any such thing as a flush toilet. All hot water had to be boiled on the one fire – for cooking, washing, bathing and clothes washing. A large brown flat circular bath was produced every Saturday night. Shoes had to be cleaned and everything pre-pared for Church attendance on the Sabbath. My father would sit in his chair studying the Lessons which he was to read in Handforth Church on the morrow.

When mother had a little time to spare she would sit down at the piano to play her favourite pieces from Chopin, Beethoven and Mozart. Sometimes she would stop and stare at the photographic faces of those great composers as she saw them on the front of the folders. Being at home more than the other members of the family I benefited very well in this respect. Sometimes the members of the family would bring in friends to enjoy a singsong around the piano with mother playing.

A paraffin lamp lit up the room each night and a candle sufficed to light each member to bed. On Sundays my father would take us the two miles across the field path to Handforth Church. We loved this for my father showed us the wonders of hedgerows and fields. He was also the Superintendent of Handforth Sunday School and continued this for over sixty years.

Later I joined All Saints Church choir, Cheadle Hulme, and attended practices twice a week (under the expert discipline of Mr Ellis Sugden). On winter nights I was always terrified of the dark when walking home the two miles through the countryside. At the top of dark and lonely Pingate Lane I always ran for dear life!

I joined the Wolf Club Pack and I shall never forget the thrill of being allowed to go to my first camping holiday, under canvas, in Adlington, Cheshire. They taught me to tie knots – a skill I've use-fully applied throughout the years, even to this day.

I was growing up into a life of happiness, adventure and promise. At the age of eleven years I passed the Cheshire County Council Education scholarship. So did another boy, Charles. Since there was only one vacancy this year, Charles, being the younger boy, was awarded the place at Macclesfield Grammar School. I stayed on at the same school, won prizes and looked forward to becoming the senior boy. This was not to be for at the age of thirteen, and to my disappointment, my mother told me I was to start work at the North Cheshire Electric Company in Cheadle Hulme. Sadly, my school days were over and I was to enter the big unknown world of work.

At school I learnt off by heart the Church of England Catechism. I consider this to have been of outstanding and lasting importance. This compulsory teaching for hundreds of years in England must have helped the nation to form a good moral heart. In my ministry, in many countries, I have taught this same Catechism over and over again.

CHAPTER 2
AN EXPANDING YOUNG LIFE

For the next ten years my life developed broadly along three lines – the Christian Faith, Further Education and Work.

Christian Faith

This became of paramount importance when I was fourteen years of age. I learned that a beautiful schoolgirl I had known (she had always been so well dressed and had golden hair) was attending All Saints Church and Sunday afternoon Fellowship. I could not resist attending! I got more than I bargained for. The vicar, the Revd Martyn Cundy, was a clerical giant. With very strong, fearless and forthright scriptural preaching he was turning upside down the fashionable, complacent, middle class parish of All Saints, Cheadle Hulme. He emphasised the nature and consequences of sin and a sinful age and bid his parishioners escape from the wrath of God through the provision of God's Son, Jesus Christ. Perhaps one text could sum up this Giant's strong ministry: '. . . let God be true, but every man a liar . . .' (Rom. 3:4).

Parishioners were converted, including my brothers and sisters. At last I realised that it was my opportunity and time and I privately confessed my sins to God and accepted the provision of Jesus Christ. My whole life's trend received new direction. Jesus had become one with me for ever. Meanwhile the parish was divided, many being up-in-arms in opposing the vicar whilst others joyfully accepted and supported his ministry and moved forward. Amongst his teachings Martyn Cundy warned of the evils of liberal theology within the Church of England. This realisation has remained with me ever since, as my story will show later. The vicar was in the parish for only four years but during that time some fourteen people decided for whole-time Christian ministry at home or abroad.

The Christian life was brisk, keen and exciting for a considerable number of people, especially the youth, for years to come. Open-air meetings, Bible and Prayer studies, singing in the choirs (for me tenor and bass) and house-to-house visiting were just some of the natural applications of the Christian fervour which blessed this area. All kinds of fascinating members of society were suddenly and often surprisingly converted and joyfully shared the fruits and fellowship of the Christian way of life.

Further Education

This was twinned with my developing work experience – mechanical and electrical engineering.

First I spent a year at Cale Green Evening School, Stockport, in order to pass the entrance examination for Stockport College for Further Education.

Four years' evening classes at Stockport College enabled me to qualify for the subjects needed for electrical engineering and to obtain the national diploma at the end of the four years. A further year was spent for advanced electrical engineering studies at the Manchester College of Technology.

Towards the end of this four-year period I also attended evening classes at the Manchester Bible College, studying church history, theology and New Testament Greek. One of the lecturers was Donald Coggan, an outstanding Cambridge Scholar, still too young to be ordained, but destined to become a future Archbishop of Canterbury.

Work

From 1926–27 I was a shop assistant at the North Cheshire Electrical Company, Cheadle Hulme. I did not enjoy this experience. For the next two years I was employed by R. L. Ross and Company, Edward Street, Stockport. They were the sole world manufacturers of the Ross Muffled Pop Safety Steam valves, fitted to steam locomotives and engines worldwide. My work was brass turning and screw-cutting. People old enough to remember the steam trains such as The Flying Scotsman would have heard the terrific hissing of the steam valve whilst the engine was stationary in the station. In every case the noise was attributable to a Ross Muffled Pop valve made at the Stockport works.

In the works a giant Babcock and Wilcox boiler raised the high pressure steam of up to 800 lb per square inch, necessary for the testing and setting of each valve. The terrifying sound of high pressure steam throughout each day created tinnitus in my head from which there has been no recovery throughout life. Also, from time to time, on working my lathe, my hand would suddenly slip into the revolving chuck, gashing the fingers or hand and necessitating a quick visit to Stockport Infirmary for stitching and care. To this day the marks on my fingers and hands remind me of those days.

Each week, for this work, and at the age of sixteen, I earned a man's pay (by piecework), which greatly helped my mother's family budget, and I was thrilled for her sake.

I travelled to and from work on a motor cycle, especially on a Sunbeam 500 cc. The people who knew me were scared at my driving of this 'monster' at such a young age.

From 1929–32 I was a draughtsman in the electrical drawing office of S. H. Heywood and Company, overhead crane manufacturers, Reddish, Lancashire. In 1931 the manager appointed me to the sole charge of the electrical drawing office. I was responsible for the design of all circuits and specifications for all cranes up to 100 ton lift.

From 1932–36 I was a student in the Power Transformer Department of Ferranti, Hollinwood, Lancashire. Ten thousand people were employed by this firm at that time. I was one of only two students. I was allowed to do no work but to observe only. Part of each week was spent at the Manchester College of Technology for advanced electrical engineering studies.

At one end of the great building was a laboratory, housing the oscillograph apparatus for testing the characteristics of electric surges up to one million volts. The jumping gap was 9 ft 6 in, miniature lightning indeed! Each surge of one million volts produced a loud crack as of canon fire.

Always of special interest to all in the transformer works was the sending away of a 100 ton 100 kVA transformer. It was loaded on to a very large and specially constructed railway waggon which stood on the railway line which came right into the works. So heavy was the weight that a standard steam locomotive could not, of itself, start the waggon in motion. The wheels of the locomotive simply skidded round. In order to help, a powerful tractor, with special buffer mountings, crashed into the waggon buffer to create an initial impact. At last the waggon began to move to the cheers of the workers.

From 1936–37 I was directed to supervise the research and first manufacture of the Ferranti electrolytic condenser, chiefly for use in the Ferranti radio sets which were manufactured in their thousands every week.

I was persuaded to take part in the annual Ferranti sports day in 1936. Thousands were present, most of them girls from the factory. The runners included professionally trained harriers from professional sports clubs who were, of course, wearing spiked running shoes. I entered for the races, wore only plain gym shoes, and came first in the mile and second in the half mile. No one knew how persistent had been my daily training. It was my daily routine to leave home at 6.30 a.m., and run or trot for two miles to catch the morning train at Cheadle Hulme station. In this way I must surely have kept in good trim, as the races showed. The girls especially took note of Edgar Pearson and I was ever afterwards noted as I walked through the works departments. Apparently my one-time weak heart was now a thing of the past and truly God was good to me.

The Meter and Radio departments were a fascinating sight to behold. Almost as far as the eye could see (and one could not see to the end on a misty day) there were thousands upon thousands of girls. They were attired in brown smocks, and sat on either side of the slowly moving conveyor belt, each girl performing one operation as the radio or meter article passed before her.

In 1936 I resigned! The time had come for me to carry out my decision to prepare myself for a future as a Christian missionary. All my engineering pursuits came to an end. I felt the parting deeply for I had passionately loved it all. Also I knew that, had I continued, there would have been good financial returns and this would have provided for my mother's wellbeing and happiness, of which she was most worthy.

From my first morning of staying at home after the resignation I felt that a fascinating, very busy and stirring life had parted from me. It was uncanny.

CHAPTER 3
PREPARING FOR
MISSION

The influence of the Christian Gospel compelled me to consider and then decide for a missionary career. I had, and still do have, a sense of logic and fair play rather than sentiment. That is the manner in which the Gospel appealed to me regarding Mission. In the Gospel I was assured that Jesus offered Himself to be the Light of the world and Saviour of mankind and, equally, his followers who believed this must do something about it and accept His challenge. This was to 'Go into all the world and preach the Gospel' (Mark 16:15); and again, 'If any man come to me, and hate not his father, and mother, and wife, and children, and brethren, and sisters, yea, and his own life also, he cannot be my disciple . . . So likewise, whosoever he be of you that forsaketh not all that he hath, he cannot be my disciple' (Luke 14:26, 33). I found these to be strong words from a strong Saviour regarding a strong salvation for a desperately needy world. To my mind the challenge reflects the unique value of a Unique Son of God.

I estimated that this was no harder than a challenge to a soldier in time of his country's need of defence from a tyrannous enemy. The soldier's life is not his own. He must go wherever commanded and often into the thick of deathly battle. His country's freedom demands this sacrifice. Also, I thought of the millions of ordinary commuters who go to work each day, leaving home in the morning, returning in late evening, to be at the disposal of a company or employer, in order to maintain a normal and wholesome financial lifestyle.

But I read also that in answer to Peter's statement of fact, 'Lo, we have left all, and followed thee', Jesus replied, 'Verily I say unto you, there is no man that hath left house, or parents, or brethren, or wife, or children, for the kingdom of God's sake who shall not receive manifold more in this present time, and in the world to come life everlasting' (Luke 18:28–30). So there I read of the harmony within Jesus, each statement balancing the other, to the great comfort of all who decide to follow Him.

Also, at this time, my decision was strengthened by the account I read of the astounding record of the Peoples' Church, Toronto, Canada, under their pastor, the Revd Oswald J. Smith. Within five years of the pastor taking over a downtown, almost redundant church, and constantly pressing home the urgent and supreme function of Mission, no fewer than one hundred missionaries had gone forth, supported by a parish income of £100 000 per annum – the equivalent of at least £1 000 000 per annum in the 1990s. (As I write this same parish has 500 missionaries in the field, financially backed by a parish income of some £5 000 000 per annum.)

For me, as a Christian, there was now no other way. God's Spirit enabled me to mentally accept the challenge and directions of Jesus and from that moment, together with all who make the same decision, I was under very special Divine orders and direction. I took action.

In 1934, while still very much involved with work, I wrote to The Regions Beyond Mission, asking whether they would accept me as a missionary. In due time they replied that whereas most of my characteristics sufficed yet, because my referees had written to say my health would not be reliable, the Regions Beyond Mission regretfully could not accept my offer. In applying to such a society I had in mind that, if accepted, I would be sent out to preach the Gospel in the minimum of time. It was unthinkable that I should apply to an establishment college. I had no classical educational qualifications and neither did I want to waste any time. I merely wanted to preach the Gospel to simple native folk quickly, and I was sure they would not require anything but simplicity from a simple Gospel preacher.

I was compelled, however, to write to the only other missionary college I could think of which would satisfy my conservative Christian thinking – The Bible Churchmen's Missionary and Theological College, Clifton, Bristol. To my astonishment my application was accepted, but with a proviso. The college had no regard for my engineering and scientific diplomas and education. No, they said, I must obtain a Durham University matriculation in order to be enrolled in the college at all. Oh, my Lord, I thought, time is going to be wasted. I asked how long the college would give me to matriculate. Answer: nine months! I was given option of college entry time and chose to wait for one more year.

Meanwhile there were at least two good significant happenings. On Saturday afternoons I and a young Christian friend went house-to-house visiting on the huge Ryecroft Estate, Cheadle Hulme. This with the permission and blessing of the Cheadle Hulme Vicar, the Revd Beccles Goodwin. There were hundreds if not thousands of houses on this new estate, with no place of worship of any kind. It was virgin soil and as we visited each home, talking to people about God and leaving Christian literature, their reactions varied; sometimes they were very pleasant and sometimes frightening! Some time later (when I was at college) a Mission Church was hastily built on the estate. From the outset it was crowded to capacity, the services having to be duplicated each Sunday. In due time a new Church – a permanent one – was built, St Andrews, Cheadle Hulme. Again, since its commencement, this church has been one of the most flourishing and vibrant in the country.

The second happening took place when I visited another house. The occupant, Miss Wilkinson, was quite taken aback to find young people engaged in Christian visiting on a Saturday afternoon instead of attending sport. There followed profitable and mutual talk about spiritual matters and I was invited to visit her on returning from my first college term. It was then that the subject of medicines came up and I first learnt from Miss Wilkinson about the homoeopathic treatment of illness. I listened, took note, obtained homoeopathic books and medicines and in due time found that they worked very well with both myself and some other people who had been very ill but who became quite all right after taking the medicines. I have often given hearty thanks to the Lord for this precious reward to me for visiting the Ryecroft Estate.

After my resignation from Ferranti I spent three months helping my carpenter brother, Richard, who was building a house in the country. It was good, healthy, but hard work, sometimes carrying a hod of bricks up those ladders! Then I fitted the house with complete electrical installation. All this being finished, it was time for me to go to the college at Bristol.

CHAPTER 4
COLLEGE

The Bible Churchmens' Missionary and Theological College was situated on the edge of the delightful Clifton Downs to the west of Bristol. It consisted of Houses known as Cranmer, Ridley, and Latimer, these being the names of Reformation bishops. It contained its own very plain but beautiful chapel, games provision and all the other arrangements which a theological college requires.

This college was founded in 1922 arising out of the division in the Church Missionary Society over the matter of liberal theology. It had been agreed by the governing body of CMS that, in order to end many theological complaints from the Mission stations, all prospective missionaries should be expected to sign a form of Christian belief. One of the clauses was to the effect that *The New Testament statements of Jesus Christ are historically accurate.* Several leading members of the society, including bishops, strongly objected to this clause and it was rejected. The conservative leaders of CMS could not accept this, and, after six months of earnest prayer, resigned from CMS, formed their own new society and founded this new college to promote Bible learning and preparation for ministry at home and overseas.

From the beginning the college life, provision and routine seemed to fit me like a glove. The college atmosphere was warm and Christlike. I loved it. This life was in great contrast to my previous very busy and active working lifestyle and greatly to my benefit. College routine was indeed a student gentleman's life in full.

The average daily pattern consisted of rising early, chapel service, breakfast, an hour for walking over the Clifton Downs, lectures until 1 p.m., lunch, prayer meditation in the common room, afternoon free for sport or leisure or study (I loved football and tennis), afternoon tea, evening studies or lecture, dinner, chapel, room study and bed.

The staff consisted of the principal, vice-principal and a further two or three lecturers, each specialising in one or two subjects. The range of subjects included, Latin, Greek, Hebrew, New Testament Greek, Old Testament history, New Testament history, Christian doctrine, liturgy and worship, Church history, and Christian ethics. In addition to these subjects, which provided for the learning demanded by the Central Examination Board of the Church of England, the college had its further distinctive studies, the most important being the Bible Diploma Course. Every student had to take this three-year study which committed him to an intensive examination of the Bible.

For those of us who were Bible lovers the critical studies of Old and New Testament went sadly against the grain. They were studies not so much of the Bible itself as of the books written by so-called scholars about the Bible. It is almost true to say that in those times a student could pass his Bible examinations without opening his Bible at all. By this constant study of many such books, the Bible faith of the unwary was gradually drained away. Whereas Holy Scripture teaches that there is one mediator between God and Man, the Man Christ Jesus, yet the many books written by the scholars so 'brainwashed' the students that Christ's influence was often surely minimal. By such influences one college lecturer, in the United States Anglican Church, boasted that he was a Christian atheist! Hence my college's great regard for their own Bible Diploma.

Open weekends were provided, with the college directing that students should get out into the country for walks, tours, relaxation. In due time I found myself organising walks into Somerset, to the Forest of Dean, Cheddar Gorge and many other lovely and interesting places. In order to pass into Somerset we crossed the impressive Clifton Suspension Bridge, completed in 1864 by the famous engineer, I. K. Brunel (1806–1859). During the construction, catastrophe wrecked the bridge, killing many workers. In spite of the public outcry the bridge was at last completed although after Brunel's death at the young age of fifty-three years. On the stonework structure, on the Somerset side, are inscribed the telling words *Vix via suspensa fit* (with difficulty was this bridge suspended).

The famous Bristol Zoo was close to the college and it took some time to get used to the constant shrill shrieking of the peacocks, the babblings of the monkeys, and the roaring of the tigers and lions. College talk had it that, once, some monkeys had escaped and made their way into the college premises. When I told my sister, Marian, about this her quick response was, 'Did they take the right monkeys back?'

The College had a superb lecturing staff. Dr A. W. Greenup, lecturer in Hebrew and New Testament Greek exegesis, had excelled in theological scholarship probably more than any C of E scholar of the century. Crockford's Clerical Directory account reveals this very strikingly. He was also revered for his saintly manner of life. Also the principal, the Revd Dodson Sykes, in his student days, had distinguished himself at Cambridge where he was honoured with every significant theological award and scholarship bestowed by Cambridge University.

In the summer of 1939 I used to look down from my window to see the principal's new twins, in their pram, in his garden. The college used to pray, of course, for God's blessing on the twins. One of them was Stephen, who followed his father's footsteps to pass through St John's, Cambridge, with the same distinctions, excelling in professorial roles and finally becoming the Bishop of Ely. And more recently a later principal, Dr George Carey, has become Archbishop of Canterbury.

For my Durham Matriculation Course I chose maths, Latin, ancient history, modern history, and New Testament Greek. It was a stiff challenge for me who, hitherto, did not know a single word of Latin; but by God's good grace, after nine months, I held the Durham University Matriculation Certificate, and was duly enrolled. Then commenced the three-year course for the General Ordination Examination of the Church of England.

There were some fifty students in the college. About three-quarters of them were men from various walks of life and the others were graduates from the universities. Some of these had already shown academic distinction. A sprinkling of students came from countries overseas. One of them was Barton Babbage – a big man, with a big heart, and mature intellectual powers. He had graduated in history in Auckland University, New Zealand. In the college for a mere nine months he completed, with distinction, the full ordination examinations which took the rest of us three years to accomplish. Barton Babbage was still too young to be ordained and so, for a time, became a lecturer at Oak Hill Theological College, London. Here he had written a thesis which earned him a Ph.D. We shall hear much more of Barton Babbage later.

Evangelism was encouraged. Every Saturday evening, weather permitting, all the students walked down to the appointed area in the centre of Bristol, near to the docks, to conduct an open-air meeting. I cannot remember anything of significance happening although it was a splendid training in evangelistic faith and duty.

On Sundays the students were happy to undertake some of the Christian duty in the parishes of the Bristol area.

During each summer vacation, teams of students travelled out to English parishes for prearranged two-week Missions. They were valuable and exciting times with surprising results. During my time I attended such Missions in Dagenham, with a parish of 100 000 people due to Ford's establishment there, and Stone in Stafford.

A small theological crisis arose in college when a few students were claiming to have received a Second Blessing of God's Holy Spirit. This, they claimed, ought to be coveted and sought for by all Christians, otherwise they would remain second class. Most of the rest of the college and staff considered them to be a little beside themselves. Little did I then think that years later I would meet with this matter on a much greater scale.

Life and studies continued reasonably and according to schedule when, suddenly – **War! The Second World War broke out**. The college, in keeping with the whole country, was stirred to the depths. Wartime instructions were given and fire-fighting teams were created. At spare times we listened to the war reports with bated breath. The college gave asylum to a German refugee. He created some panic and we suspected he might be a spy! We watched the daytime German air raids over the Filton aeroplane works where Spitfires were being made, watched the aerial dog fights and the shot-down German and British parachuters descend.

In September 1940 two of us were cycling towards college for our new Michaelmas term. Darkness had fallen when, fifteen miles from college, we saw the searchlights and heard the anti-aircraft guns and the bombs. Another raid was taking place over Filton. We would never get through, and so slept on a haystack, arriving at college the next morning to find most of the windows shattered from bombs dropped near the front walls. In the afternoon, before that bombing raid took place, incoming students were told by the tutor to sleep in the basements. One student, named Calver, considered that, because he was chosen by God to be a Christian minister, nothing untoward could happen to him. However, he decided to pray about the matter. As he knelt beside his bed, praying, the bombs fell, shattering his window and covering him with debris. 'Thank you, Lord, for the answer,' he said, and ever after slept downstairs in the basement. From then on we slept every night in the basements and during the day, for each air raid, left our lecture rooms to shelter below. In this atmosphere I sat for my final examinations for General Ordination Certificate and later I heard the glad news that I was successful.

Just before leaving the college the principal asked me if I would do him a favour. It was to travel up to his private house on the Cumbrian Coast to put an electrical fire extension into one of the cold bedrooms. His wife and family were already staying in that house, away from the dangerous Bristol area. The twins were confined to bed with measles. The principal asked me to do this knowing that I had been an electrical engineer and because, in wartime, it was almost impossible to find the usual electrical engineers.

In due time I made the rather long railway journey and in the darkness on a stormy winter's night reached the lonely house beside the roaring waves on the seashore. Mrs Sykes welcomed me to the house. Her husband, the college principal, had been forced to return to Bristol because his Church, St Mary Le Port, had been bombed to ruins.

On the next day, having brought with me the necessary cable, I started work on the extension. From the electrical source of supply I positioned the cable around the rooms towards the bedroom. Now, in the bedroom, all I needed to do was to knock in clips here and there to grip the cable. It had to be fixed over the door facing the twins' bed. Ah, I could see the wood on which to nail the holding clip. I drove in the nail when, immediately, a stream of water made a complete arch slap into the midst of the twins' bedclothes. 'Come to this side, Hugh,' shouted one of the twins excitedly, 'you'll get a better view of it here!' Mrs Sykes was not amused. I was not a plumber and there was no hope of finding one. I took my hammer and managed to hammer the lead pipe over the leak and mercifully the water spout stopped. Stephen has become the Bishop of Ely!

Otherwise I left the college for the last time and returned home with the society's instructions to stand by ready for sailing to Upper Burma. The missionary committee had allocated me to service in that land. I was to replace the Revd Roy Meadows, whose ship, on the way out from Britain, had been bombed and he had returned home.

Week after week went by with no news of a shipping passage. The Vicar of Handforth, the Revd Hugh Thomasson, enlisted me to help with his Sunday services. At last the vicar wrote to the Bishop of Chester, Dr D. H. Crick, who agreed to ordain me so that I could be suitably employed until a shipping passage became available. I was ordained on Lady Day, March 25th 1941 by Bishop N. K. Tubbs.

Following his retirement as Bishop of Rangoon the Bishop had become Dean of Chester Cathedral. He was particularly pleased to ordain one about to depart for his beloved Burma. He was absolutely the kindest of people and the memory of his charming demeanour remains with me always.

The story of my adventure that evening is given in the Introduction to this book.

Suddenly, one day in the beginning of November, 1941, I was called to answer an urgent telephone call from London. It was from a shipping company, offering me a passage East.

'How long will you give me to decide?' I asked.

'Half a minute,' was the reply.

With tremendous joy and thrill in my heart I said, 'Yes'.

Then I was charged to secrecy concerning my movements, for it was wartime. I was to travel to Glasgow, to Queens Dock, to embark on SS *City of Exeter* on Friday morning, November 5th. Hastily I said goodbye to my elderly father (who I would never see again) and close friends and relations. I visited the hospital where my dear and courageous mother had lain for three years and with a gulp in my throat kissed her goodbye. I left Handforth Station on the morning of the 3rd November. The vicar and a policeman saw me off. Not one soul knew where I was going but I knew I was travelling via Manchester to Glasgow to embark upon a journey which gave me a sense of deep anticipation of the unknown which I was about to enter. Christ was with me, of course.

CHAPTER 5
WARTIME VOYAGE

There was a thick fog as I approached the SS *City of Exeter* alongside Queen's Dock, Glasgow. How highly excited I was to see at last, through the mist, her huge bows. Customs officials checked documents, took away my wartime gas mask and ration coupons and then I approached the ship's gangway. At the foot of the gangway stood a soldier on duty who said to me, 'Once you go up there, sir, you cannot come back'. This, indeed, stressed and dramatically sealed the end of an old world, life, and country, for an unknown future as vast as the ocean. 'Go ye into all the world' was beckoning to me right there.

I remained elated with excitement as I was shown to my cabin (to share with three other men) and then to tour the liner and mingle with hundreds of passengers. They were men, women and children. Many were officers in uniform travelling for duty in the East, India and Malaysia. In like manner were civil servants. We queued for ship's registration and duties and wartime instructions. At last the ship began to be moved by the tugs and as we cruised slowly between the banks of the Clyde – lunch!

What a lunch in wartime! As we saw the provisions our eyes nearly popped out. Was this real? Would we be allowed to eat this in wartime? Is there no rationing here on board? And served with Asian waiters in their resplendent attire who responded immediately to everyone's slightest signal for attention.

The ship entered the large Loch at the end of the Clyde and stayed there for about two days. During this period wartime boat drill was rigorously practised – and woe betide any passenger who took the officer's orders lightly, as one man did to his intense embarrassment, being rebuked before all the ship's company. Each passenger was to carry his or her life jacket at all times, without fail, and not to undress when going to bed; and be ready to muster and enter the lifeboat within one minute's warning.

Early one morning, before dawn, I heard the ship's engine throbs and, going out on deck later, saw that we were cruising through the picturesque islands of the Outer Hebrides. Little did I then realise that in forty years time I and my future wife would be spending a holiday on these islands. We were a great flotilla of ships and during the next few hours many more ships joined us until I was able to count at least seventy to the north, south, east and west as far as the eye could see. Practically every ship carried wartime timber-encased cargoes on both fore and aft decks. Guns, ready for action, were mounted on the extreme fore and aft decks of each vessel.

For the first few days it was quite warm on deck because we were sailing in the midst of the Gulf Stream. Then, quite suddenly, it grew very cold as we steamed northwest towards Iceland.

All recognised that the voyage would be long. A school committee was formed, teachers volunteered and boys and girls met daily for school. I took my turn to teach arithmetic, science and religious knowledge. A returning and experienced missionary gave daily lessons to those of us who had the need to learn the rudiments of Hindustani.

The captain invited me to act as ship's chaplain – a duty which included conducting services on Sunday and led to continuous opportunities for friendly talks. So some of us were kept happily busy. Others formed card parties. Later, when we had crossed far out into the Atlantic and sailed south into a warmer climate, the deck games were extremely popular. And so far, wonderfully, there had been no ship's casualties through enemy action. Neither did we see our protecting warships, although we were assured they were around us, out of our sight, defending the ships. The huge fleet steamed on, having seemingly grown no smaller in size. After three weeks the convoy changed to a southeasterly course and in due time the fleet put into and anchored off Freetown, Sierra Leone, West Africa, for refuelling and revictualling.

After putting out from Freetown we noted with interest that the convoy was splitting up. Now our ship was able to increase speed. We were sailing a southerly course on our own, and we were now out of range of German U-boats and war planes. Undoubtedly we were heading for Capetown.

Then, one morning, we read on the ship's news bulletin, '**Pearl Harbour Bombed!**' And then, a little later, '**British Warships Sunk Off Malaya! Japanese Invade Malaya! America In The War!** The news was devastating for the world and especially for me.

What now were my prospects in Upper Burma, my proposed

destination? Once again, to use the words of my Introduction, *I was flat on my back*.

After completing six weeks of the voyage we docked at brilliantly illuminated Capetown, whose shops were bountifully filled with everything money could buy. What a contrast to war-dimmed Britain. I was invited to a Church Christmas party where the tables were laden with luxurious everything. I sadly noted all the characteristics of apartheid on the buses, in the parks, on the streets, and indeed everywhere. It was distressing.

Then on to Durban where the ship berthed for the Christmas season. The vicar of a parish there very kindly invited me to his home for Christmas. It was so strange to be celebrating in such humid hot weather. Then there was bathing in the warm surfing sea. I visited a large museum and wondered at the large and impressive exhibits – especially the large animals. Then SS *City of Exeter* put out into the now-war-endangered Indian Ocean, alone and unescorted.

Our ship zigzagged, day and night, for weeks on end, fortunately without any Japanese attack. But by this time passengers' nerves were becoming frayed, ugly quarrels had broken out and the ship's peace was difficult to maintain. And none of this was helped by the great and humid heat from which there was no escape by day or night. It was, therefore, a great relief when the ship at last entered the Hoogly Estuary, sailed up the river and finally docked at Calcutta, some thirteen weeks after leaving Glasgow.

Introduction to India

Babbling natives thronged almost every square foot of space, performing a myriad tasks, with every movement commanding my attention – raw and naive as it was.

Mr and Mrs Ingram, the returning missionaries, chaperoned me to the old Mission Church, a large Church establishment to the rear of Calcutta's main business centre. The Vicar, the Revd Gerald Westcott, and his wife could not have been more helpful in welcoming us at a time when Calcutta itself was on the verge of war hysteria. We could stay with them until our next moves were sorted out. Out came my mosquito net for the first time. I slept on their verandah, causing everyone much amusement by my incessant questions as to what to do next and why? After all, as a raw newcomer of only a few hours, I was only trying to learn to live orientally. In the early morning I awakened to the multiple hum and buzz and clamour of the most densely populated square mile in the world: the sounding of motor car hooters, the prayer call of the Muslim priests, the clatter of industrial movements and the smells of the orient!

This old Mission Centre was a large establishment which had once been Calcutta Cathedral. It now ministered to British, Anglo-Indians and Chinese Christians, and was also a caring centre for the poor and needy.

I was granted an interview with the Archbishop (Metropolitan) of India, Burma and Ceylon, the Most Revd Foss Westcott. I asked him whether he considered I ought to continue my way to Upper Burma now that the Japanese were invading. He replied that if God had called me to Upper Burma then I should endeavour to go there. I then cabled to the Revd W. Crittle, Field Secretary, Upper Burma, 'Have arrived Calcutta, do I proceed?' Knowing that the reply would take ages, I accepted the invitation to travel to Mirzapur, United Provinces, to be the guest of the Revd Sam and Mrs Burgoyne who were in charge of the Bible Churchmen's Mission there. Then came the novelty of the first Indian train journey: the appealing beggars and lepers, the never-ending hustle of Indians, the interesting villages and towns, the glimpses of Indian fields and jungle; everything so new and fascinating. Howbeit heat, poverty, smells and ignorance were frightening.

There followed six weeks' experience of Indian missionary life and activities. We sometimes travelled around on bicycles, even through the scorched Indian scrubland.

At last came the reply to my cable: 'Proceed to Kamaign!' Kamaign was Field Secretary Crittle's home and Mission headquarters in the far North Mogaung Valley. How was I to travel with the Japanese invading the South of Burma? I declined the offer of a passage on a ship travelling from Calcutta to Rangoon. (Later, I learned that this ship had been sunk by Japanese action in the Indian Ocean with the loss of all on board.) Instead, I booked my flight on a China Airways Dacota plane and left Dum Dum airport on the Sunday morning, 1st March 1942.

The passengers were seated, some twenty-five on each side, on long, straight seats in the very bare and plain aircraft. Looking out of the window I could see, far down below, the fascinating sight of the many and mighty estuaries of the Assam Delta. As we approached the Burma mountains the plane rose high into the clouds in order not to be seen by the Japanese warplanes. The Dacota had no air pressure control and we were distressed. Fortunately radar was not yet used and so we remained undetected by the enemy fighter planes. The great height had its effect on some passengers, especially the big Sikh gentlemen sitting next to me. During the next hour or two he almost passed out through high blood pressure and strain to his heart. He expected me to check his pulse rate every few minutes and I was indeed alarmed at the high rate! At last, some time in the late afternoon, we skimmed down over the picturesque landscape with colourful Burmese women working in the fields and we safely alighted at Lashio Airport on the China border, into a war-stricken Shan States. Military officials checked our documents and provided us with hospitality for the night; then it was time for us to enter the train that was to take us to Mandalay.

CHAPTER 6
UPPER BURMA

Because it was a war area the train journeyed slowly and cautiously for about two days and nights. War-scared railway officials and staff had left the stations and so there was little attention and no food supplies, but I was not afraid of a bit of starvation. One characteristic was constantly with me – I never had any sense of fear, panic or aggravation of mind. After all, no outward circumstances ought to ruffle one who was in the hands of the Almighty.

The Shan States comprise one of the most pleasant areas of Burma and I must have keenly appreciated and taken note of the ever-changing beauty of scenery of this rich and fertile land, so well supplied with rainfall.

Slowly, and at last, the train steamed into Mandalay railway station, which had already been bombed. It was not difficult to find my way to the Established Christian Winchester Brotherhood. Their brethren were simply magnificent in meeting my needs and gave me their utmost help and encouragement. We spent a day or two digging air raid shelters. They gave me further inoculations against certain tropical diseases, fed me well, and we enjoyed fellowship in Holy Communion, prayer and praise.

After two days or so they put me on the train for the north, to commence a journey to last several days and nights. So followed a fascinating thousand-mile journey into Upper Burma. This journey gave me views of the mighty forests of great grandeur, quaint and busy villages, gailey coloured Burmese and Jingpaw natives, various types of working animals, and the large river bridges we crossed from time to time. I enjoyed every minute of it. I cannot remember what I did for feeding but this must have been quite all right.

And at last to Mohnyn Mission Station – very significant for me, because here at Mohnyn was our Bible Churchmen's Mission and Hospital. Sure enough, waiting at the railway station were the members of the Mission, Dr Farrant Russell and the Revd Bill Rushton. Greetings and news were hurriedly exchanged. They wanted to know what I had to report of war conditions in the Mandalay area. They told me, amongst many other things, that all the female members of the Mission had been flown out to India for safety from war dangers. The whistle went and the train moved out of the station. I had made it to Upper Burma and the arrival of a new recruit had created much interest and talk for the Mission members.

I travelled on for the next hundred miles to reach Mogaung Station where I was to disembark at the end of my rail journey. At the station I was met by the young wife of the government official for that area and, like so many other people I had met, she was charming and kindness itself to me in my travelling needs. She had arranged for me to travel on the country bus that would take me to my final destination *and home* at Kamaign.

I was given the seat next to the flamboyantly dressed Kachin driver. And how madly and dangerously he drove that bus at top and reckless speed all the way for fifty miles or so! The radiator water kept boiling and spurting out of the top of the radiator, spraying me through the open-front windscreen. I could only assume that the driver was showing the new Englishman what a splendid and skilful driver he was.

But those giant jungle trees on either side of the road! I had never seen anything to equal their thickness, grandeur and mighty height. They seemed to be like great green and glistening cathedral pillars, so straight but interlaced on the lower parts by lesser green trees and saplings. A primaeval virgin forest indeed – and supplied with heavy rainfall to give it full vigour. And in those jungle forests roamed, in abundance, wild animals: tigers, pumas, bears, panthers, elephants, boar and jungle fowl – a far cry from the Bristol Zoo.

And now, at last, as the bus came to a halt, and some four months after leaving Glasgow, **I Had Arrived at My New Country, Home, and Work for Life!**

The Revd W. Crittle and his wife were there on the spot, to meet and greet me and then to escort me along the compound track to their house. There, in that first hour or two, many thoughts were exchanged, especially concerning the war situation, with all the anxiety it created for Mr Crittle and the Mission. My arrival must have been almost as stirring for them as it was for me.

Then I was taken to my little white house at one side of the compound. It was, like every house in Upper Burma, mounted high on posts. This was vital as a safeguard from wild animals. On entering the house the movable steps were brought up and into the house so that wild animals were not able to climb up.

I had brought hardly any of my belongings because of the limited weight allowed for the aeroplane. Even so I was told, there and then, that instead of using wardrobes, all clothes or articles not in use must be left in the airtight steel trunks. Otherwise the intense and hot humidity would cause mould in a short time. Pillow slips had to be changed almost daily and even then one could often smell the mould.

A young Burmese teacher was engaged to teach me Burmese and a Kachin to teach Jingpaw or Kachin. I was taken around to see the Kachin villages and their peoples. Rarely were journeys made at night because of the dangers of wild animals. When a journey had to be made it was with a modern oil lamp held in one hand and a sword (dah) in the other. Quite a number of Kachin men had ugly scars on their faces, most of them caused by bear attack.

The 'brain-fever' bird, sitting in a tree and screeching well into each night, was quite a devil. I used to try to shoo him away by throwing stones at him before retiring into my little house. It was no use; he returned and shrieked as soon as I went indoors! Some nights one listened to the snarls of a roaming tiger, or to the growl of a bear, as they made prowls around the compound looking for prey. One night a tiger attempted to get at the government official's cow in the next compound. The tiger was shot.

I shall never be able to forget the first Sunday! The Church was a large, sparsely erected building made of wood and with only wood strips for the raised floor. On the Sunday the huge gong, made of bronze, was sounded (and heard for miles around) to call the Christians to worship. As they filled the Church – standing, for there were no chairs – I was amazed at their looks and demeanour. Many of the men's faces in particular looked grim and stark. During the service men and women walked about. Some men chewed the red betel nut and from time to time spat out down through the spaces in the floor.

But here the Spirit of Christ was obviously at work in these primitive people, uplifting them from their previous religion of fear of the spirits, for basically they had been animists. At times, when storms were destructive, or things went severely wrong, the spirits, they believed, were angry and punishing them. A sacrifice was demanded – sometimes a cow or calf – and, failing improvements, the spirits demanded some greater sacrifice. From time to time the sacrifice was the most beautiful baby in the village! What a great contribution it was to bring to these people the love of Christ, dispelling their old fears, to be replaced with the common sense and love of Christ!

Daily we listened to the radio for war news. It was conflicting because the South Burma radio news attempted to reassure us that the Japanese would be driven back but the London BBC World Service revealed an ever-worsening situation.

After some weeks it was decided that I could be useful at the Mission station and hospital at Mohnyn and I was transferred. The Kachin handyman and gardener of the Mission was an interesting fellow. Although he had never had a lesson he could converse well in English, Kachin, Burmese, Chinese, Hindustani and Shan. And his wage per week was most modest. What would such a man be worth in the West?

Up to the time of the British conquest of Burma, the Kachin peoples had suffered greatly through their inter-warfare and especially through repeated incursions of Chinese rebels, not curtailed and indeed encouraged by the Chinese government. From 1891 onwards, until the end of the First World War, the British Burmese government acted relentlessly to curb these troubles by all possible means – persuasion, treaties, agreements and, when unavoidable, the use of force. The outcome was peace amongst all the Kachin peoples who were integrated with the rest of Burma. As a result the Kachin peoples have ever been grateful to the British. In particular, they responded well to the Christian Missions. I saw this for myself. One evening, as thousands of them mustered near Mohnyn, perhaps for their weekly pay, I had to walk through the midst of these grim looking people, every one with his sword (dah), and yet I was perfectly safe because I was British!

There was considerable war-oriented activity going on. Thousands of Kachin labourers had been commandeered by the government to erect, at great speed, dozens of large huts and at first we did not know why. But soon all was revealed. The total allied Burma medical corps, retreated to Mohnyn, set up their hospital in conjunction with ours, housed their personnel in the new huts recently made, and began to bring in allied wounded soldiers to the hospital. They were British, Indian, Anglo-Indians, Burmese and Chinese. From that time I was expected to act as chaplain to the wounded. Our Dr Farrant Russell worked almost day and night to try to cope with his own native patients as well as those of the allied army. And meanwhile the **war news was getting even worse!**

It happened very suddenly. We awakened one morning to find

that the whole of the medical corps had secretly and literally done a moonlight flit. They left all the corps' medical equipment, provisions, drugs, instruments, X-ray and operating equipment. All personnel, including their very sick patients, had also been taken but they had left us with forty-five walking wounded officers and men.

Dr Farrant Russell was a broken-hearted man when he saw so many precious medical and surgical instruments being bandied about or kicked about in the bazaar. For many years he had hoped for just a few of these valuable instruments and now, here they were, being destroyed in front of his eyes. It was for him a sad and bleak day.

But worse was to come, for positive news came that within a day or two Japanese soldiers would be in Mohnyn. Quickly our missionaries, Dr Russell and the Revd Bill Rushton, had to decide whether to try to escape through unknown, uncharted, unadminis-tered and mountainous country, and with the heaviest rainfall in the world, or prepare for the onslaught of the Japanese. It was decided to try to escape and to take the walking wounded with us. The area for 200 miles was familiar and after that we would have to try to find a way, via the opium smugglers' track, into and over the wild Naga Mountains and, if lucky, to Assam – a distance of about 500 miles altogether.

The next twenty-four hours saw feverish activity. Dr Russell had no staff now so he asked me to help him with the last operations. I helped him extract a steel pin from a man's broken thigh which had been trampled on by an elephant. All other patients were assisted, mostly by their relatives, to their homes in the jungle. We then set about destroying all possible equipment and stores throughout the establishment: generators, pumps, medical gear, drugs, food, stores, everything. We prepared what essentials we could carry and were ready to flee. Once again, I was flat on my back.

We shut the doors of our homes and walked out, knowing that the Japanese soldiers would occupy them within a few hours. We made our way to the railway station where an engine driver was waiting with the last engine and a freight van to take us quickly sixty miles up the line to Saumour and so put a little more distance between us and the Japanese soldiers. The other two missionaries were heart-broken for they had served there for many years, and Dr Farrant Russell's first wife had died in that house. As we made our way through the village and bazaar all the locals surrounded us, many weeping at what was happening, and on seeing their beloved doctor (for eighteen years) fleeing from their midst.

We quickly piled into the freight van, the engine began to move and we were away, arriving at Saumour some two hours later. There we arranged ourselves in the previously flourishing but now forsaken sugar factory. We had some food and then slept wherever we could. I slept on a billiard table but the only 'break' was my painful back! As dawn broke we began our first day's trek with good, sunny, and dry but very hot conditions. Hundreds of refugees were on the move. All day long we tramped across scrub country until, in the afternoon, we arrived at my previous Mission Station, Kamaign. There Bill Crittle was waiting for us. His wife had long since been flown out to India for safety. Again, we had good food and a good night's sleep. The Mission pony was a welcome addition to our party the next day, and in his saddle bags carried some of the walking wounded men's belongings. The rest of us who were fit carried fairly heavy loads in rucksacks.

Now, thousands of refugees were on the track as we marched along. Many were pitifully carrying loads of possessions they were not able to bear for long; and so along the way were dumped masses of articles, once of much value, but now worthless. We were fortunate in occasionally finding abandoned shelters to sleep in. Then it was our good fortune that someone came after us and offered the use of a jeep for a few miles; thus it was that the walking wounded men's belongings were again carried for them. How thrilled we were the next day also when an escaping soldier came along with an army lorry which carried us all for the next ten miles or so, howbeit in the dark, up to the banks of the mighty Upper Chindwin river. Still the question was, would the Japanese soldiers suddenly be upon us?

It was a relief to have made it to the river before the rains had set in. Otherwise the whole of this area would have been flooded for thousands of square miles which would have allowed us no movement for six months. We had at least raced the floods! That night I slept under the lorry, surrounded by Indians, and was kept reasonably dry from the heavy rain of a thunderstorm.

For several days I enjoyed the company and Christian fellowship of Canon Tidy, Archdeacon of Rangoon. Each evening we sought the shelter of some forsaken hut and there said Evening Prayer, taking in turn, priest and people.

I thought of the Revd George Appleton who, like many more, had fled to us in Mohnyn when the Japanese invaded the South. In Mohnyn, when there was time to spare, he and I had walked together through the outer environments. He was lame and would never have survived this trek. I had phoned the general of the medical corps about him and as a result George Appleton was flown out to safety by one of the last flights to leave the most northerly airstrip, Myitkyina. The whole Church knows of his outstanding ecclesiastical history since then. As I write he is still living.

Thousands of refugees lined the bank. All the river rafts but one had been wrecked by panic-stricken refugees scrambling for a place of refuge, and quite a few were drowned. For the next day and a half we organised the movement of the raft to see many elderly people and children safely over to the other side. And the other side was at least a quarter of a mile away for this was one of the mightiest rivers in the world. It was so wide – and still a thousand miles from the sea! Those of us who were able were expected to swim. Although a poor swimmer, I took my turn, swam on my back, and let the swift current carry me down river until I successfully reached the far bank. In all these happenings and in the river I never had a moment's fear or panic, for which I was thankful to God.

The track was now a quagmire after the heavy rains and going was slow. I caught up with a lot of elephants belonging to Steel and Company, Burma Forestry. Their staff was escaping by this means, so far riding in some comfort. We had watched these elephants swimming the river with a full load on their backs and only their trunks showing above the water.

Then we crossed a second large river, again with rafts operating but overcrowded by panic-stricken people. Very deep mud was the result of thousands of refugees per day walking along one rain-soaked track. Footwear disappeared. Thousands were already dying from malaria, typhoid, dysentery and other tropical illnesses.

We came to the open settlement of the last Kachin village named Shimbiyang. How delighted and thrilled we were, within a short time of arriving, to see RAF planes dropping parachutes of food on to the open space in the midst of the huts. We controlled the otherwise mobbing crowds and stored the foods and distributed rations to as many as possible – and this for a day or two.

Then came another piece of good fortune. The Mission mahout (elephant driver) turned up with our Mission elephant, 'Maggie', and for the offered reward of a shotgun and a large number of rupees he agreed to drive the elephant on our route for a week or two. So once again the walking wounded loaded their few belongings on to the elephant's back together with one or two of those men who were now very ill.

An elephant carries approximately 800 pounds of baggage. It also eats about 800 pounds of food per day. In the jungle the food consists almost entirely of bamboo shoots. For this feeding the elephant is shackled at the end of the day and allowed to move from clump to clump of eatable shoots. The elephant will not walk for more than about ten miles per day. It knows when it has done enough and nothing will make it go any further.

We commenced to climb the steep track of the lofty and rain-soaked Patkai mountains. Many refugees could not manage now and died from exposure and pneumonia. A woman was in childbirth. Dr Russell was there to help her and the next day mother, carrying baby, was walking along the muddy way. The other three missionaries and men, seeing how well I appeared to be coping, asked me to go ahead, each day, and try to find a place of shelter for our party for each night. For days I travelled along the track singing my childhood choruses:

> When the road we tread is rough,
> Let us bear in mind
> In our Saviour strength enough
> We may always find:
> Though the fighting may be tough,
> Let our motto be –
> Go on, go on, to victory.

I knew a score of similar songs and singing them was a very great uplift.

The Patkai mountains ranged from south to north and our track was from east to west. So we climbed range after range with valleys in between. Most of the refugees could not cope any longer and lay down and died by their tens of thousands. At some stages the dead lay so thickly that my pony refused to move. He would not place a foot on a dead person. What a noble creature!

And then one day we arrived at the worst valley of all, literally the valley of death. We were approaching the area of the heaviest rainfall in the world – at its peak twenty-five inches in a day. And now, as we were there, the rainfall was severe. No wonder the area produces the largest and most abundant rivers in the world. Because the heavy rains had commenced, the river in the valley was a savage rushing torrent. We spent much time trying to solve the problem of how to get people to the other side. In due time great lengths of strong jungle creepers helped a great deal. These were tied together and, with the help of the elephant, suspended from one bank to the other. By this means many people took hold of the line and crossed to safety. Maggie, the elephant, made a number of crossings to convey our walking wounded and others safely across. In the end the cane disappeared. It was then that some were left on the wrong side of the river. I plunged in myself, and let this cascading torrent rush me along like a leaf until, a mile or two further down, I scrambled out on the far bank. Once again, although I am a weak swimmer, I suffered not a second's anxiety for which I give thanks to God. In fact, for myself, I do not remember ever having experienced an anxious moment regarding my own safety. A person in Christ need not.

But hell it was to see the thousands dying, and some holding out their hands for food and drink when I had nothing to give. In the plains and lowlands people had died by their thousands from malaria, dysentery and typhoid, but now here in the rain-drenched mountains they died by their tens of thousands from hunger, exposure, and pneumonia. Neither could I speak their language. As I lay down somewhere to rest when darkness fell, my greatest comfort was in knowing that 'He descended into Hell' and hell was here now except for Him. I sometimes prayed 'Lord, let me die' for the suffering and deaths of thousands was so terrible. For me everything had gone.

Practically all my clothes and footwear had rotted away, I did not own a penny in the world, my job had gone, leeches all over the body were sucking away the last portion of blood remaining, a world war was sweeping men and women into eternity. I had come to the end. I could help no one. I was useless and less than nothing.

The pride of life and so-called learning were worthless and were swept away for ever. Only God and His Christ remained. In answer to my asking God to let me die a message from Scripture said, 'You are dead and your life is hid with Christ in God'. And with the rain falling on me I closed my eyes and went to sleep. But oh, the suffering of the multitude around me! Why has a dead Church so badly let Christ down? In the name of Christ why has the Church so miserably failed to dispel the world's terrible evils?

By this time all our walking wounded were so ill that they had to be carried on stretchers by Naga men, six men per stretcher, four carrying at any time and two taking their turn to rest. They were paid at the rate of one rupee per day per man. Fortunately Dr Farrant

Rusell was always to hand with his precious medicines and skill. From time to time I took my simple homeopathic medicines which I had been careful to preserve in my rucksack. I give them the credit for keeping me entirely free from colds, chills or fever of any kind. It was not so, unfortunately, with our other friends.

We passed over the highest Pass – Pansau – 9500 feet above sea level. Knowing that we had walked well over halfway we felt encouraged. Gurkha soldiers, who were with us, were helpful, even lifesaving. At night, in the pouring deluges of rain, they could make a fire. Having carefully preserved their matches, two of them would make the fire. One would hold a waterproof sheet over a spot; the other would split wood into the size of matchsticks and make a small pyramid of them; he would hold the lighted matches underneath the tiny pyramid, create a tiny flame, apply more small matchsticks, then slightly larger strips of wood. Then he could build more surely with ever larger sticks of wood until branches and, finally, huge jungle logs were safely added, defying all the drenching rain. In this way we warmed our tummies and backs, drank hot tea and lay down to sleep as only worn-out people can.

Then one afternoon it happened! Suddenly, a convoy of Nagas met us. They were carrying loads, strapped around their foreheads in Naga fashion, and these loads were packed with precious foods! These Nagas had been commandeered and paid by the Assam government to hasten towards the refugees in an effort to save some. Dropping food from aircraft was never possible in these mountain areas because of the thick permanent clouds.

They parleyed with us. Then they drew their swords, made buckets, cups, plates, knives, forks, spoons, etc., all from bamboo. And from their packs they produced rice, tins of corned beef, sugar, cocoa, ovaltine, butter, large biscuits and tomato ketchup. We thankfully gorged our first meal for a long time and from this point of view we were gloriously saved. Then, as the light was fading, the Nagas again drew their swords and this time they cut down bamboos, trimmed upright supports, laid a bamboo roof and laced it on top with giant leaves. I shall never ever expect to see such giant bamboo trees as in those mountain jungles. That night I lay down to sleep in this splendid shelter. There lay down beside me one of the wild Nagas with his sword by his side. In true Naga fashion he was almost entirely naked. These Nagas were wise enough to live permanently like this because they knew that the wet humid climate would rot away their clothes in no time; so why use them at all? I, too, was almost naked except for khaki shorts. All my clothes and footwear had rotted away or gone floating down a river long ago. In fact, by this time, people could be seen without any clothes at all. We were refugees in the starkest sense of the word.

But the irony! I had been sent to Upper Burma with the probable intention of someday, over the period of a lifetime, proceeding with a Gospel Presence into the areas of the wild Naga tribes. We used to pray such a prayer almost daily in college chapel: 'Send them forth, O Lord, into the wild Naga tribes.' And here I was, after only three months in the country, sleeping next to a wild Naga who had, by the food he had provided and the shelter he had made, saved my life! They whom we were hoping to save had themselves become our splendid saviours!

From this time, being strengthened with wholesome food and gradually descending from the lofty mountains, progress was more speedy and sure. In the next few days we came to more established jungle tracks and found jungle caned bridges over the gorges. We were getting nearer and nearer. Then we struck a newly made wide road being cut into the mountains. Preparations were in hand for allied troops, in due time, to be able to travel up this cutting to storm the Japanese.

Our last day's trek had arrived. As I walked down this newly cut road the sun was actually shining and the jungle glistened as with a myriad sparkling jewels. The jungle was alive with the loud chatter of many types of monkeys and baboons. They were singing for us, as it were, a happy song of welcome to Assam.

And there it was at last – a narrow railway track leading to the small mining centre. It was here that we waited for the train to come, as come it did in due time. We sat in crude trucks to be driven for some miles to Ledo. What a liberating experience that was. From there a normal gauge railway train seated us comfortably and we steamed away to Margareta where a large government refugee camp was waiting to take us in. It was a kind of homecoming. The great and terrible trek was over. We handed over to the sick-bay our wounded officers and men. Every one had been saved, greatly to the credit of Dr Farrant Russell.

We spent two days in this refugee establishment; we were well fed and cared for and I was declared reasonably fit. Like others, I was given a pair of gym shoes, socks, underclothes and a shirt. I was also given a rail ticket which would take me across India for recruitment of health. Mr and Mrs Booley, Anglo-Indians, were the volunteers who were to make me welcome in their home. This was some 2000 miles away, in the mountains, Kangra valley, south of Kashmir. What a journey this would be.

My mission field secretary, the Revd W. Crittle, provided me with a plentiful supply of Indian money. He also ruled that after the holiday I should look out for some employment. The mission stations in India were over-full, especially with the women who had been flown out of Burma. My future was just as unknown as ever.

For the first few hundred miles we four missionaries travelled together on the broadest gauge railway track in the world. Each rail coach was like a room. At the first large railway siding we waited for hours. During this time I obtained a small basin and begged hot water from the railway engine driver and bathed the painful boils in my ears. Several times the railway ended for the crossing of the great rivers by ferry. Then on again for more hundreds of miles until, after days and nights, we arrived once more in Calcutta.

The Revd Gerald Westcott and his wife were, of course, intrigued to listen to our story. From here I sent air letters to friends and relations in England who, by this time, had feared the worst concerning us.

Once more we were on the train – this time for several days and nights, travelling those immense Indian distances and seeing ever-changing oriental sights until we arrived at Amritsar. Here is the centre of the Sikh religion, with its Golden Temple which I was allowed to enter and see.

I had to take my place in the carriage of a narrow-gauge mountain railway, climbing into the Himalayas. And again, what a breathtaking journey, crossing gorge after gorge over what appeared to be slender bridges. Higher and higher we climbed. After a day's journey we arrived at the mountain terminus, there to be met by Mr Booley. From here it was necessary to journey by bus, crowded to the limit with natives, but seats were assured for Mr Booley and myself. From the bus terminus we walked, quite a mile or two, through mountain conifers interspersed with a Ghurka regiment establishment; and we saw them drilling. Then past delightful-looking Swiss-style chalets with neat diamond-style windows.

'This,' Mr Booley said, 'is the Canadian Church of England Mission.'

Mrs Booley greeted us at the house. She was just like a homely, healthy looking English farmer's wife, speaking perfect, country-like English. But she had never moved out of these parts all her life. For her, England was a dream country, a haven of her imagination; and so it was, too, with her husband. And now they had a refugee Englishman as their guest.

I was made welcome at the Canadian Mission as often as I cared to visit. A Miss Edgar said that her library was open to me at all times I cared to go. I was invited to parties attended by interesting folk including the government commissioner of the area. Their Mission supervisor, the Revd Canon Wilkinson, told me he had written to the Bishop of Lahore, the Rt Revd George Barne, concerning my recent adventures and to let the bishop know that I needed to be ordained a priest of the C of E and appointed to some work. In due time I received the bishop's letter asking me to call upon him on a certain day and to be in time for lunch with the bishop and his wife. The bishop was at his summer residence – in a town named Kasauli – away in the Himalayas at an altitude of 9500 feet.

Meanwhile, for exploration and interest, I climbed higher into the mountains up above the Booleys' house and one day came to a tribal village where the primitive natives were all jet black. From the babes to great-grandparents they crowded with wonder around a white man. They sat me down and gazed at me intently and wondered. I could only speak to them by signs. There were so many flies and, as they settled on my knee, I swatted them one by one. Each time I killed a fly the natives laughed loudly. I learnt later that they believed that to kill a fly was to shorten one's life by a day and, so they thought what a foolish man I was, to be shortening my life so much and so quickly!

Time for recruitment of health had come to an end and the interesting visit to the Bishop of Lahore lay before me. It was to be another journey of hundreds of miles, first down to the plains to Amritsar, then some hundreds of miles across country to Kalka and from there up to Kasauli situated at 9500 feet in another part of the Himalayas.

At Amritsar there was some delay and confusion because the Gandhi riots and strikes were on. The trains ran in convoys with armed protection. However, the rail journey proceeded (though much delayed), and after a very long time we arrived at Kalka in the early morning. The monsoon rains had set in with a vengeance. Links to Kasauli, by road and rail, were washed away, and so was the telephone line. I bought a large-size monsoon umbrella, hired a coolie to carry my heavy case, and set off for Kasauli to climb the mountain somehow, some way, although it was quite clear I would be very late for lunch. This would be 'cake' after Upper Burma. After walking in the driving rain, and slushed thoroughly, I knocked on the bishop's door at 4 p.m., not exactly lunch time. The bishop and his wife were delightful. He brought me in, provided a bath and changing room, listened to my story and my plight, and said he would ordain me and provide me with a ministry. This would be in three months' time. Meanwhile I would accept the Revd Gerald Westcott's invitation to assist him at the Old Mission Establishment, Calcutta. So, after a day's rest in Kasauli I left for another very long journey to Calcutta.

At the Old Mission Church I helped in the services for Anglo-Indians, Europeans and, amazingly enough, for Chinese Christians! Their service had been transcribed into Romanised Chinese. To my astonishment, after each service, they said they understood very well. A great deal of time was spent giving monetary and food aid to those in need. The huge church organ had to be tuned twice a week because of the intense heat and humidity. And, because of this, all Europeans looked deathly white. The usual ultra violet rays of the sun could never penetrate this atmosphere.

Suddenly I was struck down with a depressing illness, which turned out to be a violent attack of tropical jaundice. I could eat only oranges. A German doctor did wonders for me, coupled with much sunbathing at the Calcutta swimming club! I recovered well. In visiting the sick in the hospitals, I found one patient who was a London fire officer; he had volunteered for Calcutta service in order to give the authorities guidance on the way in which to deal with the expected Japanese bombing onslaught. He told me that the terrible, squalid, and unbelievable Calcutta conditions had caused him to have a breakdown and he was to be sent back to London.

My three months came to an end as the weather mercifully turned cooler. Another episode lay before me – ordination to the priesthood and an established job, somewhere. I wondered about it all as I boarded the train once more to take me over that long journey towards the north-west frontiers of India.

CHAPTER 7
LAHORE AND THE NORTH-WEST FRONTIER

Lahore Cathedral is well built, a blending of English and Indian architecture, and quite large. I was guided to the bishop's house to be his guest for a few days' preparation for ordination and afterwards appointment to ministry . . . somewhere . . . I knew not where. The weather was different from Calcutta. Here it was winter: cool, misty, and frosty at night. I felt cold and dressed accordingly. The bishop was splendid, I thought; understanding, patient, and possessing a most dignified and typical episcopal face and demeanour!

Nine other Indian clergy were also to be ordained. For three days we were committed to keeping total silence, attending lectures and listening to the bishop reading from a chosen book at our mealtimes.

In my quiet times I could not help thinking what an extraordinary diaconate I had served. I had in the past year learnt deep things about God and His Christ, experiencing a very cruel, terrible and sinful world. God had wonderfully spared me from the full force of this evil. I would, indeed, all the more endeavour to preach His Gospel as effectively as possible for the rest of my life.

The ordination service was quite wonderful with a full and expressive cathedral choir. Although the service was in Hindustani the spiritual sense was very real. After every ordination the cleric ordained is handed his Orders, either for a deacon or in my case a priest. On these Orders is written the title of the parish to which the newly ordained is to be committed. Some time after my service I looked at the words of my Orders. In the midst of the Order I read: **Priest of Peshawar and the Khyber Pass**. I should imagine that no other English cleric has been priested to this title.

I was duly informed that I had been gazetted into this charge by the Secretary of State for India and that I was a member of the Indian ecclesiastical establishment, a branch of the Indian civil service. I was further instructed in the basic rules and regulations of this civil service and was given further documents of authority to this end. I was to be assistant to Peshawar's senior chaplain who would guide me further when I arrived at Peshawar. At that time, so I was informed – and I was certainly able to confirm this later, when I arrived – this capital of the North-west Frontier (NWF) province was the centre of vital and strategic war efforts. To me all this was mind-boggling and hard to take in. I had not expected anything like this. I had merely prepared myself simply to proclaim the Gospel to simple souls in a simple way. But then, I thought, I am still committed to doing just this wherever God sends me. These military personnel were to be sent into the fighting areas at any time and desperately needed the comfort which Christ and His Church can give.

I was jolly tired, having been forced to change my sleeping places approximately sixty times in the past twelve months. The Good Lord would have to help me now. I believed He would.

Peshawar

The senior chaplain, the Revd Roy Beynon, welcomed me and took me under his professional wing. The first Sunday parade service was awe-inspiring with 1000 army officers and men in Church, from generals downwards and heads of the NWF government with their wives and families. The next Sunday morning 1000 Royal Air Force personnel took their turn in Church. This was the pattern each week and the military church atmosphere was a very sensitive one. Quite rightly, I was not allowed to preach! In any case, at those services, only about five minutes was permissible for the sermon in order not to make the military congregation restless.

There was much for me to do: hospital visiting, early morning communion services, baptisms and, alas, burials. The latter resulted mostly from RAF flying officers practising dive-bombing, in American-made machines, and failing to come out of the dive. Such awful accidents were far too frequent. I visited a dangerously ill army officer in the military hospital. Spinal meningitis was his trouble. He was unconscious and bent backwards in a grim way. Two days later he was approaching normality, thanks to the new sulphathiazole drugs. It was like a miracle for the patient, doctors and all concerned.

The Christmas Eve midnight Communion service was impressive, with a crowded choir and Church and an intense and beautiful Christmas atmosphere. What a contrast it was from the Upper Burma experiences of only a few months ago. True to my priest's Orders and instructions, on Christmas Day I journeyed along the Khyber Pass for a Christmas morning service at Landikotal on the Afghan border. Military transport conveyed me. The Pass was bristling with armour and military units. At that time, the German Army had marched into Southeastern Russia. The India Defence Staff considered that they would be likely to try to come down the Khyber to attack India, so unprepared for such an onslaught. Hence the Khyber defence.

What should be my mode of preaching, I thought, to so varied a congregation, some highly cultured and intelligent and some – like the humble soldier – wanting simple and good thoughts? For many of them battle and death were round the corner. It was a serious responsibility to try to minister comfort and help through Christ. How fortunate I was to find, in one of my steel trunks, some books of essays by Dr W. Boreham. I had never read them before, but now, to my intense relief and delight, found them to be ideal for what I wanted. And the congregations were delighted with this kind of approach.

One Sunday in January 1943 it was my turn to preach the sermon at evensong. The Revd Roy Beynon was in his stall, with Sir James Almond (judge of the province) at the very fine organ. The governor's wife was in her place; so also were many officers, men and others. In the midst of my sermon I heard what I thought to be a terrific hailstorm rattling the great church roof loudly. The Revd Roy Beynon stood up and instructed the congregation to leave the Church quickly and quietly, women and children first. It was an earthquake! Fortunately it did not last too long; the people returned to their seats and I brought my sermon to a brief ending.

In the vestry, after the service, a stockily built man came in, congratulated me on being so calm in the pulpit during the earthquake, and invited me to have dinner with him at his house on Tuesday evening.

'Who is he?' I asked, after he had gone.

'Sir A. G. Perrott, Chief of NWF police', I was told, 'and one of the toughest and bravest police chiefs in India!'

It was the beginning of a close and dramatic friendship. Mr and Mrs A. G. Perrott and their two young children welcomed me to their delightful home and garden. I discovered that he was a firmly committed evangelical Christian. His father had been a previous editor of the *Church of England Newspaper*. I also learnt that, every Sunday afternoon, while other government personnel were taking things easy, hunting or otherwise, A. G. Perrott and his wife were running the afternoon Sunday School for the British children of Peshawar. Peshawar has been called the city of roses and his breathtakingly beautiful garden was a very good example. But more about A. G. Perrott later in this book.

I had delightful and joyful letters from members of the family and other friends from England. From this time my adequate salary enabled me to send, each month, some money to my sister Marian to help pay towards my mother's hospital charges. There was no NHS in those days.

In April 1943 a bishop's Order informed me that I was to become chaplain of Multan District as from May that year. I examined my map and learnt that Multan was the hottest garrison station in India, with a temperature of around 120°F in the shade during the summer.

Multan 1943

Another very long train journey took me across the NWF province and the North Punjab to Lahore, and from there across South Punjab to Multan, not far from the River Indus.

The chaplain's large house was there for me to live in. It was surrounded by a large tropical garden with gardeners (*malis*) and the buffalo to work the well for drawing water. By this time, good and faithful servants were looking after my daily needs, waiting on my requests, and really spoiling me in Indian domestic fashion. My goodness, though, it was hot! The walls of the house were four feet thick, with no windows except little chinks up above, for the sunshine must be kept out. Punkahs (electric fans) were on perpetually, day and night. Each day my servant (bearer) heated up my bath water outside in the sun and before my bath each evening cold water had to be added. Great spiders, up to eighteen inches in diameter, were common everywhere. So also were the dangerous scorpions and giant centipedes. There were no flies because they could not live in temperatures above 100°F. But hornets were everywhere, as well as small, very poisonous snakes, so one had to develop a sixth sense and look everywhere, always, for safety's sake, especially in one's bed!

I slept outside every night and even then could not endure even one sheet except for a few minutes each morning. Early each morning the bearer brought on a tray, the *chota hazri* (little breakfast), and placed it neatly underneath the mosquito net. Sometimes in the night, I heard crunching noises. I whipped out my torch to shine it on a fight to the death between a huge spider and a scorpion. The scorpion always won; the crunching noise was that of the scorpion eating the spider's juicy head.

Because of the great heat by day, military work, parades and activities were curtailed to early morning, and after 6 p.m. in the evening. Afternoons were spent resting indoors out of the heat. Most parties, meetings or functions started at midnight. I travelled about the garrison on a bicycle with good rubber grips on the handlebars and the tubular metal could not be touched without blistering the hand. Neither could any vehicle, of any kind, military or private, be touched by bare hands during the day. The Church service, in the huge garrison church – a building of cathedral size – was held at 9 o'clock in the evening. Besides military personnel, some Anglo-Indians from the township loved to come to the service. For them it was the highlight of the week. What a life in such terrible heat. Occasionally a soldier shot himself because he could bear the heat no longer. Some evenings I walked along the only street, called the Mall. It was illuminated by electric lights around which there were always three or four owls.

I was asked to visit a second lieutenant's wife and baby girl. She was at the end of her tether because of the heat and chose to stay in a bath of cool water for much of the day. This was her means of survival. On her husband's pay she could not possibly afford to travel up to and live in the cool of a hill station. I visited the district commissioner about this and he came to her assistance and had her accommodated in the coolness of Fort Munro in Baluchistan, situated at 9000 feet above sea level. When I visited Fort Munro I saw her happily settled in.

To travel to Fort Munro, in the course of my duty, was quite an event in itself. First came a bus journey to the River Indus (and my goodness it was hot in that bus); then, at the river, one had to embark on quite a large river ferry with various decks and light cooking facilities. It took two to three hours to cross the mighty river, especially in August when it was swelled by the monsoons and boosted by the summer melting of the greatest glaciers in the world in the upper Himalayas. At times our ferryboat was almost out of sight of land – and this 1000 miles from the sea. From the far bank of the river, another bus took us the considerable distance, first across the desert and, after many miles, the gradual climb into the hills of Baluchistan and to Fort Munro, an established and protected summer garrison town. The cool climate was heavenly after the heat of Multan, and to require a sheet and a blanket on the bed at night was beautiful – an almost unbelievable treat. But this was all too short a joy. Soon it was time to return to Multan, its heat and its work.

The chaplaincy included far distant visits to British personnel occupied with commerce. One such place was a citrus fruit establishment. The staff always made you most welcome in their beautiful homes and greatly appreciated my ministry for them. Another settlement, Mianwali, was situated about 1000 miles to the north on the side of the River Indus. It took a day and a night in the train to reach this destination. In fact I estimated from the map that the Multan chaplaincy contained about 90 000 square miles – an area greater than that of Great Britain.

Towards the end of the summer came the bishop's notice of chaplains' transfers. I was to go to Nowshera.

Nowshera

I was beginning to get used to very long train journeys. Nowshera was a gunnery garrison, thirty miles from Peshawar and having about six outer garrisons; one, Malakand, to the north, reached into Central Asia; other stations to the east and across the River Indus, were Cambellpore and Attock.

There was a good and comfortable chaplain's bungalow, and with the help of a few servants I was quickly established. There was quite a garden, too, with a good supply of sweet orange trees. Later I noticed that, although the orange blossom fertilisation required the warm heat of the spring, the maturing oranges enjoyed the autumn and winter frosts.

By the rules and regulations of the Indian civil service, welcome or farewell ceremonies were not allowed for members. Neither could any gifts or presents whatsoever be received, not even a wedding gift. Should it become known to the authorities that a gift had been received, the officer concerned was discharged from the service forthwith. It has been claimed that the Indian civil service has been the purest of its kind in the history of administration. So no one seemed to know just when or how a new chaplain either arrived or departed. They simply took it as a matter of course when he turned up to conduct the Sunday service.

Although Nowshera Church was not nearly as large as Peshawar or Multan, it was a dignified, beautiful church and English in design and atmosphere. The surrounding church garden, well kept by two *malis* (gardeners), contained the most colourful, vigorous and beautiful sweet peas I have ever seen.

The Indian ecclesiastical establishment was one hundred per cent financed by the British Indian government. This included the original construction of a church and maintenance and care of all Christian buildings used for military, government and trade personnel. The government budget provided for all chaplains' salaries and travelling expenses, all travelling to and from the UK, and retirement pensions. Collections from Church services belonged to the chaplain's discretion who usually shared this responsibility with the commander of the station and one or two Church officers. Most of this money was given to Christian work of one kind or another.

I took lessons in Urdu from the teacher appointed by the government. I made a schedule of regular visits to the outlying garrisons and visited their various offices and messes. Risalpur, only a few miles away, was an RAF establishment. Choirs were formed, friendships established and the chaplaincy began to tick with Christian life and services.

One day, after the evening service at Nowshera, an army captain came to me and asked if I would like someone to play the harmonium for future services. I told him how delighted and grateful I would be. During the next few services he played so brilliantly that I asked him who he really was. He was Dr Willis Grant, until the war a musical director and organist of Birmingham Cathedral. He had been conscripted for the war, seconded to a truck service unit, and had spent his time happily greasing trucks and talking music with soldier pals. Then he was posted to India and here he was teaching Indian sepoys basic English. I introduced him to the Bishop of Lahore on the bishop's next visit. In quick time the organist was transferred to New Delhi GHQ as officer in charge of music. In this capacity he was sent all over India, Burma and Ceylon, on first class tickets or more, as Officer to provide British Forces with Music Appreciation.

I saw him a year later. He was thrilled. He had seen many of the wonders of India, Burma and Ceylon with all expenses paid and for a very handsome salary! Once again I was delighted to have been a catalyst.

My duties took me north, to the Risalpur RAF establishment, then further to a number of famous army scout establishments, especially Gardai, the regimental home of the famous Guides, and in the extreme north to the fort and garrison of Malakand. At the turn of the century Sir Winston Churchill was stationed here as a newspaper correspondent. He criticised the defence arrangements, was thus brought into the limelight, and from that time was known as a fearless and promising military authority.

Some brief background information regarding the Guides of Gardai, to whom I have just referred, might be of interest here. Because India is such a vast country and (during British Rule) military communications were sparse, emergencies, such as the 1887 mutiny, sometimes occurred. Vital extra military help was sometimes necessary but, from the Establishment point of view, was often non-existent. On such occasions, an officer, or officers, often met the immediate need by speedily creating a rescue force and hastening to wherever help was required in a bid to avert disaster. Recognition of such wonderful help was often conferred on a newly created force by gazetting them into a permanent and proud military unit. The Guides of Gardai were one such.

Just outside the Malakand Fort was the famous Swat River. It provided outstandingly good sport for officers on leave who delighted themselves in fishing. From this river they caught the large and tough fighting Mahseer fish. From time to time I invited a car load of RAF service men to accompany me on trips like these; and how they loved it all! These splendid young men would otherwise be cooped up in their sun-baked RAF surrounds with nothing very much to do except dream of England, mums and dads, brothers, sisters and sweethearts at home. We were a friendly lot. The big question was: when would they (and when would I) be home again?

On another occasion I took a chartered coach load of servicemen to the famous Taxila Museum, near Rawalpindi. There we saw a wonderful collection of exhibits dating from the centuries before and after Alexander the Great (356–323 BC), who had made this area his headquarters. In those far off times, carved busts (not photographs!) were made in their thousands to perpetuate the memories of family members. They were excellent, and so were all the other exhibits:

gold, silver, carvings, toys, etc. Some of the toys of those ancient times might have come straight out of Harrod's store. Frequent thick dust storms in that area had been responsible for the instant burial of the various dynasties, which remained, however, amazingly intact.

Practically every Sunday afternoon, service personnel joined me for afternoon tea in my house. I wonder where they are today? One of these men asked me to talk to him. He was a keen member of a main British communist party. Qualification for membership was never to have been inside a Christian Church. He spent night after night with me reading and discussing the Acts of the Apostles. He had never seen or known of revolution to equal what was written here! I wonder whether some readers of this story are keen on progress? If so, look no further than the Book of the Acts of The Apostles. This revolution changed, and is changing, world history in a remarkable way.

I wrote earlier that more would be said about the Inspector General of NWF Province Police, A. G. Perrott. One day a commanding officer in the RAF came to see me with a request. He asked whether I could arrange, for his men, a weekly evening service at Campbellpore which lay, of course, on the other side of the River Indus. 'The men', he said, 'are stationed in the hot and arid scrub countryside making up a large RAF maintenance unit. They are not allowed to go anywhere and certainly not to their nearest small town of Campbellpore except for a Church service. Can you give them such a weekly service?'

Sadly I could not because I had to give an evening service at Nowshera and the Attock Bridge on the River Indus was closed every evening at sundown. This bridge, I told him, could not be opened after sundown except on a pass issued on rare occasions by either the commander-in-chief north west army or by the inspector general of police, NWF Province. 'Therefore,' I said, 'I cannot oblige.'

However, he would not take 'No' for an answer and said that I must do something for his men, who were beside themselves. Without making promises, I decided to ask the inspector general of police if there would be any hope of helping these men by providing a weekly service. A. G. Perrott was deeply worried to say the least. Being a Christian man he at last agreed to let me have a book of Attock Bridge passes providing authority to cross the bridge weekly, at night. It was a very unusual permission indeed.

'You must keep the passes in a safe', he said.

The RAF officer was highly delighted; so were his men.

The Sunday evening services were to be weekly at 9 p.m. The superintendent of police, Campbellpore area, Superintendent J. C. Jameson, being himself a keen Churchman, commanded that I stayed each Sunday night in his house at Campbellpore. I found him to be a quite extraordinary person. In size and demeanour he was very Churchillian. He possessed a brilliant photographic mind and was able to converse and joke in at least seven languages. He acquired a complete command of the difficult Pushtu language without ever having had a lesson or a teacher. On receiving a new copy of Crockford's Clerical Directory he went through the 15 000 clerical histories, correcting them, and then returning the copy to Crockfords. He did just the same with the Indian Army list. He was once with an Indian Army officer when they were introduced to another officer who was wearing the DSO ribbon. Afterwards Superintendent Jameson told his fellow officer that the officer should not be wearing that ribbon for he had never received the award. He hadn't. This astounding person had also collected every public school tie, every English university hood and also all types of Church of England hoods and complete ecclesiastical robes. All of these were beautifully enclosed in fine tissue paper and kept in special wardrobes.

The interior of his large house was so beautiful, with the finest silk cushions and fittings, that one was almost afraid to sit down. His dinners commenced at about 11 p.m. and continued up to about 2 a.m. Nothing would hurry him. He trounced his servants unmercifully and they seemed to thrive on his chastisements. It was clear that they adored their great master. He was a very Anglo-Catholic type of high Churchman, but tolerated my ministry which of course was, and is, evangelical, and satisfied himself by calling me, 'The Submarine'.

I must now tell you about the first Sunday night journey and bridge crossing. Nowshera HQ provided me with a staff car and driver. This was waiting at the Nowshera Garrison Church so, after evening service, I was driven the twenty miles to the Attock Bridge. This bridge was a 'double-decker', with railway overhead and road beneath and, of course, the great steel green-painted doors were shut and bolted for the night as we drove up. An armed guardsman approached my car. I handed him my pass and requested that the bridge be opened for me. He returned and reported to his superior – the chief of the bridge guards (Frontier police for one half and Punjab police for the other). Another more senior officer came and searched my car for bombs or anything of that nature and then returned to the bridge. Orders were rapped out and bells suddenly clanged in the night. The complete guard took up positions across the bridge.

The great steel doors were slowly opened and signals were then given for the car to proceed slowly. As we passed through the two lines of armed guards, half of them faced outwards looking at the great chasm over the river. What they wanted or expected to see in that darkness I do not know, for the mighty Indus river was more than a hundred feet below. The other guards pointed their rifles and bayonettes towards me and followed the car's movement as it passed each one of them. It was quite frightening. And so we progressed to the other side and the great steel doors were clanged to and bolted. It was, after all, wartime and chances could not be taken with this vital bridge, the only one for about 1000 miles.

I proceeded to the garrison building that was set aside for use as a church. It had already been suitably prepared. The building was full of RAF personnel and a few others including, of course, Police Superintendent Jameson. It was a warm and rousing Christian service. I am sure the men were thrilled to hear prayers for their kith and kin at home. It was all quite splendid. And for an hour or two before the service the men had had refreshments in the Campbellpore restaurant and seen the few women who served them!

We proceeded to Mr Jameson's house for the rest of the night to be entertained as I have already explained. The next morning we returned to Nowshera. The bridge was, of course, open and apart from a quick military check there were no difficulties.

This programme continued for about a year. You can imagine, perhaps, the feelings of the Attock Bridge guards towards this awful Chaplain sahib. My bridge crossing coincided with their dinner time! I suppose I was fortunate not to have been shot.

About one year after the commencement of the special evening services at Campbellpore I travelled in my own large Vauxhall touring car specially suited to Indian long distance roads. One Sunday I was scheduled to take another service at Campbellpore, this time in the afternoon. I took with me a car full of RAF personnel whom I thought would enjoy this afternoon out.

All went according to plan and, the service having ended, we commenced the homeward journey, crossed the Attock Bridge and were about five miles from Nowshera when I developed a tyre puncture and stopped. As we were changing the wheel I saw an immaculate limousine car approaching from the Nowshera direction. It was Inspector General Perrot with his wife, friends and family, being chauffeur driven for a Sunday afternoon's drive. The Inspector General spotted me and ordered his driver to stop a few yards further along on the other side of the road. The chauffeur was instructed to come over and give a hand with the changing of the wheel. The Inspector General came over, too. Then, suddenly, there was a mighty crash. Two army vehicles travelling at speed crashed into the back of the limousine and sandwiched the back of the car to its front. As by a miracle the Inspector General's wife, children and friends had got out of the car a few seconds earlier to stretch their legs; they were therefore safe.

I hurried to Nowshera to inform the garrison authority of the accident and they were quick to organise rescue operations. You can imagine my grief and sorrow now that the Inspector General, who in so many ways had been kindness itself to me, had suffered so grievously in trying to help me further. He had no hope, in wartime, of obtaining a similar car to the beautiful one he had lost. We shall hear more about his young son later.

CHAPTER 8
THE HIMALAYAN REST CAMPS

The Bishop of Lahore's early 1945 postings ordered me to be chaplain of the rest camps situated in the foothills of the Himalayas around Murree. Before I left one early morning in May, Brigadier Ekin, Commander of Nowshera Brigade, telephoned me to say that Germany had capitulated. This had been anticipated for months and now there was a sense of relief at this momentous military victory. Perhaps this made my journey and ascent into the mountains all the more enjoyable. For it was indeed great joy to be leaving intense summer heat of over 100°F in the shade, to climb into and amongst the pines and cool mountain air and breezes.

The chaplain's house in Ghariál was surrounded by conifers roughly fifty per cent of which I noticed, had been struck by lightning. Soon I experienced days and nights of these thunderbolts; they were more prevalent than in any other place I have known in the world – caused by the clashing of cold currents of air from the snows and ice of the Upper Himalayas with the torrid heat of the Punjab. At least two lightning conductors were on every government structure and I never heard of any such building being struck. But in the night, all around us, these incessant thunderbolts were shattering for several weeks.

RAF and army personnel were all over these hills, living in the various rest camps. There were some RAF Arnhem battle survivors who pleaded for a memorial and thanksgiving service for their comrades who had been killed a year before in that terrible battle.

RAF men eagerly formed a strong choir for the Garrison Church making the atmosphere for them like home-from-home, and for me also. Their brilliant education officer, Dudley Clarke, conducted the Church music and choir and actually composed music for us. As a result of his experiences with the Church, in those six months, he later completed his war-broken history BA at Cambridge, achieved his ARCM, read theology at Ridley Hall, was ordained and served his first curacy at Aldershot. Some time later he became principal of the senior anglican school in Tasmania. Twelve months after I left the rest camps he sent me a letter mentioning that it was his Church experience at Ghariál, in the Himalaya Mountains, which had been his turning point. As I write he is the university chaplain, Tasmania.

There were some six or seven different rest establishments all over these mountains. I travelled almost daily to do what I could for the servicemen. The car journeys along those ever-changing twists and turns of mountain track called for the utmost driving care. To leave the track would have meant falls of hundreds of feet down the mountain side.

One of the rest camps had been handed over to the American army. They treated me with great kindness whenever I visited them. At times they welcomed my car load of British servicemen who would, after receiving bountiful supplies of American food, declare that they had joined the wrong army!

One day in August, 1945, I was standing near a rustic bridge together with a few friends when one of them produced a newspaper. There, in large headlines, was the dramatic notice of the allied nuclear bombing of Hiroshima in Japan and the account of the capitulation of Japan's war efforts. The war was over! What a wonderful day that was for which we had so bitterly fought for all those years. A divine feeling of relief fell on us. For those of us in those mountains this was followed by solemn thanksgiving services in the garrison churches. The servicemen realised that they were now much nearer home. I knew this was not so for me because of the exigencies of the Establishment Service.

The Bishop of Lahore's autumn postings list came once more to inform me that I had been posted to the Razmak garrison, situated beneath the Afghan mountains. Another very long and strange journey had to be undertaken and at last I arrived at my destination.

Razmak, Waziristan

I reported to the commanding officer at the Edward's Fort at Bannu before proceeding a further seventy miles to the Razmak garrison of 10 000 men. On this mountain road I passed some six or seven forts or garrison strongholds. These also would expect my visitations from time to time.

The history attached to Fort Edwards was interesting. In 1847, because the farmers in this part of India were not paying their taxes, the British authorities at Lahore sent Lieutenant Edwards with a company of soldiers to find out what the trouble was. The root cause of the trouble was found to be the law of 'An eye for an eye'. Each small farmstead in the fertile valley of Bannu had established a shooting tower. Any offence or murder had to be avenged. So by day and night an aggrieved farmer would watch from his shooting tower ready to shoot the farmer next door. This inter-community feuding was so widespread that the farmlands were not being worked, there were no harvests and so no taxes could be paid.

During his first winter in Bannu, Lieutenant Edwards organised his soldiers and hired workers to build a very robust and large fort. When it was splendidly completed, Edwards sent out an ultimatum to all heads of houses in the valley: 'Surrender your arms by a given time and date, or else!' The ultimatum was obeyed, arms were surrendered and the harvests were reaped in fullness once more throughout the Vale of Bannu. Fort Edwards has been a life-saver ever since and I was pleased to sleep soundly in the safety of its robust structure.

Waziristan had been a skirmishing and sniping country for some years when I went there in 1945. Free travel was no longer safe and had to be undertaken under strong military protection.

A zealous Muslim named Epi had been inspired to fanaticism by his pilgrimage to Mecca. He came back to find the Indian Congress Party pressing for the British to leave India and gleefully jumped on the bandwagon. He drew to himself rebel and discontented soldier deserters. They plundered Hindu settlements, abducted the Hindu women and began to harass the government and military forces which tried to curb them. Hence it was no longer safe to be anywhere outside the fort, of which, as I have mentioned, there were several along the Bannu-Razmak road. In the rest of Waziristan, an area about the size of Wales, were many more such garrisons and forts. In my time there were at least six battalions of soldiers guarding the forts and protecting transport and movements up and down the road to Razmak. Military food and supplies required were considerable so the protection required was also considerable. The night before a convoy was to travel the *secret* code went around, 'ROD day tomorrow', 'ROD' meaning 'road open day'. Armoured cars would proceed forth from each fort accompanied by artillery and when these reached particular vantage points further infantry units would take their places along the route. Only then would the responsible commander give the order for traffic movement of the convoy to take place.

The average convoy would consist of several dozen food and supply trucks interspersed with infantry-filled vehicles. The infantry were to be especially ready and take up their positions at any time the convoy halted. In this way the Razmak garrison and all the other garrisons were kept adequately supplied with food and necessities.

I was given permission to position my car in between other infantry vehicles and this passed off quite well for several years. But, even so, the Waziristan snipers were clever enough to kill or wound members of the forces from time to time. My car was hit with rifle fire only once, but that was enough. There was a special price for the head of a Christian padre!

Razmak Garrison was merely one mile square but it held 10 000 soldiers and housed all their guns, tanks, armoured cars and necessary impedimenta. So wherever possible all things were in miniature. Apart from 'ROD' the gates of the garrison were securely shut and bolted and woe betide any person who was foolish enough to venture out. Around the square mile was the stone wall of protection, fully manned, day and night. Even then there were skirmishes, sometimes in the night.

The consecrated burial ground was outside the garrison. When a burial of one of our soldiers took place a battery of machine gunners took up their position before, during and on retreat from the service.

Razmak Fort, and other forts in the area, were considered to be the only parishes to have one kind of register – for burial. There were none for baptisms or marriages. No women or children were ever allowed, or seen, in those areas where battles could suddenly erupt; and erupt they did from time to time.

My small house was next to the small church and on the other side, close to me, was the general's house. Previous chaplains had left a very good supply of classical music records which I thoroughly enjoyed. During the weekdays soldiers were welcome into their games room, which was the church building prepared for these weekday activities. I had friendly chats with so many of the men in this way.

One day I heard a woman's voice singing in the games room! I rushed round to see this female! I found instead a tall young infantry-man and he was still singing with a woman's voice! I asked him what this meant? His answer was that he was still a treble member of Westminster Abbey Choir! 'Before my voice was due to break', he said, 'I contracted diphtheria; my throat was so affected that my voice never did break and I was gladly kept on as a pure treble'.

Later there was a garrison concert in the cinema. In several acts my soldier friend was beautifully dressed as a woman singing women's romantic songs. He came on again several times, each time with a different and attractive dress, and brought the house down. He was singing women's songs to hundreds of men who had not seen any kind of women, native or white, for twelve months or more.

It was the first Remembrance Sunday after the terrible war which had just ended. The service took place in the open space in the garrison. The 1st Batallion, the Wiltshire Regiment, was the garrison at that time.

Although there were few leisure activities I did enjoy playing snooker after dinner and in this manner came to know some of the men very well. During the winter months the weather was extremely cold with frost, deep snow, and ice. How unusual and interesting it was to see large numbers of military camels, normally associated with hot sand and hot climates, ploughing across the snows as they pulled their lorries laden with military stores! Sometimes the officers invited me to accompany the 'mule and mortar regiment' for field manoeuvres and permitted me to take photographs. From the given signal the parts of a mortar had to be unloaded from the mules, fitted into position and ready to fire within two minutes.

For a year I continued to travel up and down this seventy-mile road, regularly ministering to the officers and men in the forts. From time to time, due to enemy action, my Christian service was held below ground level.

From the bishop came the autumn postings. I was to become chaplain of the New Delhi cantonment or garrison.

CHAPTER 9
NEW DELHI

After another very long journey – hundreds of miles across the north of India – I arrived at New Delhi just as the weather was cooling off pleasantly for the autumn.

To my great inconvenience the previous chaplain had left all his household effects in the house. Therefore, for the time being, I had to store my belongings in the church vestry. I slept on my verandah without a mosquito net because it was locked away in my boxes. I paid the price, for in the next day or two, I caught an onslaught of fever. My homoeopathic medicines were also locked away. I drove myself to the military hospital and committed myself to them. The doctors placed me in the polio ward (considering that I had all the symptoms), gave me antibiotics, and hoped for the best. I broke out into a savage itching rash and then I was put into the smallpox ward. Another doctor said it was the medicine which created the rash, so they gave me sleeping tablets and I hardly awakened for two days. But now I was better and ready to come to terms with the work of New Delhi.

The large New Delhi Garrison Church was the last of its kind to be built in British India, being completed in 1929. It was designed by Shoosmith, assistant to Sir Edwin Lutyens, who designed New Delhi from 1911 onwards. The Church was constructed from millions of red bricks. It was Babylonish in style, huge, and from the outside looked very like a large electricity generating station with a large square tower. In size it was more than adequate for a battalion of a thousand men or more. Inside the church were spacious porticoes and outside, around the church, were extensive grounds.

The Bishop of Lahore had preached at the first service on Christmas morning 1929. His text was, 'Let every man be swift to hear and slow to speak'. No one heard a word, for it had now become quite clear that this church had the very worst possible acoustics! For some years the church was virtually out of use until acoustics experts from the UK were commissioned to do what they could to help. They ordered asbestos muffling material to be applied, about one inch thick, around the walls and up to half the height of the church, which was fifty-five feet high on the inside. If there was an improvement it must have been only small. I found the acoustics to be a great hindrance and decided to do what I could to improve matters.

I invited the army mechanical engineers' department to come and advise. They sent a very intelligent young Scotsman, who spent much time trying to help. 'Two things you can do', he said. 'Cover with woollen material, the large rear balcony' (which was designed to take a full military band) 'and secondly obtain the best public address equipment possible'. Both of his recommendations were carried out. To achieve the first I visited the New Delhi cloth mills and purchased appropriate lengths of blue shade woollen tapestry. Because of the interior height of the church it was necessary to have the help of the latest New Delhi fire engine ladders. Even with the ladders at their fullest extent the workman could only just reach the summit in order to fix the hooks to suspend the material. But it was done. A first class PA system was also installed and the acoustics were greatly improved.

At this time India was in a state of dangerous tension and unrest because of the ever-increasing 'home rule' movement. Riots, strikes, fires, squabbles and great anxiety were commonplace – and important government and military measures were implemented almost continuously. The situation was very alarming and dangerous because there were now several million battle-proved Indian soldiers who had been discharged when the Second World War ended. The Indian Congress Party was ready to make use of them to back their 'Britains go home' policy.

The 2nd Batallion the Royal Scots Fusiliers were in residence at the garrison, commanded by Lt Colonel Buchanan Dunlop. There was also a strong contingent of the RAF. Colonel Buchanan Dunlop was exemplary in his support for the church services every Sunday and we became very good friends.

One Sunday morning two Rolls Royce viceregal cars drove up to the Church door. General Sir Arthur Wauchope, Colonel of the Black Watch Regiment, with his viceregal friends, had come to worship. After the service the General requested Colonel Buchanan Dunlop and myself to talk with him as we walked up and down the Church grounds. He was a church enthusiast and spoke his mind on many Church matters. He asked Colonel Buchanan Dunlop for his views on compulsory Church parades. When the Colonel replied that he supported them wholeheartedly, and gave his reasons, the general replied in his strong military manner, 'I have opposed this all my life and have won'. Compulsory Church parades had, indeed, ended two years previously. I thought the General was severely official from a military point of view and for a time we held him in awe. But as he and his party came regularly to the service we became much more friendly, even to the after-service coffee enjoyed in the outer shade of the great building, for the heat otherwise was very severe.

It was New Year's Eve 1946/47. I decided to take a leisurely stroll through the garrison area. The garrison canteen seemed to be in full New Year's Eve business even at midnight. But as I came up to the canteen I saw that it was more than ordinary business. Members of the Royal Scots were within. They were hurling glasses at one another, throwing chairs around and seemed to have gone generally berserk. The poor Indian waiters, terrified, were cringing in the corner as they watched their cafe being wrecked. I was indignant, took courage, entered the cafe (I was in battle dress with clerical collar) and called out with the firmest voice I could muster, 'Stop this, I want your names and numbers right now'. There was a dead silence. Then all made a sudden dash for the open door and open windows and within a few seconds the cafe was empty. It was a miracle because those men could have torn me to shreds! I rushed out and chased one of the Royal Scots. I did it for my own fun, really. I was now enjoying this New Year's Eve frolic. I knew I could outrun him and caught him. What he then expected I do not know. I smiled at him, said how foolish and unfair this skirmishing had been and wished him a happy new year. The cafe had been saved and those waiters and owners were relieved to have been rescued from the Royal Scots. I had taken a chance and it paid off. Courage often does.

A military hospital messenger came to me one day with a DI (dangerously ill) note. I went immediately and was admitted to the room where a warrant officer's wife lay unconscious. She was suffering from double pneumonia and meningitis. With the nurses present I offered a prayer for her and after a time departed. The next day I did the same thing and the next day, and so on. After a few days the Sister told me that the pneumonia was now under control. The results of the meningitis remained, the patient was still unconscious and this remained so for several weeks. I prayed daily. The doctor then told me that a brain specialist was coming to try to help.

Some days later I was at the hospital but could not find the warrant officer's wife. The Sister said, 'Oh, you passed her on the verandah. Yes, she is now quite all right and will soon be leaving hospital'.

The brain surgeon had performed a simple operation. He drilled small holes in her scalp, washed the interior of her skull with penicillin and the cure was immediate. I then talked with the joyful warrant officer's wife. She said that for most of my visits she had realised what I was saying and doing but had no power of response whatsoever. It had been a case of one-way communication. I have never forgotten that. The same could apply to so many people, especially the elderly.

The chaplain of the central New Delhi parish was granted leave and I was gazetted to take charge. Because the care of the two parishes demanded too much from me, I met and invited the Revd Francis William Cocks, Chaplain-in-Chief, Royal Air Force, India, who was stationed at HQ New Delhi, to take the services at the Church of The Redemption. He agreed and the services of both parishes were smoothly maintained. Many years later I met the now retired bishop, the Rt Revd Francis William Cocks, who had become Chaplain-in-Chief, RAF, in 1959, sometime after his New Delhi days.

In January 1947 the tension throughout India had become very serious. The main danger was of a possible uprising and mutiny against British people, for there were now some two million returned battle-proven Indian soldiers who might strengthen the trend of the Indian Congress party.

Felicity Wavell, the viceroy's daughter, was married in the Church of The Redemption early in the new year. It was, of course, a very notable occasion. As chaplain I was present at the marriage ceremony in the Church and afterwards at the reception on the lawns of Viceregal Lodge. It was, in effect, like a splendid royal occasion. Amongst those present were maharajahs, rajahs and all kinds of heads of Indian state affairs, delighted to be honouring the viceroy's daughter in this manner. Felicity had married a young and handsome army Captain.

The reception, though truly notable, was strange because there were refreshing drinks but no food whatsoever. This was because, at that time, there was a widespread food shortage, bordering on famine, and the viceroy-in-council had decreed that, for the time being, food parties would be unlawful. The viceroy was bound to honour his own law.

The wedding gifts were arrayed on tables which filled the great ballroom of Viceregal Lodge. They must have been very valuable, especially the gold, silver and jewellery gifts, displayed in glass cabinets, at one end of the ballroom and guarded by Bengal Lancers. This ballroom was and is, reputedly carpeted with the largest single Persian carpet in the world.

During the ever-increasing national tension in February 1947 we held our usual Sunday morning service in the Garrison Church. As usual, General Sir Arthur Wauchope, with his viceregal friends, were present. After the service we sat outside, in the shade of the Church to share in coffee. It was then that the general said to me, 'Padre, I expect you have heard the news'.

'Sir', I replied, 'what news?'

The general replied, 'Lord Wavell had been given the sack by Prime Minister Clement Attlee. The viceroy and all his staff have been given three weeks' notice. Lord Wavell does not mind for himself, but is perturbed and grieved for his aides and their families who sacrificed their previous careers to become his aides and assistants'.

Perhaps I did not realise it immediately but those sombre words marked the **beginning of the end of British India and, indeed, of the end of the British Empire.**

Within the given time Lord Louis Mountbatten arrived as the new Viceroy of India. From the outset he made it known that he had come to arrange for the speediest possible hand over of power to India.

General Sir Arthur Wauchope had now gone. (He actually died a few months later.) I missed him and his inside information and now could hear only the ordinary news of the unfolding dramatic events. Lord Louis was obviously working very speedily. Now that he had declared the British Government's decision – to give India her independence as soon as possible – the national tension eased considerably and we welcomed a period in which there was reasonable good will towards the British people in India.

We were approaching Easter Day 1947. Colonel Buchanan Dunlop told me there were plans for the disbandment of his regiment. Could there be, he asked, a commemorative Church service on Easter Morning? I agreed, and preparations were put in hand for this great service to be. Members of the Indian GHQ defence staff would be present and the viceroy, Lady Mountbatten and their daughter Pamela would grace the service also.

By this time the public address equipment was in excellent working order and the large band balcony had been draped off with wool material. I had received from Harrods, in England, a recording of English Church bells which could be sounded through our large loudspeakers in the great tower of the Church.

But who would preach for this auspicious occasion? I knew I must not. Then who? I knew that Lieutenant General Sir Arthur Smith, Chief of India General Staff, was not only a renowned soldier but also a fearless and dedicated and committed Christian. I knew he would fearlessly preach the Gospel at the service. I was granted an interview with him and Sir Arthur was pleased to accept my invitation. I thought, then, that we would have a great service. We did.

It was, as expected, a glorious warm and bright sunny morning. One thousand officers and men of the 2nd Battalion, The Royal Scots Fusiliers, were ceremoniously paraded to and entered the Church. Officers from GHQ, with their wives and some members of their families took their seats. The bells were duly ringing, as in England, and the large congregation sat with deep concern and anticipation regarding the service about to begin. I waited at the large west door for Their Excellencies, conducted them to their seats, and the great service commenced. Perhaps then no one considered that this was to be the last Easter Day service in the capital of British India, bringing to an end the Church's faithful Christian service of this kind for over 150 years. Well known Easter Day hymns were sung heartily, especially by those 1000 men who had survived bloody battles not so long ago and had left some of their slain comrades on the battlefields of Burma. Soon, no doubt, they would be returning to their native land and relations. And some men of that congregation would remember this padre who had broken up their rough New Year's Eve party!

Lieutenant General Sir Arthur Smith had been appraised of the previous problem of the acoustics. There was a microphone in the pulpit. Before he began to preach the sermon he asked any man to put up his hand if he could not easily hear. Not a hand went up. The General then preached a very moving sermon. Otherwise there was not a sound in that Church as he preached. After the service Lord Mountbatten took the salute of what was thought to be the last parade of the 2nd Battalion of the Royal Scots.

Two weeks later the disbandment was cancelled!

CHAPTER 10
LAHORE, KASHMIR AND WAZIRISTAN

But now the Bishop of Lahore's postings for 1947 ordered me to proceed to Lahore Cathedral and to be there in time for the Holy Week services.

It was a nightmare journey all the way to Lahore, a distance of several hundred miles. For the transfer journey, my car and trailer were filled with my belongings. This heavy load, plus the intense heat, were too much for the vehicle and the clutch snapped just as we were leaving the outskirts of New Delhi. Just then an army lorry appeared and the driver agreed to tow me to Lahore. I bought some rope from the local bazaar nearby, we hitched up and away we went. But the rope was not strong enough, kept snapping and, each time we re-tied it, it became shorter. This made me steer extremely cautiously. The temperature was well over 100°F and I had been up for most of the previous night, packing. I was repeatedly on the verge of falling asleep as I was towed. It was a nightmare journey and I think it was one of my miracles to have arrived safely.

It was now my duty to conduct the daily morning and evening cathedral services, as well as the choir and to precent for the main Sunday services. The cathedral was served by a society known as The Grey Ladies Society. Their service resulted in the smooth and beautiful harmony of cathedral life. They gave attention to detail, maintained the linen in perfection and prepared the service books for every service. The book markers were in the correct pages without fail. One of the Grey Ladies was the young Dick Turpin (as we used to call her). She was the headmistress of the Cathedral Girl's School. And what a magnificent and beautiful solo soprano she was.

As news told of the ever-closer approach of the ending of British India, chaplaincy postings became liable to change overnight. The bishop was evidently deeply concerned and worried. After only a few weeks of my time at the cathedral he found he needed someone for the summer chaplaincy of Gulmarg, Kashmir. I was instructed to prepare and go forthwith.

Gulmarg, Kashmir

On leaving Lahore I knew that I was destined, climatically, for a beautiful cool summer in some of the most glorious scenery in the world. If I had thought of choosing this chaplaincy I would have felt guilty. However, I had been ordered to Gulmarg, so that was that, and I would now seek to serve to the best of my ability. Indeed, to be leaving the scorching heat of the Punjab and to begin to climb the Himalayan mountains was heavenly in itself. The air became cooler, heavenly breezes blew, the green and majestic conifers were everywhere and the rivers, when we passed over them, were gushing cascades. All went well with this journey for hundreds of miles with scenery becoming ever more refreshing and exhilarating.

Tangmerg, the end of my car journey, was reached at last. From here Gulmarg, another 3000 ft higher, could only be reached by walking, riding on a horse or being carried in a chair by coolies. Coolies were waiting in abundance to carry my packages up to Gulmarg. So we left, with each of the coolies carrying on his head one of my cases – cases which I found difficult even to lift. How hard some people have to work for their money! Up and up we climbed through the stately and lofty pines, at night the roaming ground of bear, panther and other wild animals, until at last we emerged through to the Bowl of Beauty, for that is what Gulmarg means.

This bowl of beauty, situated at an altitude of 9000 ft above sea level, consists of several hundred acres of undulating emerald green grassland. The grass is interspersed, in the summer, with endless colourful wild flowers including anemones, orchids and other species.

In the centre of this grassland, and on a hillock, was the most typical looking English Church you could wish to see. A fairly large stream twisted its way here and there through the grassland. And this grassland had been divided up into three 18-hole golf courses. To one side of the area was the large and well-constructed country clubhouse where residents could come, meet one other, have meals and relax. On the perimeter of the grassland, and nestling amongst the pines, were Swiss-like chalets. They were quite large, as was the chaplain's house. These chalets were summer-time homes for officers and their families who were able to afford this summer haven.

From this plateau, and especially from the verandah of my house, could be seen the mightiest range of mountains in the world, with many peaks over 25 000 ft and interspersed, in their valleys, with more glacial ice than anywhere in the world except for polar regions. Each evening the setting sun illuminated these peaks with vivid crimson. During the day the whole range is snow white. One of the peaks, Nanga Parbat (26 660 ft), is the queen of the region, with one sheer five-mile upright face. To see this illuminated with glowing crimson each evening was glorious.

Two of my house servants had journeyed with me and they were thrilled. They were good, dependable and loyal servants. My main servant (bearer) on arrival, was quick to organise the rest of my domestic requirements. It had to be remembered that, in India, a servant would do one type of job only, and hence the need for a number. So my bearer (Nobby) organised a dish washer (*masalchi*), a house cleaner (sweeper), a bringer of firewood (*lacri walla*), a bringer of water (*pani walla*), a night house guard (*chaukidah*), a messenger and private postman (*chaprassi*), etc. In Gulmarg practically all my salary was spent on servants' wages!

The Church services were typically and traditionally English, using of course, the Book of Common Prayer. Every Sunday morning there was an early children's service. Children came riding on their ponies – even the tiniest – and all had glowing pink complexions. One morning a child was crying and when I asked her why, she replied, pointing to her horseman, 'He won't let me gallop'! The Church and holiday life was a touch of England with glorious environment added.

For games of golf a ball walla was always taken on. He had a tin and it was his job to clap the tin over the ball as soon as it landed. Otherwise it would be quickly seized by one of the many crows which were always waiting in the area. When occasionally a crow did pick up a ball the ball boy would run after it crying '*Peinkdow, peinkdow*' (drop it, drop it) and the crow usually did so. So there were many 'Birdies'!

How could I resist arranging a mountain climb on one of my days off? I set off with rucksack, a very worthy messenger chap (who could speak several languages) and two other guides. We climbed and climbed. Once more I marvelled at the infinite variety of beautiful wild flowers growing everywhere – anemones, orchids and many others. We came to a vast treeless area on which cattle were grazing for as far as the eye could see.

Having just crossed this plain, a violent mountain storm struck suddenly. We took shelter in a cave and had to remain there for a considerable time. Then my men persuaded me to cross even further to the next village, down into the Province of Poonch. When we reached there my men explained my predicament to the natives (who appeared to be half Chinese). They pushed me on to a kind of bed, massaged me all over and then brought some kind of egg food. Then, because I must return before tomorrow and it was now dark, they prepared torches and some of them accompanied me back over the mountains. Higher and higher we ascended. At 2 a.m. they ran out of flares. There was nothing more we could do except sit there at about 13 000 ft, in freezing cold, and wait for the dawn. Then followed a very long, hurried trek back to Gulmarg. We reached there at 4 p.m. just before a search party was to set out to try to find us. The bishop, who was at Gulmarg on holiday, had taken three services in my absence. I had made two mistakes. First I should not have left on a Saturday, the day before Sunday, and secondly I should not have agreed with the other men when they persuaded me to go further to the next village in the State of Poonch.

This Gulmarg summer community consisted mostly of officers and their families of the British Indian army. These officers were part of the largest army units in the whole of the British Empire. That is why a Bishop of Lahore had to be the right kind of person to match this very considerable military strength and it was expected that the chaplains also should know what they were supposed to do. The bishop himself was in my congregation for much of the summer. I suppose he would quite often consider that I was the one who, a few years before, had straggled up to his door at Kasauli as a refugee from Upper Burma. The Bishop was now observing my ministry in this, the choicest of the summertime hill stations in the north of India.

I always tried to preach Christ's Gospel as faithfully as I could and with much joy. At this time Russian communism was rearing its head in much of the world and I did not hesitate in my sermons to warn of this and how only the Christian Gospel would be able to face it. Since then the world has known, so bitterly, the evils which I used to mention in my sermons. And now, in 1992, many are rejoicing to witness the downfall of communism.

During these summer months Lord Mountbatten worked ceaselessly to create acceptable terms for the handing over of British India.

He was defeated in his efforts to maintain a future United India and therefore had to accept the formation of two new countries to be called Hindustan for the Hindus and Pakistan for the Muslims. At last terms were agreed and the date of handing over was announced, 14th August 1947. A shock shivered throughout the land for no one had expected such a speedy termination of British control. The Bishop of Lahore was now deeply worried for, above all others, his church and churches were bound to be deeply affected. His chaplains would be gone and many of his garrison churches would become empty shells with no more state funds to maintain them.

One day General Whistler approached me with a request. He had just been appointed commanding officer for the sending home of British personnel. His wife, who was with him in Gulmarg, had sustained an abscess following medical inoculation. Would I take her in my car to the nursing home in the capital, Srinagar? Of course I agreed. On the morrow Mrs Whistler was carried down the mountain to Tangmerg where she was transferred to the back seat of my car and suitably propped up with cushions. General Whistler sat beside me at the front of the car and away we went, some fifty miles to the outskirts of Srinagar. There we were stopped by state police who said we must stay there until Lord Mountbatten's car had proceeded. He was on a visit to the Maharajah for constitutional talks.

We waited for quite a long time. Then, possibly because we had explained that Mrs Whistler was in pain and needing urgent attention, the police chief suddenly gave us permission to proceed. The main road through the capital was lined with troops and police. As my car proceeded they all, in turn, gave a royal presentation of arms and salute. General Whistler was highly amused, especially when I said to him, 'Sir, you have had many a General's salute but this is your first Royal one.'

We reached the nursing home, near cross roads, where more senior police were stationed. They, too, had given us the Royal Salute! When they saw the car stop to let Mrs Whistler alight, they were furious indeed, ordered us off the road immediately and two minutes later Lord Mountbatten's official fleet of cars went by.

The month of August arrived, the month of the great deadline of the 14th when all British personnel's duties would be terminated and they would all be moving towards home. This, of course, included all chaplains. But the bishop told me I could not be spared. He had promised Lieutenant General le Fleming, Commander of the Waziristan Army, that he would provide him with a chaplain for the time to be taken for the official withdrawal of the Waziristan Army. I was to leave for Bannu immediately, said the bishop, before the mass riots, already widespread, made it impossible for me to get through.

I successfully made the long journey down and away from the Himalayas and across the Punjab to Bannu Fort, there to report to Brigadier Cariappa, Commander of the Bannu area. Meanwhile there were reports of wholesale massacres of both Hindus and Muslims. At first the massacres took place mostly on the railways. In one direction trains were carrying Hindus. In the reverse direction they were carrying Muslims. A line would be blocked, the train halted and no one would be spared. Retaliation followed retaliation. Mass transmigration was taking place on the roads, too. In fact this was probably the greatest transmigration of human beings in history. Cholera, smallpox, typhus, and dysentery ravaged the masses who made nightly camps consisting of tens of thousands of people. The dead were bulldozed into open pits. The Holy War in Kashmir had commenced and within three months it was estimated (and so declared by Winston Churchill in the House of Commons) that four million people were slain as the result of this war alone.

Waziristan is about the size of Wales. Along three prongs of military roads lay numerous military garrisons and it was my duty to try to reach each garrison in turn to minister as best I could. Also it was my government duty to pay the caretakers of military cemeteries, and there were about fifteen of them. The caretakers, locals, could not write, and so, for a receipt, I had to take their fingerprints. The cemeteries contained the graves of hundreds of British soldiers who, from time to time, had given their lives for the cause of British India.

The great day, the 14th August, dawned a few days after I arrived to make my base in the Bannu Fort. On that day I witnessed the appropriate military and other ceremonies, functions and celebrations in and around Bannu Fort. The central ceremony, in the afternoon, was the deeply moving final lowering of the Union Jack and the first hoisting of the new Pakistan flag. After an historic 150 years, British Rule and control suddenly came to an end, like the snuffing out of a candle. This also was to mark the beginning of the end of the British Empire, the greatest empire the world has ever known.

Kipling, of India, had written one hundred years before:

'Lord God of Hosts be with us yet,
Lest we forget, lest we forget!'

Brigadier Cariappa, who supervised these ceremonies and took the last British salute and first Pakistan salute, soon after was appointed the first Indian Commander-in-Chief, Indian Army. He spoke impeccable English, and was always very gracious and kind to me personally.

One particularly devout Churchman, always attending a Church service whenever possible, was Lieutenant Colonel Brian Montgomery, G.S.O.1 of the Waziristan Army and brother of Field Marshal Lord Montgomery of Second World War fame. He was the director of the withdrawal operation for this army under General le Fleming. The colonel particularly asked me to pray for the success of the withdrawal of the army and the handing over of several dozen forts and garrisons with all their valuable construction and materials within.

If an officer or soldier was killed or died I had to travel to the place of burial the same day. Sometimes this urgent journey was taken with my car sandwiched between two armoured cars and we made a dash for it, believing that the unsuspecting enemy tribes would have no time for action. There was an alternative method which I sometimes used. A political escort was provided. This consisted of some dozen tribal warriors, each representing a major tribe. They placed me on a seat in the front of their coach and they travelled on top of the coach, always with their rifles at the ready. If anyone dared to attack, then, by political agreement, all the tribes would unite in punishing the offender.

The Fakir of Epi was giving great trouble at this time with telling effect. He had now acquired several 25-lb shell field guns. With these guns he and his warriors roved the heights above and around the various forts and from time to time he shelled the forts, almost as he wished. The official army could not get at him and they knew it. Should there be any attempt to do so Fakir Epi, his men and guns, would just go over the boundary into Afghanistan. In some ten years or so Epi cost the British Indian Government many millions of pounds. The Fakir was never caught.

I was in the Razmak Military Hospital when he shelled Razmak. It took place in the late evening. At the sound of the first shell exploding I left my hospital bed and with others went down and outside. Once we detected the position of the cannon, by the sight of the flash, we knew how to take cover. We then watched each explosion on the mountain above us, and knowing that it would take so many seconds for the shell to land and explode, we were able to take appropriate protective cover. That evening the shells damaged the house of Jos Donaldson (the political agent), a store and the garrison cinema. One shell hit the side of the hospital and immediately afterwards I moved from my cover and picked up a part of the fragmented shell while it was still hot. The general and brigadier stood in the middle of the main road, laughing their heads off. Within a few minutes all the garrison guns were blazing away at Epi and his gun; he was quietened and retired for the night.

Very sad news arrived concerning the Grey Ladies of Lahore Cathedral. One of them, Dick Turpin, had returned from summer leave in England. She had not been inoculated against the epidemics raging throughout the Punjab, and caught cholera and died. The Mother of the Order caught the infection from her and also died. So did a third member. The bishop, who officiated at these funerals, was shattered and became a broken man.

At this time, I was instructed to visit our various churches scattered throughout tribal territory, collect as much as possible of the silver and any other precious items, lock the churches (for ever) and return the precious articles to Lahore Cathedral for safe keeping. It was of course a traumatic experience marking the end of an era.

The role of political agent in India at this time was a very exacting one. India as a whole was controlled by the viceroy and his council. The land was divided into provinces, each controlled by a governor. Provinces were divided into areas known as Districts, controlled by a district commissioner and other certain areas, such as the princely states or tribal territories, were divided into political agencies where the district political agent was in charge. He was a man of supreme administrative ability and authority – especially in law. His judgement was final and he was answerable only to the governor. Supported as he was by the police and the army, the political agent was an important and key figure.

Jos Donaldson was the political agent for the Razmak area and when he was not on touring duty he lived in his residence in the Razmak Fort. He was held in high esteem by all who knew him, tribesmen and British alike. One day, while he was travelling on duty, recalcitrant tribesmen from the Data Kail area kidnapped him and kept him in a cave for weeks. Eventually the government paid the ransom of rifles and a large sum of Indian rupees which the kidnappers had demanded. Jos Donaldson was released and returned to his house in Razmak. Severe government reprisals followed. Twelve inch naval guns were brought to Razmak and mounted and sighted at Data Kail, some twenty miles away. The inhabitants of Data Kail were warned to leave their area and farms and houses, as a non-stop bombardment was about to begin against their area.

I lived in my house in Razmak at the commencement of the shelling. With each salvo, Razmak seemed to rock and my windows rattled, until I was sure they would crack. This shelling continued for several weeks. In the end the recalcitrant tribesmen surrendered entirely and returned the ransom.

Soon after this I had just ended a Church service when a member of the congregation, Jos Donaldson himself, asked to speak with me. I took him into my house. 'I am ill,' he said, 'I cannot do my work, I cannot fulfil my government duties, I am afraid, what do I do?'

I suggested it was the effects of his kidnapping and captivity. He declared that this was not so, for he had been feeling like this for quite some time. He then swore me to secrecy and especially that I would divulge this matter neither to the general nor the governor of the Province. I said I would do everything to help. Would he kindly come again to see me after my next tour of the garrisons; and he promised to do so.

I should have immediately sought an appointment with either the general or the governor for it was obvious that Jos Donaldson was under great stress. Two weeks later I attended the regiment's summer farewell party in the general's house. The army officials were to leave the cold regions of Razmak for the winter quarters in Dera Ismail Khan. At the party a brigadier said to me, 'Have you heard the news, padre?'

'No,' I said, 'What news?'

'Jos Donaldson has shot himself.'

It was, of course, a very sad burial of a very brave man who had given his life for British India as so many had. It was a particularly sad funeral for me. I should have tried to prevent this.

Kohat was another army centre to be regularly visited. Brigadier Ekin of Nowshera days was now the general of the area. Over the years the British authorities had made this area look like an English village green and township. Now it was nearly deserted and soon it would be entirely so, as far as the British were concerned.

Well known to the officers were a brave missionary and his wife, Mr and Mrs Nicholson, called Nick and Nicky. Mr Nicholson conducted the services in my absence with great acceptance by the congregation. But now he was in great trouble because no monies at all were coming through to him and he and his wife were becoming hungry. I knew I must do something about this and found an opportunity when I went on my next visit to another garrison, named Parachinar, underneath the Afghan mountains.

The fifty-mile road from Kohat to Parachinar runs, at one place, through a deep road and river gorge. Here, a few days previously, Muslim tribal warriors had successfully ambushed a Ghurka convoy, inflicting heavy casualties and securing rifles and loot.

I hurried through this gorge as fast as possible and with some trepidation. I arrived at Parachinar safely and reported to the commander, Colonel Harry Garland, who happened to be a most committed Christian and Churchman as well as an expert officer. When he heard my story of the plight of the Nicholsons, he said he would have them both up here to stay in his garrison quarters for some time to give them adequate and full care. And he did. But more than this, my request to some ten or so remaining British officers, produced sufficient and ready cash for the two Nicholsons to pay for their return to England. They actually returned even before I did! In many matters such as these I rejoiced because God was making use of my ministry amongst men and women.

It was almost too terrible to be believable, but on my return journey, just as I entered that dangerous gorge, I developed a tyre puncture and had to stop to change the wheel. Never did anyone, I think, change a wheel so quickly in all the world. Thank God, not a shot was fired.

My next tour was to the extreme south of Waziristan ending with a visit to the garrison and stronghold named Wana. I had been there for only one day when again the warrior tribesmen successfully ambushed another Gurkha convoy leaving for the long journey to India. The Gurkhas suffered severely. Our military road was then closed for nearly two weeks. I found some of the adventure books of John Buchan, first Baron Tweedsmuir, in the army library and read nearly all of them. Whilst there an army telegram was handed to me. My aged father had passed away in far off Cheshire, England. At last the all clear was given for travel down that road. My car was sandwiched between infantry vehicles, in the powerfully armed convoy. So we proceeded for some miles to a junction with one road going to Dera Ismail Khan and another going my way to Bannu. The convoy was ordered to remain here for some time. I thought to myself, why wait? I have been delayed for so long, I ought to go. I told the convoy commander, who thought I ought to stay but he could not give me the order. I moved away from the convoy towards Bannu. When five miles from Bannu I saw before me some twenty or so warrior tribesmen straddling the road with their rifles directed at my car. Their leader stood in the middle of the road with his arm held up for me to stop. I was travelling very fast and before I had time to think, I was upon them and into and through them. The leader jumped back just in time to avoid being hit by my car. I was through, and accelerated away; and, thank God, not a shot was fired. The next day, the Muslim political agent, who had been penned up in Wana Fort with the rest of us, travelled along this same road with another car and with his several wives and relations. He had valuable goods in his car. The warrior tribesmen stopped his cars, looted all that he had and took the rings from all the women's fingers, even though he was a fellow Muslim.

It was Christmas Eve, 1947. By invitation I was the guest of the CMS Station at Tank. The Station had been controlled for years by Dr Madeline Shearbourne, Vera Studd (daughter of the late Kynaston Studd, at one time Lord Mayor of London), and a Danish nurse. They nursed and cared for tribal Muslim women and especially cared for their babies. The tribal people thought the world of them and they were safe. Now that the British were to leave and because of widespread unrest, murder, looting and danger, the authorities advised them to leave. They declared, 'Over our dead bodies'. They had been and were 'The Salt of the Earth'.

In the early hours of Christmas morning, just before daybreak, tribal nurses, trained by the CMS Station, sang Christmas carols in their Pushtu language just outside my window. At 7 a.m. I celebrated Christmas Holy Communion for all Christians on the Station.

We were having breakfast together when a messenger came for Dr Shearbourne. After a while she returned to say that some warrior tribesmen, who had been fighting in the Holy War in Kashmir, had brought a warrior who had been wounded and was very ill. He had tetanus. Could I take him to the hospital at Dera Ismail Khan? I was about to leave for that town to celebrate Christmas Holy Communion for the last few British soldiers there.

'And, most important,' said Dr Shearbourne, 'could you make sure that anti-tetanus serum be sent back to save the staff from infection?'

The very tall 6 ft 6 in warrior was seated at the back of my car. Two other warrior friends piled in as well, together with their huge rifles, belts of bullets and daggers fastened around them.

There were literally thousands of camels on that forty-mile road. The Pawinders from the Afghan mountains were making their annual winter migration into British India for their winter trading. I hooted and hooted but it made no difference and our journey was a very slow one. Eventually the sick warrior was handed over to the hospital. It was too late and some time later he died. The anti-tetanus serum was sent to the Tank hospital to comfort them in this respect. Wonderfully, I was preserved from catching the tetanus fever.

The military Christmas Service in Dera Ismail Khan was the last of its kind in British Indian history.

Two days after Christmas another political agent, Colonel North, a brilliant young Scotsman, who also lived at Tank, was shot dead by a rebel Muslim. With the greatest of difficulties did I try to offer spiritual consolation to his distraught wife. Previously I had stayed at their house during my tours in that area. Another brave life had been given for India, now Pakistan.

Just another few days and it would be time for me to leave Pakistan on my journey home. A few weeks before, Colonel Montgomery had asked me to take him as a passenger, all the way down to Karachi and he would provide two army trucks to carry our baggage. It was to be another very, very long trip and a hot one too.

By this time the colonel was very pleased concerning the success of the Waziristan Army withdrawal operation which had proceeded entirely successfully and without a single loss of life.

On January 1st 1948 we passed through the great iron gates of Bannu Fort (Fort Edwards) for the last time. As we cruised along the frontier roads I noticed that Colonel Brian Montgomery, sitting beside me, was sad and all but weeping. He acknowledged that he was reminiscing. Several of his forebears had given their lives for the wellbeing of British India. His grandfather had helped to design, plan, and build the many garrison towns, especially in the Punjab and on the frontiers. He had been particularly determined, in the planning, that a good Christian Church should be built in the centre of each garrison or garrison town and the government must adequately provide for the Christian worship of the soldiers and of all concerned. I was the last of those chaplains to be leaving. The others had left on August 14th.

For these dangerous parts of the frontiers we were accompanied by adequate armoured cars and were met by even more as we approached the next Guides' post or garrison. At each place the colonel and I were treated with the greatest warmth and care.

After some days we were approaching Quetta. With about five miles still to travel, there was a sudden sharp left-hand turn, into the bright rays of the setting sun which helped to blind the sight. I only just managed to guide my car over the narrow concrete crossing over a *nullah* (deep ditch). There were no side rails to the crossing, but we were safely over. Not so, unfortunately, one of the following trucks which happened to be carrying my baggage. The driver missed the concrete and plunged into the deep ditch, my baggage being scattered all over its bottom. The other truck carried the injured driver into Quetta where rescue operations were quickly organised and the army engineers did what was needed. We were delayed in Quetta for two or three days.

For the next week or so we travelled those long distances along the mighty Indus valley and then through the Sindh desert; and how hot it was! The city of Hyderabad, perhaps one of the hottest cities in the world, is a sight to be seen. On every structure or house is a wind catcher, similar to the large dust extractors seen on flour milling factories. These catchers are turned with the breeze to take into the building whatever breeze or wind is available. It rains there for not more than four days per annum. When it does rain the life of the city comes to a halt so that the inhabitants can rejoice in the rain.

We arrived at our last halting place for the night before Karachi. We bathed and changed before going into the dining room for dinner. It was then that Colonel Montgomery said to me, 'Padre, can we kneel down to thank God for the great success He gave for my Waziristan Army withdrawal operation?' We did so. Here is an example of how British India government public servants possessed the qualities of Christ and took those qualities naturally and firmly into the very woof and warp of their profession.

We arrived at Karachi where I handed over my car which had served me so well over those thousands of miles of roads up and down mountains and across the vast plains of India.

Then came the shocking news which swept through India and Pakistan – **Gandhi Shot Dead!** Fortunately the assassin was a Hindu. Had he been a Muslim there would have been a mighty war between Hindustan and Pakistan. Only a spark such as this would have been required.

I boarded the SS *Castalia* which was to carry me back, after seven years of almost unbelievable and dramatic activities, adventures and service in Burma, India and Pakistan. As the ship swished through the gentle waves of the Arabian sea, India was behind, but her memories would be with me for ever.

The mysterious India of a myriad shades of life; of sorrows so terrible, of joys so great; of fortunes and misfortunes, opportunities and tragedies; of brave and noble people and some the opposite; of the glorious Indian Army of the past; shades of all the colours of the spectrum; of gigantic mountains, glaciers, rivers, torrid heat, intense cold; of love and cruelty. All of this life was behind me now – finished.

And to use once more the words of my Introduction, *I was flat on my back*. Now, once again, I was facing an unknown future.

CHAPTER 11
RETURN TO ENGLAND

The main impression of the voyage home was of incessant and tumultuous seas continuing from one end of the Mediterranean to the other. It all began as soon as SS *Castalia* steamed out of the Suez Canal. From time to time I stood on the plate-glass-protected upper bridge deck admiring and photographing the mighty waves as they cascaded almost completely over the ship. When the sun was shining the cascades were illuminated with all the colours of the rainbow. When we were steaming in the vicinity of Crete I thought of St Paul's epic voyage in this area. No wonder he went out of his way to describe it so markedly. He named these ferocious winds *Euroclydon* (Acts 27:14). It must have been terrible for Paul and those with him in their small wooden vessel compared with our modern steel Castalia. Even so, I wondered at the mighty strength of the Castalia to stand up to all this pounding day after day and night after night.

Most of the passengers were hardly seen for a fortnight because of sea sickness. I was fortunate, for although often susceptible, on this occasion I seemed to be quite all right and enjoyed splendid meals and every bit of the voyage. The weather became more subdued as we steamed past the Rock of Gibraltar, across the Bay of Biscay and through the Irish Sea until early one foggy dull morning, in early February, we pulled alongside the dock at Liverpool. Oh, the drabness and lifelessness after the sunshine and stirring life of the Orient! At least that was my impression. How could it have been otherwise?

My brother-in-law, the Revd G. E. Bottomley, had kindly come for me and, after customs were completed, he drove me to his rectory at Bucknall in Staffordshire. I remained there for some weeks feeling like a fish out of water.

The British Government's ecclesiastical secretary for Church appointments arranged for me to see him at No. 10 Downing Street. During that interview he offered me, in acknowledgement of my past service to British India:

- A vacant Crown Living anywhere I chose in England;
- A chaplaincy with the Royal Navy, Army or Air Force;
- A place at either Oxford or Cambridge University; or
- A curacy at Leeds Parish Church.

I took some time to think about these generous and attractive possibilities. Some influence was preventing me from accepting any of them. Again, for the time being, I was like a fish out of water, waiting and hoping that some vocation would open up before me.

Then I was pressed into a temporary ministry by my previous vicar, the Revd Dr Hugh Thomasson. He was in retirement at Weymouth where the sick and busy Vicar of St John's, the Revd H. Jameson, urgently required an assistant, especially for the approaching summer. So I went there to help for six months only, being persuaded that my future work was yet to be determined.

St John's Church, Weymouth, has a beautiful and tall spire and is situated prominently on the sea front. Summer weather and bright sunshine came, and happy holiday crowds filled the town. Eight hundred people filled the large Church every Sunday and I tried to act as a good assistant, but it was all so different from the past. The vicar was a very tall and sick man. One Sunday morning, in the middle of the service, with some 800 people in the Church, as he was giving out the notices, I thought he looked unsteady and hurried to him as he fainted into my arms. There was a stunned silence in the Church until I asked the churchwardens to come forward to help carry the vicar out into the vestry. I then continued and completed the service. After all, I inwardly thought, this is a small matter compared to matters in the East!

During evenings in the week I gave talks and showed films of some of my ministry in the East and the audiences seemed to be most interested and told me so. I was, apparently, a very welcome help in more ways than one. They could very well realise what lively experiences had been mine.

Sports days with the young people and playing cricket with them was always jolly good. I thought how pretty and charming the girls and women were. The flowers in the sea-front gardens were out of this world. But my mind, secretly, was still restless. Past grim experiences of the East kept filling my thoughts. Delightful parishioners invited me to their homes and gardens to play croquet and chat with them and have tea on the lawns.

I was instructed to take harvest services for four parishes at Tollard

Royal near the New Forest. When I arrived for the weekend, the vicar's wife looked after me in the huge and rambling country vicarage, still having to use its own well for water supply. I felt so dull. 'Lord, make something happen,' I prayed, at the end of Sunday when the services were over. And of course the Lord did. Later that night, just before bedtime, some people came to the rectory door. Had we any petrol for their stranded car? We had not, so I walked with them through the length of the village searching for petrol. No one had any. Most people had already gone to bed. It seemed clear now that the people must stay in the village for the night. But where could they stay? It was now midnight. We went to the large village pub, and asked if they could put up this family.

'So sorry, no,' said the publican, 'the pub is filled with Prince Hussein's bodyguard. Prince Hussein is a pupil at a school near here in the New Forest.' (Our Prince Hussein, here, is, of course, the present King Hussein of Jordan.)

We took our family back to the rectory, and the rector's wife agreed to accommodate them for the night. She could not do otherwise by this time. There was not enough bedding without going up into the third floor which was usually closed. It was somewhat eerie, but we managed to find sufficient bedding materials for the extra family, and they were bedded down for the rest of the night (it was now 2 a.m.). In the morning, they enjoyed the country breakfast, and were most grateful and charming. They managed at last to obtain petrol and depart. I had had my fun. The Lord does answer prayer, I thought, even in England. I returned by bus to Weymouth.

During August of that year my mother passed away. Yes, she was still alive when I returned from India but, alas, no longer recognised me or anyone else. She had been in a hospital bed for ten years. How I took a little part in the funeral service I do not know. The service took place in Handforth Church where she had been married and the school at which she taught was just over the road. I considered that Katherine Beatrice had been one of the most wonderful and courageous mothers in the world.

Having completed my summer and temporary curacy, I spent the next few months visiting my brothers and sisters and their families in various parts of the county, and was able to take them presents from India. I took some of the younger members for holidays to places such as Newquay in Cornwall. In particular I spent much time with my sister Marian and her family. She was the 'fairy godmother' of the family: delightful, patient, kind and understanding.

Then I accepted an invitation to be chaplain to a party of senior schoolchildren for their skiing holiday in Switzerland. Their parents were in professional occupations abroad.

As we were crossing the English Channel and were mingling with the passengers I could hardly believe it. I bumped into Mrs North, wife of the political agent who had been shot dead in Tank in Pakistan shortly before I left. Of course we had so much to consider when we talked, both on the ferry and on the train journey across France. She cried, bitterly. What a cruel world it can be for some! And how much we need the help and influence of the Prince of Peace and Comfort, Jesus Christ Himself, the Son of God. Other passengers who passed to and fro in the corridor must have wondered what I had said to this woman to make her cry so much!

It was a good skiing holiday although I did not appreciate or understand all the demeanours of those modern teenagers! We learnt to ski on the snows and to skate on ice, and we enjoyed the wonderful lunches in the midday bright sunshine on the verandah of our hotel. The winter weather, however, was unusually dry with not much snow.

I must climb that Dom peak, I thought. The climb should give me a bit of a thrill! I was provided with the best guide of the area. He agreed that there was not much snow at our level but much more on the heights and we might have a good trek unless more snow fell. This kind of winter climb of Dom is rarely undertaken, he said. I was delayed for another day or two waiting for a colour film to arrive, and then we set off, supplied with food and gear for the day.

Up and up we went. It was, as expected, exhilarating. But then the sky darkened and later the snow began to fall, becoming increasingly heavy. In this snow we were crossing a very large, wide snow face, on a steep slope. Here the snow, piling up on previous falls, was deep, as our steps and ice axes showed. From time to time there were sudden strikes across the whole snow area, like a flash of lightning. My guide stopped, said how sorry he was, but we would have to retreat and return to base. Otherwise, he said, the alarm will be raised down below and expensive operations taken to come to our rescue on this mountain. By that time we were about three quarters of the way to the summit. We turned and safely descended the mountain in the midst of increasing snow falls. Bad luck, Dom, I would like to have reached your summit.

The train for home, across France, was like an ambulance, or a war-casualty train, because there were so many, of various ages, with broken limbs, now in plaster. I was thankful that not one of my party had been injured at all.

A telegram was waiting for me on my return. It was from the Bishop of Lahore: WISH YOU TO COME TO BE CHAPLAIN TO GENERAL SIR DOUGLAS GRACEY AND HIS FOUR HUNDRED BRITISH OFFICERS.

It did not take me long to believe that I was possibly fitted for this role. My previous years had provided the experience required. I sent a reply accepting the invitation and saying I was coming immediately.

I went aboard a flying boat from Southampton waters. This was another new experience. Indeed it was thrilling to feel the double-decker giant rev her powerful engines to full roaring strength, plough through the water, and raise huge waves on either side. How could she rise out of this, I thought? She did, and presently we were flying over the Solent and heading for France. The flight veered southwards, then along southern shores of the Mediterranean, and in due time we skimmed down into a bay at Augusta, Sicily. I thought the customs officials there were extremely anti-British and uncooperative and I would have liked to know why.

From here the flying boat crossed the Mediterranean to land at Alexandria where we stayed in a hotel for the night. Throughout the flight I had an open atlas before me, gazing down at each place and letting its history speak to me as it wished. The absolutely perfect steadiness of the flying boat interested me very much. There could have been a glass, full to the brim with water, placed on the window ledge of the plane and not a drop would have come over the edge of the glass. As we flew across the Suez Canal area, and then across Sinai, I wondered which of those mountains Moses climbed to obtain the Ten Commandments which have so affected the moral and spiritual history of much of the world. Visibility over Arabia was cloudy, no doubt due to dust storms and, after a very long flight, we glided down to Kuwait waters where a brand new super-hotel had been opened for service only a few hours before.

We then flew along the Southern Baluchistan coastline with its many great estuaries carrying waters from the mighty Himalayas. And so down to Karachi waters, with familiar peoples, sounds, smells, and railways and the long journey to Lahore.

The Bishop of Lahore was very ill. His worried wife could not allow me to see him on my arrival, but perhaps tomorrow and then only for a few moments! I talked with the Archdeacon of Lahore. I tried to learn of plans for my work, for which I had travelled all this way. No one seemed to know very much. Where would my house be? No one seemed to know. We think, they said, you will have to live in a school room! The next day I was allowed to see the very sick bishop but only for a minute or two and he was incapable of making serious conversation. I stayed there for some days, gleaning all the information I could. It then became known that before long British officers in Pakistan might well be fighting British officers from India over the Kashmir dispute. To my mind the situation appeared to be increasingly unstable. My future role as chaplain appeared to have been given little professional and legal thought. After some days of further discussion and prayer I knew that I could not stay. I regretfully announced my decision, packed my bags, bought my tickets and sadly left for the return journey to the United Kingdom. At Karachi I boarded a regular flight plane flying direct to London.

It was not long before the war in Kashmir flared up afresh and was destined to become worse. Neither India nor Pakistan would even accept the United Nations conditions for a truce. At last the British Government realised the dangerous and absurd situation for the British officers in both Pakistan and Hindustan, about to face each other in war! Their contracts were cancelled, and they were ordered home.

The Bishop of Lahore had become a broken person; and no wonder, considering all the terrible burdens and momentous changes of those past two years. Before long, after a great, noble and distinguished life, he passed away. He was always superb towards his chaplains and, as for myself, when I was, as it were, down and out – a refugee – he had set me firmly on a new career rejoicing.

Once again, I was flat on my back, as I returned to London.

Caring for a South London Parish

Almost immediately I accepted the invitation to care for St John's Church, Lewisham Way, South London, for their interregnum. It was a strongly evangelical parish of some 17 000 people and, until recently, had been in the care and ministry of Canon T. L. Livermore, one of the foremost evangelical ministers in the country.

I was firmly tied down by the busy services and necessities of the parish. Not least, I had to take my turn at the London cemetery of that area, and for a whole week be responsible for many funerals. At times, and especially at holiday periods, there were also many marriages. I found it quite intriguing to take note of the different characteristics of the couples who came to be married. Some were ever so good, some laughed, some cried; occasionally the bridegroom was so drunk he could hardly respond to the questions. Their marriage attire varied greatly, too. Quite often the nature of the bride's dress, mostly beautiful, made it easy for me to base my comments on this alone. On one occasion a bride was dressed in red and white and, of course, her bridegroom in black. They were quite delighted when I based my address on their liturgical colours. I think most clergy are very happy taking wedding services.

The services were very strictly Book of Common Prayer, but all this I liked and supported. Nevertheless, on arrival it was clear that there were sad divisions amongst the parishioners. I did not consider that I had sufficient theological skill or learning to help directly. What did help were my weekday evening talks, with coloured slides and cine-projector, concerning the recent unfolding history and affairs of the Indian subcontinent. After each fellowship evening the people enjoyed refreshments and meeting each other and we all seemed to become great friends and rejoiced.

During this time at St John's I took the opportunity to taste of the London music concerts. Though not very classically minded, I enjoyed those concerts very much and marvelled, as I still do, at the skill, dedication, and discipline of people in an orchestra.

I had become a life member of what used to be known as the Royal Empire Society, (later to become the Royal Commonwealth Society) and attended lectures given by distinguished commonwealth specialists.

I was much honoured when the society invited me to give a lecture on *The Closing Days of British India*. Later, the Commonwealth Cambridge Branch invited me to give a lecture on *The Problems of Beautiful Kashmir*; afterwards I was to give this same lecture to their Brighton Branch. In all such matters I always endeavoured to emphasise the influence of the Christian way of life.

At this time, when my spirit was striving to decide on my future, the Revd Canon Goodwin Hudson came to see me. He had recently returned from a schoolmaster ministry in Santiago, Chile. He was sure that my experiences in the past would adequately fit me for a ministry in Chile where they were in need of a new chaplain for the British speaking people of the South American coast. He supplied me with names and addresses of people to contact. In due time communications resulted in my accepting the post of chaplain of Valparaiso and Vina del Mar. This chaplaincy had been written into the Chilean government constitution many years ago.

St John's interregnum had ended and I would not be leaving for Chile for another three months or so. My brother-in-law, the Revd G. E. Bottomley, had just resigned as rector of Bucknall in Staffordshire and begged me to take this interregnum for three months before I left for Chile.

Bucknall was one of the largest parishes in the diocese of Lichfield, in the Potteries area, with a population of over 40 000. My sister Vian, his wife, was to stay in the rectory for the time being, together with her three boys, so I was to be well looked after.

I moved in, took a deep breath, and commenced to minister to the three parishes. George Bottomley's two previous curates left when he left, so I was to look after these three parishes on my own. (After my departure the new rector was to be supplied with six curates!) In addition to this ministry I was expected to act as the official chaplain for the Stafford Crematorium. During those three months, therefore, I officiated for sixty-four cremations or funerals. It was traditional for mourners to attend the service at Bucknall Church on the Sunday following the funeral. It was normal, therefore, for the church to be half-filled with the mourners and of course my ministry had to help them in their spirit of sorrow as well as trying to be helpful to the non-mourners also.

During the same three months I married well over sixty couples. Each marriage required at least two interviews and each marriage service required four marriage entries. On one August Bank Holiday weekend twelve marriages were solemnized, two on the Friday, eight on the Saturday and two on the Sunday. I had written to each bride asking her to be ready for the service five minutes before the stated time so that all parties would be pleased and none disappointed. They complied in a most excellent way so that all went smoothly.

On average there were eight services each Sunday and on one Sunday there were ten. This was indeed a non-stop life and ministry.

It was a great relief when a new incumbent arrived and was inducted. I handed over to him the keys to the rectory, gave him my report and notes, left for Stoke railway station, and boarded the train for Liverpool ready to embark in the morning for Chile – phew!

CHAPTER 12
TO CHILE

This was not like my departure from Queen's Dock, Glasgow in 1940. This was peacetime. And so quite a few of my brothers and sisters and some of their children were waiting at the Liverpool quayside to bid me bon voyage as I embarked on the SS *La Reina del Pacifico* (Queen of the Pacific). She was a stately vessel of more than 20 000 tons.

The month-long voyage included stops at Bilbao (Spain), Bermuda, The Bahamas, Cuba, West Indies, Panama, Guayaquil (Ecuador), Callao (Peru) and Antofagasta (North Chile); and we finally docked for disembarkation at Valparaiso (Central Chile). *Valparaiso* means Vale of Paradise.

For the sake of those who have never been there I can affirm that the Panama Canal is a great marvel of marine engineering. It was completed in 1912 and cost a great number of lives, mostly from disease amongst the workers. In order to make it possible for ocean-going vessels to cross an isthmus much higher than the level of the ocean, various locks, at different levels, were cut from the ocean inwards, and supplied by water from the lakes in the centre of the isthmus. As a vessel steams from the ocean into the first channel it is roped up to moving machinery on either side (called donkeys) which pull it into one lock after another. The vessel is then pulled along and up through more locks, until it is on a level with the great lakes. The vessel then sails through the lakes, is passed through locks on the Pacific side and then steams away into the Pacific Ocean. It was intriguing to behold the movement from start to finish for our SS *La Reina del Pacifico*.

At Guayaquil in Ecuador we had a most unusual experience. I was one of three men from the ship who decided to visit the town, and we entered into their largest and quite modern store. Before long we were concerned and embarrassed because the store stopped trading and hundreds of shoppers crowded around us, staring and laughing – and pointing to our legs! Because of the intense heat there (near the equator) we were dressed in khaki shorts which, unknown to us, was forbidden by Ecuadorian law, and punishable by imprisonment. So we were considered to be quite daft, irresponsible and stupid types of gringos. They did not often have the opportunity to see men's knees!

The mighty range of the Andes was clearly visible to us for much of the cruise down the Pacific coast. I might not have been aware of it then but the fact is that the Andes mountain range is a range whose highest peaks are over four miles in height, while the Pacific Ocean, over which we were cruising, is five miles deep.

As we were tugged into the deep Valparaiso harbour it was obvious that the country was 'navy' minded for there were many warships. Standing out clearly, as the pride of their fleet, was the battleship *Latorre*, bought from the British Royal Navy years before.

Immediately behind Valparaiso harbour and city the land rose sharply and was closely housed for the inhabitants. I could see elevators by which the people were carried up or down, to and from this residential area.

I went through strict customs and then was met and greeted by some of the chaplaincy trustees. Everything was indeed very strange and different from any previous experiences. One of the trustees explained that, for the time being, they had found a Roman Catholic family willing to accommodate me. They took me there, that is to Viña Del Mar, a modern residential area, some ten miles away from Valparaiso. The very demure and conservative Senorita could speak no English, nor could I speak Spanish. Fortunately there were two grown up daughters who could speak sufficient broken English to make matters possible. How careful I had to be with my steps in order not to transgress their set traditional Roman Catholic customs and habits. Somehow I managed to survive this initial and difficult role.

There was no chaplain's residence. This was because, for the last five years, the Valparaiso Seamen's Mission chaplain had also been the constitutional chaplain and was content to live in his Seamen's Mission house. The trustees had been happy to sell the chaplain's official house by which they bolstered their depleted funds.

There was no time to lose, for in a few days the annual remembrance service was to be held in St Paul's Church, Valparaiso. I was informed that this was the great and outstanding service of the year and that the church would be full – with about five hundred people. It was full. Of course I was used to services like this and all went according to plan. The people had all seen the new gringo chaplain and I had seen some of the potential of the area. Howbeit I was soon to discover that it was a very flimsy potential. These five hundred people consisted of a very mixed racial group. A small proportion were basically Anglo-Saxon, and many others were Chilean-British or Anglo-French or Anglo-German. In fact there was no limit to the variety of inter-European and Chilean breeding.

After the service I was warned, I suppose quite lovingly, that the congregation next Sunday would be very different and might give me a shock. I think it did, for there could not have been twelve people present at the service. I realised that it would be my interesting role to find out the reason – and perhaps also the answer – to this problem. After all it was for matters such as these that I had travelled such a long way.

It took some weeks for me to discover the basic working of church life in the area and why there were so few people attending services.

First of all the colossal earthquake of 1906 had a basic bearing. Until that time there had been so many British or British associated people living on the hills around St Paul's Church, that it was called the English Hill. There were thousands of them, apparently, acting as business people for the many British business concerns in what was then a very rich and thriving Chile. It was chiefly British business enterprise which had made it so.

But then came this terrible earthquake. It happened at night which made it all the more ghastly, for not only did the earthquake bring down most of the houses, but all the oil lamps overturned, the oil spilled, and there were fierce fires everywhere. Marvellously, St Paul's Church remained unscathed and was used as a refuge and place of salvation for many who were thankful for its shelter. The English Hill, however, became a ghost area and was deserted, especially by British people. Ten miles away, in virgin and open country, Viña del Mar was designed and constructed. In the centre was a large sports area, consisting of a race course, playing fields, tennis courts and a country club. Around this, new and architecturally attractive houses were built in Chilean style. They were pleasant and very varied in design. So the well-to-do, in fact nearly all the British people, lived now in Viña del Mar. The businessmen worked in Valparaiso city during the week and at weekends they loved their Viña del Mar dwelling places. Certainly only a minority wished to go back to Valparaiso city for a Sunday service. St Peter's Anglican Church of Viña del Mar was built. Of course, in structure, it could not compare with St Paul's Church, Valparaiso. No one wished it to.

There was another outstanding and contributing factor for the falling away of the St Paul's congregation. On the death of Queen Victoria in 1901, that is before the earthquake, the British people decided to honour the Queen's memory by buying and installing a magnificent organ, which was to be the largest and finest in South America. At the time a talented organist, Mr Hill, was appointed; he helped with this initial installation and then became the honoured and official organist of St Paul's. From then on a kind of new religion took over at St Paul's Church – the religion of the organ!

So, even after the earthquake of 1906, when the majority of Protestant people had gone to live in Viña del Mar, the chaplaincy trustees (who still lived on St Paul's Hill) were determined that the main Sunday Services should take place in St Paul's Church, with Mr Hill at the organ, and nowhere else! When I arrived, some chaplaincy trustees still lived on the English Hill, and this was the situation I found – the religion of the organ.

There were further major reasons for the decline in worship compared with the pre-1906 or even pre-1912 and pre-1918 periods.

I now describe, as briefly as I can, Chile's world rise and fall in commerce and also how, at one time, it became very British at heart.

During the nineteenth century a Briton named Mr North reconnoitred the north of Chile and in due time was sure that there were unlimited supplies of nitrates contained on the surface. When he felt completely assured of this, and without giving his game away, he bought great areas of this land from the Chilean government at a very low cost. He then set up a worldwide structure for promoting sales, and money began to roll in to Mr North and his company. He initiated various supporting enterprises for his flourishing trade in nitrates – bankers, business houses, miners, engineers, works, and builders. He brought out, largely from Great Britain, great numbers of people, professional and otherwise, to staff his enterprises. Chile became one of the richest countries in the world, and very pro-British. Her basic currency was a large gold coin, the peso. This great success naturally involved itself in Chilean/British politics, relationships and intermarriages. In due time the British Royal Navy became responsible for the overall training of the Chilean Navy. It is not difficult to imagine how this large influx of British people opened the way for the Anglican Church to create chaplaincies, in different parts of Chile, for the spiritual care of all these people. These chaplaincies were written into the Chilean constitution. Many British people set up their permanent or semi-permanent homes in Chile.

This great commercial success lasted until 1918. The nitrates trade had received a terrific boost from the 1914–1918 war when nitrates were in great demand, especially for war purposes. But at the end of 1918 the Chilean nitrates industry dramatically collapsed. Germany suddenly announced its discovery and then its provision of scientifically produced nitrate at a much cheaper cost than that obtained from Chile. Many very rich (and some not so rich) Chilean people lost their fortunes overnight and there was great lamentation. From that time onwards the British population diminished rapidly and was continuing to do so during my time as chaplain (1950–1955). My ministry was to be to this depleted and mostly poor community.

Chile also experienced another commercial rise and dramatic and sudden fall: in shipping. The opening of the Panama Canal in 1912 put an end to what had been, for a very long time, a lucrative shipping trade. Ever since European vessels had begun to come west with their cargoes of merchandise for the western coasts of both North and South America, they had discharged their European cargoes and restocked with supplies from the port of Punta Arenas in the South and then the further ports of the Island of Chiloe, Concepción and Valparaiso. From there they would continue north for their trade with North America. The opening of the Panama Canal brought an end to the greater part of this commerce in shipping. Chile suffered severely.

I found a sad, poverty-stricken Chile, then, whose inflation by this time was perhaps the worst in the world. Not only had it lost all its benefits but there was another factor which greatly reduced the British presence there, and that was Chilean nationalism. Whereas in the past, British business houses and concerns had been free to import their British staff and workers, now, in my days, some ninety-five per cent of staff had to be Chileans.

When I arrived for my work in Chile in 1950 there were six Anglican chaplaincies. When I left, less than five years later, there were but two – my own chaplaincy of Valparaiso and Viña del Mar and the chaplaincy of the capital, Santiago.

Within the first two months of my arrival I had reasoned out these causes of a falling Church life. I knew that unless I took quick action this chaplaincy of Valparaiso and Viña del Mar would soon be terminated. I took action!

It was clear that I had to end the religion of the organ. In any case it is surely the ABC of any Christian denomination that we worship God, His Christ and the Holy Spirit. Worshipping a Church organ was idolatry in the extreme.

Therefore, after the Christmas services, 1950, I told the few people at St Paul's that, as from the beginning of the New Year, the main morning Sunday service would be at St Peter's Church, Viña del Mar, in the midst of the majority of the Anglican people. Sparks flew! They complained; they protested; they asked the bishop to remove this unworthy chaplain; but it made no difference. I commenced my new schedule of Divine services.

At St Peter's, a children's service was initiated at a time before the main morning service. Very quickly, interested parents showed their appreciation. An organist offered to play for both the morning services and the congregations began to increase steadily. There was such an opportunity for the children that a Sunday morning coach was chartered and brought them to Viña del Mar regularly, and the children were extremely happy with their Church service. From time to time they put on Bible plays, with great effect, David and Goliath being one in which I played the part of Goliath. The Church was usually filled for these occasions and it seemed that we had won. Necessary funds were coming in very well and the majority of trustees and churchwardens were more than satisfied. And so was I. A chaplaincy had been saved. Finally, when I did say farewell in 1955, the chaplaincy fund was strong and worth the 1992 equivalent of £50 000.

The Director of the Chilean British Institute appointed me to conduct English classes twice a week. This put me in touch with young Chilean people, who were most interesting. Their main reason for learning English was so that they could better understand the British and American films at their cinema!

The president señor of Valparaiso University invited me to his house once a week to converse with him in English; and I found him to be a very learned and charming person seeking ever so eagerly for knowledge and truth. He believed that new knowledge was the key to any good progress and he was always able to show me the latest American brochures and magazines along these lines. He was also quite happy to discuss with me religious philosophy. In due time I was a guest at his daughter's marriage which took place in the house. The service, conducted in dog Latin, began two hours late. Mañnana (tomorrow will do) characterised Chilean life and thinking.

There were several large schools, senior boys and girls, and I was called in to teach Christian knowledge. The standard of behaviour in these schools left much to be desired.

The Scots had their own chaplaincy and church with Chaplain George McLeod as their minister; and he was an excellent pastor and we were good friends.

Inflation continued to be the curse of the country and currency values deteriorated swiftly. At one time the value of the Chilean currency decreased by fifty per cent in two weeks. Always, on receiving my salary, I immediately bought English pounds, American dollars or currency in gold. The chaplaincy trustees, who were shrewd businessmen, kept the chaplaincy funds invested in inflation-proof shares and they did quite well and were safe.

Chile had virtually the world's worst record for child sickness and mortality. Proudly the government resisted the many offers of help from the United Nations. Masses of Chilean people were poverty-stricken, disease-ridden and unemployed; neither were there any free medical or hospital services for anyone. The cost of any private medical attention was prohibitive except for the few wealthy people. Communism was a severe threat.

It was absolutely essential for me to look for and partake in some form of relaxation from my duties. I lived in 'digs' having only my bedsitting room; and I sat with the family for meals. I had no garden. For a stroll I could walk along to the sea front near the Cassino, but that was not nearly sufficient relaxation for me.

However, the countryside of Chile afforded excellent relaxation in full measure and I revelled in country walking and mountaineering. This was always exhilarating, exciting and satisfying. From this point of view Chile is perhaps one of the unique countries in the world.

Chile has no poisonous snakes nor spiders and in the central part of Chile no dangerous wild animals. In the mountains and further south, however, was to be found the Chilean puma or lion. This beast was a cattle stealer, but would not normally attack people. It was wonderful to be free from this anxiety when in the open or mountainous country. I nearly always went off alone and could even lie down and go to sleep in peace and security.

My favourite outing was to climb a mountain called La Campana, 'the Bell Mountain'. It was so called because higher parts of the mountain were, indeed, bell-shaped. The summit was about 9 000 ft above sea level. For such a day out I caught the 6.30 a.m. train which took me to Limache. From here I boarded the country bus which took me quite a distance and then I was ready to commence the walk and climb. Immediately it was delightful to smell the various shrubs and trees and to see the flamboyant blossoms. I carried with me, of course, drinking water and food for the day. However, it was impossible to carry sufficient water because the weather was usually very hot and the distance and height were very considerable. I knew that three quarters of the way up there was refreshing cool water running out of an old disused mine. It was always so delicious and my water container was also very satisfactorily replenished.

Near here, too, was a plaque, permanently mounted on a rock, commemorating the fact that Charles Darwin climbed La Campana more than once. In his memoirs, as Recorder on HMS *Beagle*, he declares that, in his opinion, the vista from the summit of this mountain is easily the finest in the whole world.

Normally I would reach the 9 000 ft summit by about 1 p.m. From this summit, looking eastwards, is the object of Darwin's enthusiasm – the majestic sight of a lifetime. Here the mighty ever-snow-capped Andes mountain range towers some 20 000 ft above sea level. Gazing from left to right the distance must be approaching 1000 miles. In the immediate centre of the range, facing the observer, is the 'queen' peak, Aconcagua, approximately 23 000 ft above sea level. Its summit creates its own storm clouds, always visible. Another massive group, to one side of Aconcagua, is the Leones (Lion) range, so called because the massive upper strata seem to take the form of a crouching lion. The view down below me, which appeared to be green grass, actually consisted of thousands of square miles of palm trees, from which the inhabitants derived a good living by extracting and trading the honey of the palm.

Usually I would recline on this summit while eating my lunch and mentally drink in this unbelievable scenery. I would let my thoughts run where they wished, and occasionally I would ask myself whether I ever had had a weak and undeveloped heart? If so, how was I able to climb so quickly (in three hours) and so often, this 9 000 ft mountain? Often, too, I would talk to God as though he were a Friend by my side. I would ask Him about His amazing world. I did not forget to mention the miseries, evils and sufferings as well, and why we had failed Jesus Christ in failing to bring in the Kingdom of God He had proclaimed and foreshadowed. And I would remember my brothers and sisters, too. Sometimes I would put my head on my rucksack and go to sleep. This kind of a day was bliss.

O Lord my God? When I in awesome wonder
Consider all the works Thy hand hath made.
I see the stars, I hear the mighty thunder,
Thy power throughout the universe displayed.

Then sings my soul, My Saviour God to Thee,
How great Thou art! How great Thou art!
Then sings my soul, My Saviour God to Thee,
How great Thou art! How great Thou art!

On turning one's gaze through 180 degrees one beheld the other half of this vision. It was a vision of the endless expanse of the Pacific Ocean, glimmering with a million flashes of gold, with green foothills down below. Quite often I returned the way I had come, and so was able to watch the ocean sparkling as I made my way down. Occasionally, however, and time permitting, I would circumambulate the mountain on the far side. They were splendid days.

Approximately once a week I would be away somewhere, not always in the mountains, but sometimes along the plains instead, seeing Chilean farmsteads and country hamlets and lanes. I wish I had seen more of these because they looked very fertile. Over the months and years I learned a good deal about the country for miles around.

I was invited by a fishing family to go tunny fishing with them. They went out with long and fairly narrow, almost skiff-like boats, each carrying two or three men. Each boat suspended two fishing rods on either side, but the lines were not let down into the sea until conditions were right. The fishermen had chosen a time when dense shoals of sprats drifted into the area. The boats travelled out about ten miles. They watched, not at first for the fish, but for the sea birds diving for the sprats. Once this evidence was seen by the fishermen they baited their hooks with sweetcorn sheaf, let down the four lines, speeded up the boats' rear engines and skimmed at speed through the bird attacking area. In quick time they were hauling in their lines and at the end of each there was a bonny tuna. The fishermen repeated this exercise until they were satisfied they had a sufficient haul of fish for that day. A very lucrative pursuit, I should think. The fishermen's fat tummies confirmed this.

To the north of Valparaiso was a large whaling station and factory and by the smells one could sense it from even several miles away!

I saw how they worked this industry, cutting up and commercialising these great creatures of the ocean.

The captain of the whaling fleet agreed to take me out and I was instructed to join his ship near midnight. All night long the fleet of vessels sailed and bobbed up and down across the Humbolt cold and deep current. Oh how violently sick I was! It was awful. And when the harpoon guns started to fire I just couldn't care less and stayed in my bunk, wretched. But later, when the vessels had become still, I saw a good deal of what was going on. Each vessel towed a good many of these sea giants back into the whaling station harbour. I did not go awhaling again!

My parish visiting was done mostly by walking. Each house was enclosed by a wall or hedge and inside the perimeter there was the German guard dog; and they were indeed ferocious. Usually, by each gate, was a bell-push which the visitor rang to bring someone out of the house to first secure the dog and then open the gate for admittance. One day, when I was walking to visit the doctor and his wife, who were very keen churchpeople, a German guard dog, free on the path, approached me menacingly with a foaming mouth, and I could see that the dog was rabid. He edged nearer and nearer, his teeth bared and snarling, and I could see he was about to attack. I dared not turn my gaze away from him for even a moment for he was looking for the moment to attack. I knew that if he did attack I would have to fight back and try to strangle him to death in order to save myself. I backed little by little towards the doctor's gate, not daring to take my challenging gaze from the dog. At last I was at the gate and rang the bell. And oh, what a relief it was to be admitted and see the gate shut the rabid dog outside.

Thieving happened to be one of the prevalent crimes in Chile. Mothers would sometimes approach me with regard to their children at the children's church service, asking me to be sure to teach the children the Catechism. The horror of thieving was uppermost in mothers' minds. Thieves would sometimes use long hooked rods and poke them through windows to withdraw some valuable article from within the room.

When King George VI died in 1952, Chile, being both pro-British and having a national characteristic of compassion (*simpatico*), desired to show national grief and sorrow. The Chilean newspapers were full of it. So, too, were the radio announcements. I called on the British Consul General, Alan Price. He agreed with me that there must be a memorial service and he also agreed that it would be on such a scale that St Paul's Church, Valparaiso, would be too small to accommodate the people expected. It was the consul general's influential friend, Mr Kenrick, who came and agreed that he would approach the University of Valparaiso to ask for their permission for us to use their *aula magna* (great hall). This permission was readily and warmly given.

When this decision was announced in public, members of both the Scottish and Anglican churches expressed their horror that such a service could ever be held anywhere but in the sacred St Paul's. In vain did we try to reason with them. They sent a telegram to the bishop, who lived 2000 miles away in Buenos Aires, capital of Argentina. He sent me a telegram instructing me to have the service in St Paul's. The consul general agreed with me that we should keep to our decision for the *aula magna*. Plans were made, and all kinds of societies and organisations were to help with car parking, ushering and guiding in the hall, etc. The Revd George McCleod, of the Scots' Church, agreed to take the prayers, I would present the main structure of the service and the consul general, Alan Price, agreed to give the address. The day of the service arrived and the great hall of the university began to fill. Heads of the Valparaiso Province and of the City of Valparaiso were there in numbers; so were the heads of police and various other services. Before the time of the service the hall was filled to capacity with 1200 people. (St Paul's Church would have seated only 500 people.)

The trained choir of the two churches proceeded on to the large stage followed by the Revd G. McCleod and myself; and with the singing of a hymn the service began. The service sheets had been printed and everyone had a copy. The Chilean Broadcasting Company was broadcasting the service, live, throughout the 2000 miles of Chile. The consul general gave a suitable and excellent address and at the end of the service everyone declared that it had been a most impressive memorial service.

Many people expressed their appreciation and, in particular, leading members of the two churches, who had previously expressed their disapproval, now came forward and made their profuse apologies. It is surely one of God's gifts to His clergy that they should be able to judge and assess situations such as these and then be firm to see the matter through.

During the years I was in Chile I made friends with at least two mountaineering men. One of them was a professor of English at

Valparaiso University, Jack Ewer, and the other was the English manager of the wool factory on the outskirts of Viña del Mar. We planned a major four-day trek to the central range of fairly high mountains. This was to be a summer trek when the snowline would be at 12 000 ft.

We had spent a year or two making several small climbs reconnoitring this region. There were no maps to guide us. We travelled from the capital, Santiago, in a country bus and after some miles were ready to alight from the vehicle and begin the trek. We had, of course, carefully considered what would and would not be required, and were carrying in our rucksacks full provisions, including tent, spirit stoves, sleeping bags, food, etc. We also carried our climbing rope and ice axes. Jack Ewer was an experienced mountaineer and on previous climbs I had found him to be very tough.

We walked the first miles up a long and easy valley with a gushing river running down its middle. Gradually, higher and higher we went until, by evening time, we had reached the first snowline. We camped for the night just beneath it. Very early the next morning, as soon as daylight appeared, we commenced our upward climb through the snows. By mid-morning we were in the midst of fairly deep snows. Vivid blue lagoons were to be seen everywhere. The mountains around us were copper-coloured, striped with the white snow and looking like strange zebras. The light was dazzling white with ultra violet rays. The sky was electric blue with not a sign of cloud to be seen; and the air was blistering hot. For protection our bodies were completely covered either with cloth or with thick cream, and dark goggles were essential. The long distance views were tremendous indeed. Many hours before we arrived we had seen the top shoulder which we were going to cross. It looked so very near, because of the atmospheric clarity, but took us eight hours to reach. Walking through the deep and semi-melting summer snow was very hard going.

From this shoulder, at some 15 000 ft, we felt as if we were on top of the world and were astounded at the mountain vista, structures, and general scenery before our eyes. Huncal peak, 22 000 ft, and its glacier of 12 000 to 22 000 ft, seemed almost near enough for us to touch. This was mountain sight delusion for those mountains were many many miles away.

As the afternoon was waning we pressed on quickly, and now easily, down the other side of the mountains, knowing that by nightfall we would be able to sleep beneath the 12 000 ft snowline. The weekend was approaching, and I knew I must return home in time for the Sunday services. It was agreed that I should forge ahead towards Rio Blanco, the place of the country bus terminus.

I must have walked extremely fast and covered many miles but I could see no trace of water streams at all. Everywhere was dry, burning, blistering summer heat; I was dehydrated, and there was still not a sign of a drop of water. And then, as the shades of darkness began to fall, I suddenly saw it. A small sparkling stream flowed out of the mountain side, making a little pool, about the size of a large wash basin, around which were growing the most perfect wild orchids. How thankful, delighted and relieved I was. I drank from that life-giving stream, and washed in the basin of ice-cool water. I prepared for the night by first making hot soup and eating other food. Then down into my sleeping bag I went, fully clothed, for the frost was now setting in, and I would be sleeping at 10 000 ft. Before going to sleep I prayed that the Lord would keep away the mountain puma.

It was a delightful but still long walk the next day, down to beautiful Rio Blanco (White River), onto the country bus, then the railway, and down to my home in Viña del Mar in time to take Divine services on the morrow. My face was the colour of copper. The people thought I looked well!

I made several high climbs, some in winter and some in summer. One of the highlights of such climbs was the vision of the night sky when preparing for sleep at about 12 000 ft. Imagine being already fully clothed with woollens and a balaclava on the head, and lying snugly in the sleeping bag with one's head on a stone covered with garments, and then looking up into the sky. The sky was one moving mosaic of streaks of light, made by particles of matter constantly striking the earth's atmosphere, and many shooting stars in addition. I wish I had used my camera, with open lens, pointing up at the sky, to recall this fascinating sight.

Another glory of the mountains was the flowers, with many species, I am sure, otherwise rarely seen or known. On one climb, at about 8 000 ft, on rocky ground, were acres upon acres of golden clusters of flowers, somewhat similar to golden crocuses but much larger and more prolific. We sent some specimens of these to the curator of the botanical gardens at Adelaide, South Australia. Growing at about 6 000 ft there was another very robust dark red trumpet-shaped flower on long, straight succulent looking stems about 3 ft in height. I wondered whether these could be poisonous, or very poisonous? They looked as though they could be. Some of my photographs of these flowers are set in the book. I am indebted to Royal Kew botanical experts, who examined my photographs and told me the yellow, crocus-like flowers are *Tropaeolum polyphylum* and the tall bell-shaped red flowers are *Hippeastrum bicolor* (also known as *Physella igneá*).

Sixteen-year-old Mary Hyslop was pretty, attractive, and a physical training teacher – and she was engaged to be married to a young lieutenant of the Chilean navy. She asked if I would be willing to marry them in our St Peter's Church, Viña del Mar. 'But', said Mary, 'there could be difficulties. I am a member of the Anglican Church and my fiancé is from a conservative Roman Catholic family. I expect', she said, 'his family will give permission for him to be married in St Peter's if we go about this matter carefully. One thing will be absolutely necessary – that our marriage service is conducted in the Chilean Spanish language'.

I agreed to this for we had our Anglican marriage service copies printed in Spanish. I rehearsed my Spanish, planned the service and the day of the marriage arrived.

The choir stalls were filled with Chilean Navy officers and their wives. The officers were dressed in their resplendent black uniforms with gold emblazonments. The ladies, in true Chilean fashion, were arrayed in gorgeous black with gold adornments. The Church itself was filled to overflowing and others had to stand outside.

The service appeared to be proceeding well. By arrangement, between the various marriage promises and vows, the organist played a few strains of Bach's 'Jesu, joy of man's desiring'. I happened to take an occasional quick glance at the congregation and was puzzled to see quite a few of the ladies crying! Were they pitying me for my poor Spanish?

At last the service came to an end and in due time I was in the midst of these people at the reception. The Chilean ladies kept coming to me with much affection and declaring that this was the most beautiful Church service they had ever attended. Something had moved them deeply. It was, mainly, that even for their own marriages, their service had been in dog Latin, which they did not understand at all. Now, for the first time, they had heard our beautiful Anglican marriage service in their own Chilean Spanish. They had adored the service.

Why, oh why, had the Roman Catholic Church betrayed Christ

and their congregations and gone against all common sense for over a thousand years by denying people the right to have the Gospel and their services in their own languages? Strangely enough it was not to be long before the Roman Catholic Church did make the appropriate changes. What a price the people had paid for so long!

Colonel and Mrs Parry Jones were good members of the parish. Their elderly father was still with them. So also was their married daughter with her husband, a successful shipping merchant. It seemed that, whereas most people had lost their wealth and fortunes over the nitrates industry collapse, Parry Jones had escaped. Anyway, they were obviously very well-to-do. They spent six months in England and six months in Chile each year. We became very good friends – so much so that, each summer, the colonel invited me to stay with them in their country setting in the Chilean Lake District. The Lakes and rivers were ideal for trout fishing and for the colonel partridge shooting also.

Like most lake districts, the Chilean one was beautiful. The Parry Jones homestead was situated near to Lago Villarica. This was a huge lake reputed to be 1000 ft deep in parts. It was lovely. The weather was warm and sunny, the scenery idyllic, the lake perfect for swimming, fishing and boating. It was teeming with large brown and rainbow trout. A 10 lb fish was quite usual. We caught plenty.

Sometimes I accompanied the colonel on a partridge shooting day. He had three of the best black labradors money could buy. All were highly trained except 'Rough', who, although a big dog, was not yet fully trained nor obedient. I saw his other senior hunter stalk and retrieve a live partridge without any trouble.

One day the colonel was river spinning with a six-fold hook called a kymen. He cast the hook far out into the fast-flowing river. Rough went in and swam towards the kymen and would not come back despite his master's frantic calls. The large dog grabbed the kymen and swam back. The frenzied colonel wondered how ever he would open the dog's powerful jaws, to try to release the hooks. The nearest vet would be several hundred miles away. Rough came out of the river and dropped the kymen at the colonel's feet! The colonel's relief (and that of his wife for she was there) knew no bounds.

Volcan Villarica, 9 640 ft, was in the immediate region. During previous years it had belched forth awesome destruction. This was not so much destruction of human lives, because very few people lived in the area, but of the farmsteads around the volcano. I saw and photographed an apparent huge river bed some 10 ft deep and 100 yards across. It was not, however, a river bed at all, but a lava flow bed from the volcano which had scooped out, within a few hours, this massive channel – a channel which went for miles. The countless tons of rocks, boulders and water were carried by this stream and scattered over a wide area, ruining farmsteads hither and thither.

I decided to try to climb this savage monster which now appeared to be tranquil. With my rucksack on, I set forth and found the lower slopes quite easy and good progress was made up to about 4000 ft. Then ice blocks began to appear and their large shapes had to be circumambulated, which was time-consuming. In addition to the snow and ice, black volcanic dust covered the ground. Higher and higher I climbed and considered everything was going reasonably well. But at 6000 ft climbing conditions worsened. From this altitude the volcano was creating its own very strong wind currents. I kept on, determined to persevere against the elements. However, at around 7500 ft, gale-blown volcanic dust was so thick and strong as to fill my ears, nose and eyes. Also the ice blocks were now huge – up to 100 ft deep – and very difficult to circumambulate, with lesser ice fillings in the gaps. It became impossible to proceed further. Volcan Villarica had won. I bowed to her great might, admitted defeat and returned home. It was very refreshing to wash away the dust from eyes, ears and nose!

On another occasion, and with my friend Jack Ewer, we climbed the central volcanic ranges and this time reached a height of about 12 000 ft. We sat and enjoyed lunch in the middle of a spacious upper valley literally full of steam clouds from hot volcanic course streams. On one side of us was a sulphurous steaming stream and on the other side was a fresh water stream.

The whole Andes range, for thousands of miles, is earthquake- and volcano-prone and sometimes vicious and destructive on an awesome scale. Untold volcanic powers lie within the bowels of all these mountains, perhaps more so than in any other region on earth.

CHAPTER 13
AUSTRALIA ON THE HORIZON

Colonel Parry Jones received air mail copies of *The Times* from Britain. In reading a copy one day I saw an article about the Very Revd Barton Babbage who had been a fellow student of mine in my theological college days at Clifton. The article praised him for his brilliant Church accomplishments so far. He had been the youngest and very successful Dean of Sydney Cathedral. Later he had accepted the invitation to become Principal of Ridley Theological College, Melbourne, but during the past week Barton Babbage had been elected Dean of St Paul's Cathedral, Melbourne. The Cathedral happened to be the largest in the southern hemisphere, seating some 3000 people.

This article about Dean Babbage planted a seed thought in my mind. Shortly my five-year Chilean contract would be coming to an end, and so far I was not sure of my next appointment. Being out here on a limb no one knew anything about me. Would the Australian Church of England be pleased to offer a vocation? I decided to write to the dean for I had known him so well in college. Quite some weeks went by before I received his reply. This said how interested he was to hear from me and, '**yes**, come to Australia. I will be your nominee!'

My future, after Chile, appeared to be directed and I felt so happy. Besides, I was getting on in life and Australia might give me the opportunity to marry and settle down. My goodness, I thought, it is time I did. But I did not know just then what vital and crucial experiences were still to be mine before I left Chile.

Journey to the World's End

I planned and set out for an autumn visit to Patagonia in Southern Chile, an area not so very far from Antarctica. There was now no remaining Anglican chaplaincy down there nor, so far as I knew, any other form of Christian ministry.

Correspondence with the consul stationed there, and the sheep farmers, confirmed that they would be pleased for me to visit them and that they would contribute towards the considerable cost of a journey of some 1500 miles each way. I booked my passage on the Chilean regular shipping service which plied to Punta Arenas in Patagonia. The vessel was to call at Concepcion, Valdivia, Puerto Montt, the Isle of Chiloé and then through 1000 miles of Archipelago to Punta Arenas in Patagonia.

From the commencement of the voyage there was so much to see at every movement of the ship (of some 8000 tons or so). But I had little conversation with the Chileans aboard and neither did I relish the Chilean food. Life within the ship was rather dull. But the scenery and movement outside was wonderful and always changing.

The ship remained for some time at Puerto Montt, affording one time to take walks around. The golden gorse flowers on a hillside were the most blazing and perfect ones I have ever seen; I took colour photographs, of course, and these projections have been admired by many people in many parts of the world.

On our next port of call we anchored outside Castro, the capital harbour of the Island of Chiloé. We watched barge load after barge load of potatoes being loaded on to our ship to be discharged at the end of the voyage at Punta Arenas. It was from this island, which grows potatoes so well, that Drake and others brought some back and introduced them to England and Europe.

I would very much like to have conversed with the islanders, knowing they were the descendents of many European sailors who, being wearied of the hazardous long voyages from Europe, decided to settle here and go to sea no more. Inevitably there would be a fusion of British, Dutch, Spanish, Portuguese, and French blood.

Chiloé is a highly volcanic area and island. This could be one reason for the excellent crops grown there. From time to time parts of the island disappear through violent earthquakes, none being so terrible as the one which happened in the early 1980s, when quite a large part of the island disappeared into the deep Pacific Ocean.

After putting out from Chiloé our vessel cruised towards the mainland and into and through the Archipelago of thousands of islands varying in size, height and scenery. Because of the shelter provided by these islands the waters were always comparatively calm and, presumably, that is why vessels choose this route. Day after day and hour after hour, the ever-changing beautiful scenery was breath-taking. I took many coloured transparencies. It was also thought-provoking to know that no one lived on these beautiful islands. There were, I was told, only some Indians who lived in boats. As we advanced ever further south the waters became increasingly turquoise in colour due to the influence of glaciers and snows.

The English Narrows call for some comment. Discovered by British seagoing reconnaissance, they provide the only and narrow way through the Archipelago at this area. The Narrows call for the most exacting and precise navigation. The passengers of our ship watched with bated breath as, at one time, it looked as though the vessel was about to strike the steep rock face and then, swiftly and suddenly, the vessel was manoeuvred through ninety degrees, and then through the straights. At one stage it would have been possible to have thrown a stone on to the rock faces from either side of the ship. And we were safely through. In general, as far as I could judge, the ship proceeded by night as well as by day, probably due to the excellence of the radar, even in those days.

We cruised into the notorious Straits of Magellan, also with our first sights of the Island of Tierra del Fuego (the land of fire) to starboard.

Until fairly recent times Tierra del Fuego was inhabited almost entirely by natives peculiar to that Island. These natives were remarkable. Charles Darwin's description of them was later proved to be erroneous. He considered them to be almost sub-human savages. This was completely untrue; they were, on the one hand, some of the fittest and hardiest people possible. They wore practically no clothes and were hardened to all weathers including Antarctic severe winters. Whereas Charles Darwin considered their utterances were similar to dogs they actually communicated by a language rich in word imagery and descriptiveness. For instance, they had a number of different words relating to different kinds of seashores or beaches, even richer than Anglo-Saxon words. They also practised splendid moral codes.

But very suddenly awful tragedy struck this race of people. Argentinian Christians decided that they should offer greater care for these Indians. Part of their well-intended goodness was to send quantities of clothes (including woollens of course) so that these natives might be warmer and more comfortable. The garments contained measles germs which, in the shortest possible time, wiped out some eighty-five per cent of the population of Tierra del Fuego. How sad it is in life when the best intentions can carry, in this way, the greatest dangers.

After another day's voyage we docked at Punta Arenas. This is the southernmost town (or city) in the world, being some 400 miles further south than the southernmost New Zealand town, Invercargill. Until the opening of the Panama Canal in 1912 Punta Arenas was a flourishing port, harbour and city. For here came a continuous flow of merchant vessels, exhausted after their long voyages, especially across the South Atlantic, and eagerly taking on precious victuals. How Punta Arenas obtained these stores would make an interesting story in itself, for the area all around the town appeared to be storm-ridden or bleak country indeed. But the town had obviously been prosperous. There was proof of this in some of her elegantly marbled old banks, and public buildings and clubs which remain to this day.

I took services in her churches, and baptized infants. I gave to members who assembled in their clubs talks of recent British Eastern history.

Then I was taken away into the country to live for a few days at a time on sheep farms. A 40 000 acre farm was a small-sized farm for this Patagonia area. The sheep farms were wonderful because their homesteads were spacious, well-equipped and supplied with the most up-to-date facilities. This compensated, I suppose, for the sheep manager's otherwise lonely and restricted life.

I was taken to spend a few days on what was claimed to be the largest sheep farm in the world: 600 000 acres, raising 300 000 sheep, or one sheep for every two acres. The manager of this vast farm was an Englishman; and his wife, also English, had been a boarder at my mother's school, Queenswood, Hatfield, Hertfordshire.

'Would you like fresh trout for breakfast?' asked my manager host.

'Yes, please.'

'Why, then, Edgar, go out and catch them!'

He handed me a fly rod, took me outside, and there, about twenty yards away from the house, was a freshly flowing vigorous stream. To my surprise and delight I caught half a dozen fresh and fine trout in no time and we enjoyed them for breakfast.

I was shown the extensive, modern and fully-equipped station storehouses, sheep sheds, electric power generating stations and water pumps. There seemed to be no end to them. This had to be, for each of those sheep farms was isolated (except by telephone) by snow for six months of the year. They were forced to be completely independent in all manner of living. Theirs was a strange and rare type of life, indeed. The farm managers of the area came from England, Australia, Scotland, Wales and New Zealand.

My host took me in his Land Rover one day and drove me many miles on his huge estate; eventually we arrived at the great and beautiful lighthouse on the shore of the entrance to the Magellan Straights. To the left was the South Antarctic Ocean.

'It was here, on this spot', said my host, that 400 years ago, Magellan finally confirmed that the world was indeed round.'

Two of his flotilla had been instructed to reconnoitre the extent of the Magellan straights. After some weeks they returned and as they raced past this spot they shouted to the waiting Flagship, with Magellan on board, 'We have found the Pacific, the world is round, the world is round!'. That discovery foreshadowed, perhaps more than any other event, the geographical wonder of our world, and prepared the way for untold and unlimited progress in the future. But oh, as I stood there seeing and hearing my host's description, the raging gale, always blowing there, nearly froze me and how glad I was to jump back into the Land Rover. I have a photograph of the lighthouse and myself, in this gale, as I pointed to the lighthouse and historic spot.

His sheep station had eighty shepherds, scattered and living all over the 600 000 acres. In winter time, when the snows were deep and the storms raged, each shepherd moves around, looking for stranded sheep and seeking to rescue, feed and tend them as required.

Flamingoes and geese were there, seemingly in their millions. What did they live on? They must have known or they would not have been there.

It was time for me to return to Viñar del Mar – and quickly. The return trip would have to be very much quicker than the boat journey. I boarded a Chilean Airways plane which flew me for about 1000 miles along the Chilean/Argentinian border to the next northerly airport. During the flight, looking down through the plane's window, I saw many lakes some of which must have been at least 200 miles long. All this territory is largely virgin and unknown to this day. The region's severe weather and terrain forbids ordinary human attempts even to explore. The plane's next stop was Santiago, which I did not want, and that is why I disembarked there, while still in the wild part of the southern region. From here there was a rough road connection back to the southern civilised world of the centre of Chile. I hoped to find a truck whose driver might take me aboard for what would have been some days' journey. By this means I hoped to enjoy the rare and almost unknown mountain scenery of this vast area. But I was very fortunate. I spotted a small Chilean Air Force reconnaissance plane. I found the young German/Chileno pilot and asked if there could be any possibility of a plane lift back to civilisation? After telephoning his superior officers the answer was, 'yes'. He would be leaving very soon! He was to make tests of flying distances between a number of emergency Air Force secret defence landing strips along the boundary with Argentine. Would I help him do the timing?

Away we went into the air, flying at about 100 mph and, oh, the wonderful views of this unknown, unadministered, virgin and mountainous region; and what skill the pilot showed as he took the plane along and around the mountain gorges. After a while he took special measures, cleverly manoeuvred the machine, and we taxied and came to a halt in a hole in the mountains. There was a man there who had been expecting the plane and helped refuel. Then we took off again, flying over lakes, rivers, snow-capped mountains and then with scaring twists and turns and dives we were down and landed. For some five hours this programme was repeated. We must be getting nearer civilisation! On the last intermediate stop the air felt warmer, the terrain showed some signs of cultivation and a farmer came forward with a hamper of food. This food was quite delicious and contained some freshly baked homemade farm bread. Within the next hour we circled around a smart-looking town, Llanquihue, on the shores of the vast lake of that name. I had taken photographs from time to time from the plane and now the flight was over. I stayed the night in a very good German-type hostel and the next morning boarded the train for the north. I stopped at Valdivia. At the next stop, Concepción I conducted a harvest festival service in the Church which had on its walls a plaque commemorating the sinking of British warships off her coast during the first world war.

I returned to Viña del Mar and resumed my routine ministry and service. Little did I think that, in this insignificant land of Chile, I was about to see the most revolutionary event of my ministerial and theological life.

CHAPTER 14
JESUS CHRIST AT WORK

Someone told me there was a special healing mission taking place and that the whole area was excited about healing miracles as a result. I had heard about previous similar Missions and I decided to attend one of these meetings. I cannot remember just by what means of transport I reached the Mission area which was in the country between Valparaiso and Viña del Mar. It was a lovely evening with a warm cosy air. I found a large crowd. In front of the crowd area had been erected a very large wood dais or platform. On it were a lot of men and to my astonishment some were evangelical pastors. I had not known there were such people. And then, as he stood up to begin to conduct the service, I had my first glimpse of **Pastor T. L. Osborn**.

I noted that he was fairly young, had a good, normal slim figure, possessed a thick crop of jet black glossy hair, a fine bone structured face with a firm and decisive look. If he was going to control and influence this large crowd of about 100 000 people then, I thought, he could be no fool. Behind him, sitting on the platform, was a young and smartly dressed young woman, his wife, with their two young children of about ten to twelve years of age. Pastor Osborn had beside him an interpreter who was completely fluent and translated the pastor's words without a moment's hesitation.

Pastor Osborn gave his address. It was about one of the miracles of Jesus Christ, such as we observe regularly in our Anglican services. So far so good, I thought. He preached well and effectively. But so could many preachers and so could I, were my thoughts. But then I had to be fair; this pastor was dealing with 100 000 people. I had never done anything like that. He was certainly one up on me there. There was a beautiful Christlike atmosphere on this warm and lovely evening with the birds singing and the great crowd listening eagerly to every word of the service. It was a New Testament scene all over again. I could see only one policeman away at the back of the crowd. Peace was everywhere.

I noted that he did not wear a clerical collar. I mentally agreed that such did not necessarily confer Christian ability, so there was really no great difficulty for me in that respect.

As I've mentioned, he was speaking with the aid of an interpreter. I could see something important here. He had come out from his home country as fresh as a daisy and had begun to evangelise effectively immediately. He had wasted no time and money in learning the language. He would be able to apply his preaching immediately in this way to any country and any language. I compared this with the normal procedure for typical missionaries who had to spend much time and money on years of training and years of language learning before they could become effective. This was for me a very striking thought.

Perhaps I did not realise just then to what extent this meeting was going to have an effect on the rest of my life, giving me no peace with some of the theology and practices I had so far been taught.

But then came the explosive theology which, at a stroke, was to change a large section of my thinking. For T. L. Osborn went on to say, '**The miracle of healing which I have preached about is about to happen now with you people before me.**' He went on to quote the words of Jesus, ' "Greater works than these shall ye do because I go unto my Father".' After all, I reckoned, there is no denying that statement. He is very sure about this, with no sign of weakness nor apology. Yet, I said to myself, very good theological teachers were always quite sure that Christian miracles ended with the Apostles.

Then the time of healing arrived. T. L. Osborn asked for sick people to be helped on to the platform. There was a blind woman. The pastor asked for witnesses and these testified to her blindness. Then, in the Name of Jesus, he prayed for her healing. He then held his fingers before her eyes and asked the woman to say how many fingers he was showing. She answered correctly every time! The people were amazed and thrilled.

I still thought there was some weakness or deception. Then a cripple was healed without a doubt. Other healings took place, I suppose about twelve. Then T. L. Osborn said he could not possibly deal with so many people individually. He asked them to place their hands on their bodies just where there was pain or discomfort and, as they did so, he prayed for the Lord's healing. No one will ever know just how many received healing.

But one thing was abundantly clear. It was that from this pastor flowed the most profound compassion I had ever known.

At this time it became common knowledge that open air services were taking place in almost every village and hamlet in Chile. Even the Roman Catholic priests were being converted to this new out-pouring of the Christian way of life and were publicly testifying to the new light and joy they were receiving. I was able to take a photograph of one young and very gracious priest as he made his public witness through the microphone.

Also it was made known at that time that the Roman Catholic Church found it difficult to find sufficient clergy to fulfil their parochial requirements. The Roman Catholic Church, also at this time, as previously stated, surprised the world, especially the ecclesiastical world, by ordering all services to be held in the vernacular of the congregations.

At the end of the Osborn service I managed a short interview with the pastor. He was gracious and totally unassuming. I do not remember a word of our conversation except that he hoped to go to Indonesia for his next Healing Mission and that he would write to me from there. He did.

It must have been during the next day or two that T. L. travelled with his wife to Santiago. He was to describe in his book, *Java Harvest*, the events which ensued:

'**The Lord Alone Did Lead** . . . It was a miracle . . . the way we went to Java! We were in South America. Our campaign in Paraguay had been closed by the president after we had spent almost all we had. We had gone to Chile and had begun a mighty campaign there. For over two years Indonesia had been on our hearts. One day as we walked down a street in Santiago de Chile, we passed a steamship company office. The Lord impressed me! "This is the time. Go in there and book your passage to Java".

'We had no money . . . not even enough to get home. It seemed foolish to book a passage at such a time, but I knew that obedience was the secret in a life of faith. I nudged my wife and said, "Honey, we're going in here to book our passage to Java! Are you ready to go?" She beamed with delight. It was a dream coming true.

'Our inquiry revealed that one boat was sailing the month we wanted to leave. Only one cabin with accommodation for four was left unreserved! The Lord said to me: "That's your room. Book it!".

'I said: "Reserve that cabin for us. We will take it." The agent informed: "Upon confirmation of this booking from the Buenos

Aires Office, be prepared to purchase your tickets. that will be in about three days."

' "How much will it cost?".

'He figured the fares. "About 2380 US dollars, sir."

The most unusual feeling swept over my soul. The Lord seemed so near. I knew He was guiding each step of the way.

' "Request the reservations. Write up the tickets, and I will be back in three days to pay the fares!" I affirmed. And as we walked out of the door, we could hardly keep from shouting. Two days later a letter arrived from South India. A Canadian Missionary in that far away country had been praying. God spoke to her to send T. L. Osborn and his wife $2400 immediately and urge them to come to the Orient for evangelistic and healing campaigns. The cheque was enclosed! Praise the Lord! On the third day, we returned to the steamship company; a cable confirming our passage was there, the tickets were written and waiting. We paid the passage and boarded the SS *Tegelbert* in Buenos Aires, Argentina, on schedule . . . The Lord alone did lead . . . (Deut. 32:12)'

Obviously T. L. Osborn was in the centre of the influence of the Spirit of God, being by God motivated and inspired positively to act in such a way of daring faith.

For the last forty years I have kept in touch with T. L. and his mighty work. I prayed at that time that God would send this fullness of Gospel blessing and healing into the hearts of the clergy of the Church of England. God had already begun to do just that.

On New Year's Eve 1953/54 a terrible and tragic fire occurred in Valparaiso. The Chileans always celebrate New Year's Eve in a fairly big way, especially by setting off fireworks.

An exploding firework landed on a Valparaiso warehouse and started a blaze. The blaze was such that nearly all the town's fire engines mustered to fight it. Valparaiso's fire brigades were made up of fire-fighting units individually promoted and maintained by the various major national communities living there: British, French, Dutch, German, Spanish and Chilean. Each service could count on the strongest and best of the men in its national community.

On this New Year's Eve they were all there, some fifty or more firemen and at last they had brought the fire under control. None of them knew just then that within that warehouse were large dumps of sawdust, and near the sawdust were stored many oxygen cylinders and near these cylinders was stored a large quantity of dynamite intended for mining purposes. Suddenly everything blew up like a terrible and mighty inferno – a mixture of exploding dynamite, oxygen and sawdust. The inferno enveloped the firemen and thirty five of them were blown into eternity. Great was Chile's grief and mourning.

In 1954 the chaplaincy trustees and I were very much exercised over the problem of St Paul's Church building. As previously explained, the main Sunday services were held at St Peter's Church, Viña del Mar, in the midst of the churchgoing people. There could not have been more than about six churchgoing people in the vicinity of St Paul's Church. What, therefore was to be done with that large major building – a building hardly used yet costly to maintain? In due time, and after much thought, we decided to sell the Church. The legal conditions were put in motion, the sale was publicised and the Roman Catholic Church offered to buy. But then adverse things began to happen, chiefly due to great delays. Because of intense inflation our sale price had now been nearly halved. It was clear we were going to lose the historic Church and lose its reasonable money value also. And we were conscious it contained the largest and best organ in South America. Was it possible to retrieve the Church from sale? Yes it was; we found a legal way out. The sale notices had not been made according to constitutional requirements and we were saved. The sale was cancelled. Not in my days there, but since then, abundant use has been found for an unfolding and developing evangelical churchgoing community of Chilean Christians. My successor but one, now the Rt Revd David Pytches, was consecrated Bishop of Chile, Bolivia and Peru in that very St Paul's Church, in 1970.

My time and ministry in Chile came to an end. The chaplaincy had been saved from the danger of termination and I left it financially stronger. Many people had now taken it to heart and valued its ministry. I had found good friends. Above all I had met T. L. Osborn and observed his way of ministry. From his ministry I saw that **application of the gospel** was the essential way of producing fruitfulness for God and His humanity. I was beginning to see that all other aspects of theology could be a waste of time or even counterproductive. My life, especially theologically, would never be the same again, and the implications would be prodding me in the future.

I felt assured that Providence had intended me to witness the glorious fruitful ministry of T. L. I shall be for ever grateful to the Lord.

CHAPTER 15
RETURN TO ENGLAND, 1955

After the chaplaincy Easter Day services had been completed, and following painful and drawn-out Chilean emigrating permissions, I stepped aboard an Al Italia Airlines plane for the return flight to England. The route took me, once again, over the Andes, which was wonderful, Buenos Aires, Montevideo, São Paulo, Rio de Janeiro and Recife, then across the South Atlantic to Tenerife, Lisbon, Rome and London. What a long and thrilling flight it was!

I visited my theological college at Clifton. My special reason was to tell staff and students of how Christ and His Gospel were being so eagerly and widely received throughout the Latin Americas, how great numbers of people were being miraculously healed, how communism was being rejected, and how good were the prospects for evangelism.

Students were very interested but the college staff just did not want to know and intimated that I was giving theological news which was contrary to the college's theological structure. The need to show great compassion for Chile's disease-stricken and poverty-stricken masses did not appear to register or greatly matter. Good orthodox theology took precedence. It was still, as when I had studied at college some years before, standard theological teaching that Christian miracles ended with the period of the Apostles.

All this was deeply disturbing. In this way it appeared that my mind was going to be greatly agitated for the rest of my life.

I had always loved simple good church music and noted, and seized the opportunity to attend, a Royal School of Church Music instructional course at their headquarters, Abingdon Palace. In this delightful building, with beautiful surrounding parkland, I spent a profitable week. The various music experts and exponents there knew me only as one of the fifty ordinands who were taking this course and treated me accordingly. I liked that and was amused.

Throughout the course we enjoyed beautifully rendered and varied services, and received special lectures on various aspects of Church music. I noted, with great satisfaction, the basic, down-to-earth common sense recommendations. For example, we were instructed that it is sometimes advisable to say, rather than sing, services and psalms in order to let people know it is the words and message which are more important than the music adornment. Good stuff, I thought.

One morning an ugly situation arose. Those of us being instructed stood around one of the large rooms. We were to be tested, and checked, on the reading of a Collect. The idea was that such a reading should be with a natural, clear and expressive voice. One ordinand read his collect with what was obviously a hopeless parsonical sing-song voice. Obviously his theological college had been at fault in allowing his voice to go uncorrected. The instructor, who was precentor of one of our major cathedrals, trounced the ordinand mercilessly. He told him how terribly wrong his reading had been and how dare he go forward into the ministry with such a voice as that. More followed. I was furious, not with the ordinand, but with what I considered to be the proud, thoughtless, and merciless precentor. Of the two, I considered he was easily the more guilty of misdemeanour. I intended to go to the director of music and complain about his manner. I hesitated, and in the end did nothing, which I have regretted.

CHAPTER 16
TO AUSTRALIA

Once more the time had come for me to face another unknown future in Australia. Once more I said farewell to all my brothers and sisters, whom I thought the world of. I travelled to Liverpool Street Station, London, and from there took the train to London Docks. There, the huge P & O oceangoing liner *Himalaya* was about to sail the long voyage to the antipodes.

It is strange how, at our English ports, visitors are not allowed on the ship prior to its departure. They have to stand, sometimes for hours, just shouting out to their friends on board or waving to them over and over again. The ship sailed away.

Sometimes, as I lay down in my bunk and heard the throb of the ship's engines leading us remorselessly away from England, there were deep and sad feelings in my heart regarding the members of my family I was leaving. This had been my experience four times already.

We sailed the normal and usual way via the Suez Canal and Ceylon, and eventually docked in Melbourne Harbour a few days before Christmas, in the height of the Australian summer. Dean Barton Babbage came on board to find me. One would never have recognised him as dean of the largest cathedral in the southern hemisphere. To cope with the heat he was dressed in open-neck shirt with rather tight shorts – tight because he had such a huge frame! Could anything have been more different from the English ecclesiastical and academic sober college clergy of England, never to be seen in the college precincts without academic gowns and mortarboards and never to be seen without full clerical dress anywhere else? Yes, this was an entirely different world.

After I had passed through customs, Dean Babbage drove me away for about ten miles to a Melbourne suburb named Parkville, and so to his Ridley Theological College and to his principal's house.

One of the first things I noted, from the sound of the animals, was the proximity of the Melbourne Zoo! It was just across the road.

From this point of view it was like being close to the theological college at Bristol, England.

Everything was very hot, new and strange. The theological college was closed for the long summer recess and so I saw nothing of students or staff. During the next day or two the dean took me with him to several official functions. I was amidst crowds and strangers and clergy of this Church diocese. Christmas Eve Holy Communion took place in the great cathedral and I was guided to my seat near the front. The dean's wife sat on one side of me and an Aborigine Christian on the other. There was a large and strongly voiced choir and a large congregation.

Before New Year's Day, Dorothy Esther Redgrave, on holiday from New Zealand, was staying as guest of the principal and Mrs Babbage. I was asked to escort her to the New Year's Eve Outdoor Show, in a public park, not far from the city centre, with a view to returning to the cathedral for the midnight service which demanded my presence. It was, of course, mid-summer. The whole area thronged with masses of people. Outside the cathedral, in the heart of the city, was what is claimed to be the busiest street crossing in the world, with a million people crossing every normal day. The traffic control at this spot always needed police, traffic lights and mounted police.

It is a punishable offence for any pedestrian to cross against the lights or police signal. Dorothy Esther Redgrave stepped into the crossing path at the wrong signal and I was forced to follow to rescue her. Oh! The language of those Australian police and in front of the great crowd of people!

After the cathedral service we walked back to the college together. Dorothy Redgrave insisted in taking her shoes off and walking barefoot. Neither of us realised then that some ten years later we were to be married! And it was only after another thirty years that it was discovered that Dorothy Esther had always had defective eyesight. Possibly she had not even seen whether the traffic lights were green or red.

Soon the dean somewhat mystified me by saying that he had had trouble with the archbishop and that he could not just yet introduce me! I would have liked to have asked him, 'What trouble?' but knew this question would have been out of place.

Then the dean told me that his precentor, the Revd Hugh Girvan, was about to leave for his sabbatical to England and he would like me to be the acting precentor in his place. After a very brief voice test, which satisfied the dean immediately, I became precentor, commencing this ministry straight away.

This precentor's ministry consisted of precenting for the main Sunday morning prayer and evensongs and for any other special services during the weekdays, to take the daily 7 a.m. morning prayer and Holy Communion services with the litany said on Wednesdays and Fridays and to visit members of the cathedral congregation, wherever they lived in the Melbourne area. This area, I found, was forty miles across; travelling in Melbourne was very costly and practically all my monthly salary was spent in this way!

When the new college term commenced the dean asked me to give the lay students evening lectures on the New Testament epistles. I liked this very much and thought that the students were typically English and delightful in manner. I enjoyed the cathedral services and in addition to precenting took a pleasure in singing either tenor or bass with the choir. The large choir sang with very considerable volume indeed. I suppose this was necessary if they were to be effective in that large building designed to seat up to 3000 people. As far as I can remember there was no amplifying system so the natural voices had to be strong.

The dean was a dynamic person and preacher and his outspoken sermons were quoted, almost weekly, by the press. His midweek services, too, provoked considerable response. In addition to the dean's ministry, outstanding people from different parts of the world, came and preached at the cathedral. One morning Lord Mountbatten read the Lesson at morning prayer in the presence of a large congregation! I remembered him, of course, from New Delhi days when he came to that last Easter Day service as the last Viceroy of India.

So far the archbishop had not spoken to me nor acknowledged my presence. At the services he must have noted my presence as precentor as the choir and clergy processed in and out of the cathedral. I thought how strange things were! Neither did he appear to speak to the dean.

Early in the year, at the commencement of the new college term, the archbishop came to the college for the annual Founders' Day and to present the academic honours. I watched him in this ceremony and noted him particularly as he handed out the academic honours to Frank Anderson. Frank Anderson had previously graduated from the University of Queensland with a B.Sc. in chemistry. His thesis had been largely in Russian from Russian scientists. Later he became senior demonstrator in science, Melbourne University. It was during this time that, being a committed Christian, like his wife who was a doctor, he approached Principal Barton Babbage, saying that he felt drawn towards the C of E ministry. The Principal arranged that Frank should adopt a dual role in the college. He should study for himself the Australian College of Divinity course and secondly he should teach the students the same subjects, being a few lessons ahead of them.

The results were remarkable. In one academic year Frank Andersen passed in fourteen papers with an average of over ninety per cent successes in each paper; he received the Australian College of Divinity citation, 'The most brilliant scholar ever to have been enrolled in the Australian College of Divinity'. He received every possible honour and award. He was awarded research scholarships to either Oxford, Cambridge or the leading colleges in the USA. Six months afterwards he had completed, by correspondence, his London B.D. His subjects had included of course, Hebrew and Greek. I was fortunate to be given some of his typed lectures in Old Testament. They were impeccable and explicit to a degree.

Even after handing him these honours and awards the archbishop **refused to ordain him!** I was informed it was because he was an associate of Dr Babbage.

The vice principal was the Revd Leon Morris: the archbishop of Melbourne **would not license him to a Melbourne parish**!

When these facts were made known to me I wept and wondered what kind of ecclesiastical world I had come to? Unfortunately worse was to come.

One evening Frank Anderson and I were walking back to Parkville after a cathedral service. 'Tell me, Frank,' I said to him, 'what exactly is going on between Dr Babbage and the Archbishop?'

'Oh, don't you know,' said Frank, 'when Dr Babbage was appointed principal of Ridley College and began appointing members of his staff for lecturing, the archbishop stepped in, claiming that it was the prerogative of the archbishop to appoint lecturers to the college. Dr Babbage could not accept this, the matter was taken to court and Dr Babbage was given a decision completely in his favour. Following this decision the archbishop would not speak to his dean and principal of college, neither would he award any diocesan faculty or diocesan position to any person who was nominated in any way by Dr Babbage, no matter how able, scholarly or justified they were. I was shocked. But even worse was to come for me.

The Revd Hugh Girvan was shortly due to return to his precentor's role. Something now must take shape for my future ministry. The archbishop at last requested me to meet him in his cathedral office. Without a smile, and without asking me a word about my previous experiences, he curtly said, 'I have nothing to offer you in this diocese, you had better return to England.'

I was shattered! Having come all this way to offer the Australian Church the fruits of my previous hard labours, and to face this, once again, *I was flat on my back.*

Once more I had nothing left, not even any respect for church leadership. The situation was cold, cruel and repulsive. Once more I had only God and His Christ for my solace. Why had God not helped me? I would now book my passage and return to England, I had no alternative.

I received a letter. It was from the Bishop of Grafton (I did not even know where this diocese was) inviting me to see him regarding a possible appointment. Although it was a kind letter I replied that I was now booking my return passage to England realising that the Australian Church was in no need of outside clergy. The bishop sent a further letter asking that, at least, I would be willing to meet him and could this be at Church House, Sydney, before I finally booked my passage to England. I could not refuse, I thought, and agreed to meet Bishop Clements.

I kept the appointment and at first could not recognise anyone like a bishop at the entrance to Church House. But, yes, it was Bishop Clements. He was warm, smiling, asking me questions; kindness beamed from him. 'Come,' he said, 'we will sail along the beautiful Sydney harbour to Manly and have lunch there and talk on the way.' After the delightful cruise through that beautiful and world-famous water inlet the bishop took me into a fish and chip restaurant at Manly, on the sea front, and paid for the lunch. On the way there and back I took into consideration all the pros and cons of his proposal. He had a group of parishes in his diocese which were now hoping for an evangelical incumbent. The parishioners were basically from Northern Ireland, keenly protestant and evangelical. He thought I would fit this role very well indeed. The bishop's appeal sank in, I fell in love with this bishop, I accepted, cancelled my plans for a return to England, bought a motor vehicle and prepared for my journey to Grafton, 200 miles south of the Queensland Border.

I said farewell to Principal Babbage and his staff and left for a new life in still unknown Australia.

Six months later the Most Revd Frank Woods was elected and consecrated Archbishop of Melbourne. In very quick time he righted the wrongs which I have mentioned. By this time Frank Andersen was studying in the USA with Professor Albright. The Archbishop of Melbourne caused him to be immediately ordained by letters dimissory.

It was another long car journey to Grafton, where the bishop lived in his pleasant bungalow. I stayed for about twenty-four hours, being briefed by the bishop concerning my new ministry. During our talks, and because he was interested in my previous ministries, I mentioned the miraculous Healing Missions of T. L. Osborn. The Bishop simply could not understand nor believe that body tissues could be renewed in this way. I once more realised that some spiritual knowledge or belief was absent from Anglican theology and practice. How fortunate I had been in seeing those miracles in Chile. Obviously the impact of the Gospel in this way would be most important for the life and wholesomeness of humanity. I would not let the matter drop from my mind. I made another mental note.

I left the bishop's house to journey to my new Australian home and parish, full of new excitement, and anticipation. Soon I would be entering my own house, meeting parishioners, organising and loving the parish and people – and perhaps there would be a garden to tend. The sense of freedom and church appointment spurred me on. Freedom! Once again to be in control, like a conductor conducting his orchestra. New life was resurging in my soul. Oh, what a wonderful feeling! 'Whose service is perfect freedom!'

The country I was passing through was good beyond words; there were forests, miles and miles of grazing lands, rivers, open spaces and a lovely climate, albeit perhaps a little on the hot side. I was approaching the area which was to be my home.

At last there it was, in front of me, at the bend in the country farm road and just up and on a hillock, my rectory. I pulled up on the grass between the rectory garden gate and the Church on my right hand side. All structures in this region were made of timber only. I opened the rectory door and entered. It was quite a spacious structure with numerous rooms all now completely empty. The house was built entirely of solid teak from top to bottom. There was a fine teak tree growing in one corner of the front lawn. I looked through the windows to see the spacious garden with flowering shrubs, frangipani and poinsettia. The area was rich in bird life, especially the parrots with their vivid colours of red, purple, blue, and green.

I visited the house of the nearest neighbour and parishioner some 200 yards down the road and found they were happy to allow me to join the family for my meals for the first few days at least. On that first night I slept on the floor. It would certainly take me some time to buy furniture and become domestically organised and so, quite quickly, down to parish work.

The parish was some twenty miles square or 400 square miles. The parishioners were about ninety-five per cent dairy farmers with a few pineapple estates. I soon discovered that practically all the milk was turned into and sold as cream for the butter- and cheese-making factories. The herds of cows were a mixture of Jerseys and Herefords. The grasses were very different from English, having a very thick texture. Snow was never seen in this area. One of their sayings was, 'This is the country which winter forgot.' There were no English type cow shippens, the cattle remaining comfortably outdoors throughout the year.

The main danger was the cattle tick which, unless controlled, was a sure killer. For prevention the Australian government had created an important Tick Control Department which was most strictly administered and woe betide any who broke the rules. All animals were anti-tick dipped once a fortnight. Areas were divided up, the roads being sealed with anti-tick controls like our level crossing gates. All vehicles were held up at the tick gates until the tick officer (like a level crossing officer) examined the vehicle for possibility of any plants, animals, birds, etc. Any such were immediately confiscated. Pet dogs, indeed all dogs had to be checked, morning and night or else they would live very short lives. People, too, had to be careful. Poisonous snakes were prevalent also. Therefore, unlike the friendly earth of Chile, picnics on the grass were mostly out.

There were five main parish centres: Eureka (where I lived), Clunes, Eltham, Pearce's Creek, and Rosebank. Each of these centres had primary schools. There were only three churches: at Eureka, Clunes and Eltham. Area Halls served for Divine services in the other centres. So, on Sundays, there was a busy schedule of services, morning, afternoon and evening.

There was one very good and interesting monthly ecumenical joint service at Pearce's Creek. At the turn of the century the leading immigrant of this area, Mr Jameison (a Presbyterian, who was still very much alive), had built the fine wooden hall at his own expense and made a plan of Church services which all agreed to keep. In turn there were to be, each month, an Anglican, a Methodist, Presby-

Tropaeolum Polyphyllum growing at altitude of 8000 ft on
Los Leones mountains

Gorse at Puerto Mont

Students and staff, B. C. M. & T. College – 1937

Clifton Suspension Bridge

College soccer team 1938 – 39

Nowshera Garrison Church Choir – 1944

Typical Waziristan Country

Sir A. G. Perrott,
Inspector General of Police,
North West Frontier Province

Remembrance Day Service at Ragmark, 1945

All my worldly goods on transfer, 1947

Gulmarg Hill Station Church, 1947

Chaplain's Tribal
Bodyguard – 1947

Lord Louis Mountbatten
taking Salute for the 2nd
Battalion, the Royal Scots
Regiment on Easter Day,
1947

Volcano Villarica and Lava Scoop

St Peter's, Vina del Mar Children's Church – 1953

Cruising through Chilean Archipelago

Magellan Straights Lighthouse

Chilean Air Force plane, pilot, farmer and officer

Pastor T. L. Osborn in action at Valparaiso – 1954

A Chilean R. C. priest testifies to his newly found Christian Joy – 1954

Wedding day

Loading Christmas trees galore for the London Market – 1976

A section of Maendy Christmas trees – 1991

Aconcagua 22 834 ft (photographed from the Huncal Glacier)

terian, Salvation Army and, on the fifth Sunday, Presbyterian service. It was also agreed that all the residents, regardless of denomination, would normally attend the service every Sunday. These services were excellent. On my Sunday, I found a small table suitably covered with pure white linen, ready for my chalice and paten. Candles had never been used, neither did I mind, especially since so many people were originally from Northern Ireland. The hall was well filled with practically every person from this area. And how well they took part in the service! It was perfect worship, I thought.

The annual Harvest Festival displays in the churches were out of this world. Two aspects in particular promoted all the products. First, the perfect climate and secondly all these farms provided all gardeners with garden manure. Fertiliser in this part of the world was unheard of. Every kind and shape of melon, marrow, pumpkin grew easily to perfection. There was an abundance of oranges, lemon, plum, peach, passion fruit, banana, but no crisp English type of apples. The flowers were plentiful and exotic. Great splashes of poinsettia always provided a colourful background. These plants grew almost wild in gardens and up to 10 ft high. All kinds of lilies grew profusely too. You could see them everywhere in their season. The scents of these plus the aroma from the vegetables always filled everyone in Church with a sense of thanksgiving for a very lush and productive region.

I suppose ninety-nine per cent of the populace were Protestants. There was one Roman Catholic family living in Clunes. Knowing that many of the Northern Irish folk still commemorated their Orange days and the Battle of the Boyne, with quite a degree of enthusiasm, the Roman Catholic, who was the only baker in the area, and from whom nearly all bought their bread and pastry, used to jovially boast that he could poison the lot!

Teaching Christian knowledge in the schools of Australia was most rewarding. From the early days of the establishment of Australia an Agreement was drawn up between Church and State concerning the teaching of the Christian Religion in the schools. By this agreement, any minister of a recognised denomination had the right to teach Christianity, as understood by his denomination, for one hour per day, in every school in his parish or prescribed area. There was another important aspect to the Anglican teaching. The Central Board of Australian Anglican control had created graded teaching manuals to be used throughout the length and breadth of the Australian Commonwealth (I still have a set of these splendid manuals). So every Anglican child in Australia was taught the same good lessons in scripture no matter where he or she might be or would be moved to. By this means it would be true to say, I think, that the Australian children were (and are) the best instructed in Christian religious knowledge in the world. My children in these classes used to love being helped to learn the Catechism of the Book of Common Prayer which I had learned in my youth, in the Cheadle Hulme C of E School.

CHAPTER 17
LIFE IN NEW SOUTH WALES

Like any normal person I needed a hobby in order to relax, especially as I was a bachelor, with no family life. With a good deal of spare time I would occasionally spend hours in prayer. Also I was in the habit of fasting for three days or so at a time. I had been in these habits for many years, especially in India where fasting, in that hot climate, made one feel fit and comfortable. Often I looked forward to fasting almost as one looks forward to food.

My rectory garden at Eureka provided some relaxation. The climate and soil would grow things profusely. It was a pleasure, therefore, to enjoy luscious peaches, plums, oranges, lemons and passion fruit from trees which had been planted only last year. In the garden, rock melons grew and ripened quickly. They were delicious. On the large patch of garden I tried dwarf runner beans and to my delight they brought forth their abundant crop in no time at all. I soon grew three crops a year, selling many hundredweight to the greengrocers.

I was also keen on fishing, and Australia provided full opportunities for this although, in this area, only sea and tidal river fishing. Most of my sea fishing took place from the rocks around Byron Bay Lighthouse, the most easterly point of the Australian coast. It was a car journey of forty miles to this spot, a very short distance in Australian terms.

Even the car journey provided one with exciting anticipation. Fish rarely could be expected before 4 o'clock in the afternoon. I would fish from that time until about 11 o'clock p.m., sometimes later. I did not have to report back to my wife! Fishing success from these rock-surrounded bays varied. And so did the weather. Best results were on moonless nights. Rough weather could cause difficulties. Once, at around midnight, a sudden large wave swept me into the sea. I had some difficulty scrambling back up to and on to the barnacle-encrusted rocks, but all was well and I returned home.

One Monday saw my best fishing ever. The day before, after taking the Sunday morning service at Pearce's Creek, I was invited to lunch at a farmstead. During conversation I light-heartedly suggested to the young farmer that, because snapper were around, would he like to come fishing tomorrow? His mother jokingly objected, asking who would do the milking? I said to her, will it be worthwhile if your son brings back sufficient fish to fill your fridge? In the same spirit, she agreed!

We fished for some time in the deep water for snapper and caught none. Then I noticed a man, who had been fishing at my favourite bay, leave with what appeared to be quite a bagful of fish. The three of us went to the pool and immediately saw extra fish activity. A shoal of sprats had come into the bay and, underneath, larger fish were feeding on them. We baited our hooks and almost immediately there were savage strikes. Soon a large fish had run out the whole of my reel, snapped it, and ended my fishing. The other two men, with stronger lines, pulled in fish after fish, some Jewfish and others tailor. We were returning home with their bag filled with fish. So heavy was it, plus the weight of their tackle, that they had to rest several times as they climbed the steep short hill towards their waiting car. I followed and found them half exhausted with carrying fish and gear. The young farmer's mother had far too many fish for her fridge and was glad to share them with neighbours. It then became commonly accepted that anyone wanting good fishing should go with the rector!

At Eureka, not far from the rectory, lived an elderly farmer and his wife. Because of old age infirmity they could no longer leave their home nor come to Church as they used to. When we had become friends, through my visiting, they invited me to come to their home once a week to play a card game with them (I think it was rummy) and, before leaving, enjoy a cup of tea and cake. It would be hard to imagine anyone more English in looks and manner than this dear elderly couple. They were so glad to hear the latest Church news or any other news I might he able to share with them. In ways like this one felt pleased to be in close touch with God's people and members of the Church of England, 12 000 miles from Canterbury.

On most Saturdays, tennis matches, very well organised, were greatly enjoyed by all. Men, women, boys and girls looked very smart dressed in white, glistening in the brilliant Australian sunshine. Sumptuous lunches were enjoyed and, as a result of the vigorous exercise, good health was boosted. Every farmstead had its own abundant, almost unlimited, supply of cream and butter for making cakes.

From the four parishes we built up an attractive and lively church youth club. The members met regularly once a week and for other special occasions. Christian instruction, games and fun all took their part each club evening. At other times trips to the seaside were thoroughly enjoyed. There was sunbathing on the beaches, but no bathing in the sea which was shark infested. Instead, on the other side of a narrow strip of sand, was a large freshwater lake giving full opportunities at all times for as much bathing as desired. From time to time the young people organised parties which were always thoroughly enjoyed. These people lived away in the farming country and the only enjoyment in life was when they made it or organised it themselves. They were a splendid and lively lot and helped to keep me young at heart.

One day one of the farmers told me that a few of them were travelling tomorrow to Brisbane to see the first of the Test Matches versus England. Would I like to join them? I would. I packed my food for the day and, thinking of sitting on some hard seat or the hard grass for hours on end, I packed in my rucksack all the cushions I could, until the rucksack was bulging. I had cushions for some of the other members also.

We arrived at Brisbane cricket ground where we had to walk past a crowded stand holding 10 000 or so Aussie spectators. When they saw me with the bulging rucksack on my back they all roared and shouted, 'Spare us some of your tucker' (tucker being the Australian word for food). Then I was surrounded with photographers who thought this picture would be a very telling one for the occasion. I felt such a fool!

I think it was this match which ended in a terrifically exciting and rare tie, each side having an equal number of runs. The last Australian batsman was bowled out with the last ball of the match. Some people, I heard, died from heart failure.

In 1955 when I came to these four parishes, the Anglican Church in Australia was financially burdened. At top level it was agreed that something radical must be done. A chosen representative was sent to the USA, Great Britain and other countries to study and bring back reports of any successes. A very good report of the USA church was brought back and this included the American way of stewardship of money and of talents. The Australian bishops then united in commending stewardship campaigns to all parishes. Various reasons were given for the necessity for stewardship, and so were details of how to prepare. For example, we were told that the average financial giving to the Church was merely the price of *one cigarette per week* per electoral roll member! This shocked most churchpeople who increasingly began to see the need for stewardship. At last it was put to our four parochial church councils that we must embark. There was considerable debate with some tough opposition. More efforts were made and eventually a stewardship campaign was decided on. Wells Company of the USA were to be the directors. Their system was tough, thorough, somewhat expensive, very directive and educational. A Gestetner duplicator was provided and was regarded as essential, not only for the campaign but for parish use afterwards.

We had been told of the successes of other parishes. What would happen here? When at last the results were known the parishes had quadrupled the Church giving! It was an outstanding success and put heart into all churchgoers.

My relief was great. For I was conscious of what had been going on before in order to raise sufficient money for the parishes to keep going. Unlike the Church in England, which relied on considerable Establishment funds, an Australian parish had to find all the parish costs, including the incumbent's stipend, all travelling costs, all costs of renovating and maintaining church buildings. And as for giving to missionary societies, this was hardly thought of.

In order to raise needed funds, each of the four parishes held about six money-raising functions during the year. Each of the Presbyterian and Methodist parishes did the same. Since churchgoers of different denominations attended one another's functions, it meant attending something like twenty money-raising functions a year. Many cakes had to be made, and there were jumble sales and the sale of vegetables, flowers, products, arts and crafts. A short concert item accompanied each function. The three clergy and others had to be on the platform, crack a joke, make speeches, and offer encouragement and congratulations. How everyone stood up to all this for so long is a mystery. Now a better, more Christian and much more satisfactory way had been found. The Churches, in this sense, were moving forward and breathing much more freely.

Four years had gone by and I had taken no holiday and decided it was high time I did. Where could I go for this holiday? Hardly any Australian places could be so good as the area I lived in. What about my beloved England? That was it. It was so appealing to my mind that the decision was made. I would soon be able to see my own beloved brothers and sisters again! The bishop agreed, I packed my belongings, booked my ticket. At Sydney I embarked on another P & O liner – this one bound for the UK.

CHAPTER 18
A GOOD HOLIDAY.
RETURN TO AUSTRALIA

It was another P & O ship, but the route was to be different. This ship was to travel east, first of all to Auckland, New Zealand. It made a comparatively short stay here, but I did have time to visit the museum and was particularly interested in the Maori section.

The next long voyage – to Hawaii – was truly Pacific, very calm, and peaceful. So we reached the most isolated group of islands in the world and stayed there for some time. I visited a pineapple plantation knowing that Hawaii produced more of them than any other country. The volcanic structure of the land could be one of the reasons for such prolific crops.

The shopkeepers of Hawaii enchanted me. I have never seen or known such courteous people. In whatever shop I entered they were always the same, quite delightful.

The cruise to Vancouver, via Los Angeles was pleasant but uneventful. But from Vancouver the journey on the Pacific Railway was, for me, something new. To begin with there was the long slow haul up the western side of the Rocky Mountains, the railway track leading up to and through what must be some of the finest pine forests in the world. At one spot, where the train came to a halt, I read a notice which pointed out the depth of the river nearby. Here was one of the deepest freshwater rivers in the world. Then the easy coasting down to the beautiful Banff area. I had arranged to leave the train at some of the major mid-Canada cities, look around the cities, towns and environments, then catch the next scheduled train. In this way I planned to travel step-by-step to Quebec. The whole route really demands quite a long time for one to be truly satisfied with some of the splendour of this vast and great grain-producing country.

At Quebec I embarked on one of the modern Cunard Liners.

Though not very big she was lovely in her design both inside and out. The voyage was cold; there were icebergs everywhere it seemed. I wondered just how the ship's navigator could so often and confidently avoid them. I thought of the *Titanic*!

So once more, after years away, I came home to visit my brothers and sisters and their families. My mind had received more impressions of God's amazing world and His amazing people. It had been wonderful, these past four years, to see the extent to which the British Anglo-Saxon race had spread and influenced so much of the world. And how well this influence had brought so many blessings to so many people.

Through the great kindness of my sister, Marian, and her husband and family, their house in Levenshulme, Manchester, became my base. However, I moved around considerably for one reason or another. The theological implications of the modern world were always in my mind. I mentally wrestled with the mysteries. On the whole it seemed that Church life in this dense population of Manchester was not what it ought to be, but was almost dead. Comparatively few people were interested in Church attendance. My sister told me of the impact of a Pentecostal Church which was not far away. I attended several times to find this Church always packed to the doors and the worshippers extremely joyful and thrilled with their adoration of Christ and His Gospel. Christ was alive and working here.

With my brother-in-law and his son, Derek, I went on a number of fishing trips, mostly to Cumberland. They were very happy occasions although we failed to catch many fish. I also spent a good deal of time in North Wales where I caught several 14 lb salmon.

The Bishop of Manchester kindly afforded me some of his precious time to discuss theology and its modern implications. He did not have much regard for modern professors of theology and I was pleased about this.

As the year 1960 was drawing to a close I received an invitation from the Bishop of Vancouver to visit his diocese with a view to receiving an appointment if I wished. I accepted the invitation.

The air route was interesting. I flew from Manchester Airport to Amsterdam. Here I boarded the scheduled flight for Vancouver via the Arctic Circle. My mind reflected on what I had heard so often at 2 a.m. in the early mornings as I lay in my bed at Levenshulme – the sound of an aeroplane flying overhead. I used to wonder where it was going. Now I was on that flight. Truly enough the plane flew over Manchester and, looking down through the window, I could clearly see the main Kingsway, Manchester street lights and other surrounding lights.

We touched down at an airport, half way up the eastern coast of Greenland, in a temperature of about 50°F below freezing. Even for the minute or so of transfer from the plane to a coach it was cruel until we entered the well-heated rest centre. We stayed there, on bunks, for a few hours. The plane had some defect which caused the delay.

The aeroplane then took us across snow-and-ice-bound Baffin Land and then across the frozen Franklin District of Northern Canada, and over the Rocky Mountains, before gliding down to our terminus at Vancouver.

I spent two weeks in the area. During that time the bishop gave me a tour of his diocese. The weather was reasonably mild and pleasant. One Sunday I preached at a bright and enthusiastic service at the People's Church, filled to capacity by committed and eager worshippers. That evening I preached at what was known as The Millionaires' Church. This was a large and robustly built edifice, but there were only a few people present. Evidently the morning services were well attended. At the conclusion of the service I was accompanied to their church hall – and what a hall! It was huge, almost palatial, and served the whole of this wealthy community for all their community activities, Church and otherwise. There were two main levels of structure with full facilities for sports and auditoriums. On one level were built about twenty smaller and fully-equipped rooms for educational and Sunday School activities. I have never ever seen anything to equal this most adequate provision for the community. Their Christian involvement was most evident.

I realised that this area of ministry required clergy who were more or less brought up in the climatic conditions. Months of winter weather necessitated months of central heating. I had, for so long, been used to tropical climes and felt this ought to continue for the time being. So I booked my return flight to London, travelling via San Francisco and Philadelphia.

I had been impressed by what had appeared to me to be a significant round flight. My scientific mind appreciated the progress and modern achievements of aeronautical science. Mine had been merely one flight. But now, I reflected, thousands of air pilots were travelling hourly and daily to all points of the world and thought nothing of it, or, perhaps, were somewhat bored by it. From a travel point of view the world had become a village. Also, I reflected, all this modern travel and international hurry and bustle must have its effect on Church attendance and Christian perception.

God's Holy Spirit was constantly motivating my way of life and way of thinking. Perhaps there was hardly a second when this was not happening to my mind. Many Christians experience this sense of guidance without being able to explain to others just why they make a specific decision.

Communications from my Bishop of Grafton assured me that he would be very pleased for me to return to his diocese. In due time I booked my passage by ocean-going liner. In travels such as this it is usually the weight of the baggage which determines whether air travel is ruled out.

At last I was with the Bishop of Grafton, once more in his house and being briefed for my new ministry. The Bishop said he was sending me to a parish named Dunoon. It was an area alongside my previous parish of Eureka Clunes although my new rectory would be some thirty miles or more from my previous Eureka rectory. 'Dairy farming, pineapple growing, banana plantations and forestry are the occupations of the parishioners,' said the Bishop.

As he gave me more details about the parish of Dunoon the bishop explained that, a few years previously, a cyclone had wrecked the Dunoon Church and that a new church had been erected with the help of a bank loan. The bishop went on to say that the parishioners were finding it hard to raise money for the promised and scheduled return of this loan. 'Please try to help them,' he requested, 'when you arrive there.'

I travelled the 200 miles or so, settled in the rectory and studied my new parish, its peoples and requirements. I found the people, as expected, the good, hard-working and delightful types common to the whole of this area.

The rectory garden was much smaller than the one at Eureka but there were some fully-grown plum trees. The churchwardens told me they produced excellent plums, 'but, look out,' they said, 'or the flying foxes will have them all!' A few weeks later, when the plums were ripening, I followed instructions and suspended electric light bulbs on the branches of the trees. Each night, from darkness to dawn, there was the loud noise of flying foxes swishing as near as they dared to the plum trees but not a plum was taken.

Parish life and activities got under way. I was happy, the people were happy, and the youth club was thriving with quite a number of sons and daughters of the farming community. As usual I loved the services on Sundays, always finding it a great joy to preach the Gospel and its implications for living.

Now came up the subject of raising money for the repayment of the bank loan. 'What can we do?' everyone asked. Amongst other things it was suggested that, for the Christmas season, we might sing carols around the many halls and churches. Everyone was keen. 'Will you help us practise?' they all said. I knew how much I would enjoy this. It was decided, further, that, as from the coming September, the hoped-for choir members would meet in Church every Sunday evening and, instead of attending evensong, learn to sing the carols.

We had no carols sheets and I could only find one or two of my own copies of such publications as the Oxford Book of Carols. We did have one copy of Australian carols.

I had a Gestetner printing machine and a typewriter to cut stencils. There were no such things as photocopiers at that time.

On wax stencils I carefully draughted the music lines, drew the treble and bass clefs . . . and then . . . ? How could I possibly draw the music notes – quavers, semiquavers, crotchets, etc? There was only one answer – type them in! I practised . . . and after a while I began to see that this could be done. But it would take a long time. I thought the expected outcome would be worth the time and I persevered. After this I fitted in the tails and typed the words in between the treble and bass clefs. In due time I had completed, by this method, some eighteen carols, traditional and Australian. I printed on the Gestetner some twenty copies of each. It was a mammoth task!

A greater task lay ahead as some twenty members came for the first practice. These members were dairy farmers, their wives and sons and daughters. They were keen, although none of them had ever been in a choir before. Most of the men did not even know the meaning of tenor nor bass. But they were friendly and willing to learn. There was a harmonium in the church; I had no piano or any other musical instrument except a tuning fork.

Judith, fourteen years of age – a wag of a girl – was to play the harmonium and try to teach the ladies, sopranos and contraltos, to sing their parts. I left my tape recorder on 'record'. I would take the men into the rectory and try to teach them tenor and bass with only my tuning fork to start me off in every case.

That Sunday night I got into bed and switched on my tape recorder to hear how Judith had persevered with her members in the Church. Judith's mother was one of the choristers. The recording was so funny that I rocked with laughter at the manner of that fourteen-year-old girl and the responses and the sounds which came forth. At the end of the recording I wound back the tape to the beginning and listened all over again – and rocked with laughter once more before going to sleep a happy man!

After several Sunday nights it was evident that some progress was being made. Those dairy farmers had good strong voices, tenor or bass, and they continued to persevere. They were keen and this was going to be the reason for success, I felt sure, at the halfway stage.

Then came the first Sunday evening when all were to meet together to try to fit in their parts. At first the noise was awful. But by sheer good will and determination the blending slowly began to take shape – and there were still a few weeks to go. Improvement continued.

One day I went to Lismore to see Archdeacon Robinson. Lismore was an Australian farming city of about 15 000 people. It was some twenty miles from Dunoon. The archdeacon said, 'I hear you have a good choir. Can you help me for our major annual Christmas carol service to be sung outside the Church? My choir,' he said, 'has fizzled out.' He would not be put off by my apologies and excuses. Christmas in these parts, as in the whole of the southern hemisphere, is celebrated in what often turns out to be the hottest time of summer. All the summer flowers are at their best with their delicious scents and aromas. So, once a year at the Christmas season, practically all the inhabitants of Lismore city assembled on the grassy slopes of the Lismore Church, brightly illuminated, and with the Crib, to observe and take part in the carol service.

The Dunoon choir could hardly believe that they had received such an invitation. They were spurred on to greater practise efforts and made further progress. The carol dates were getting nearer. Then came another startling request, this time from the Australian Broadcasting Company for the whole of New South Wales. Would our Dunoon choir sing Christmas carols for them on Christmas morning at breakfast time? Again the Dunoon choir could hardly believe this. They practised even harder. At last the time for the Lismore festival arrived.

On that lovely, warm summer evening the Dunoon choir sang eighteen Christmas carols, unaccompanied and note perfect, with counter parts and descants.

All the people were thrilled; so was the archdeacon; so was I. Three months before, few of the splendid Dunoon choir members knew what choral singing was. They had been magnificent. They had enriched themselves and the whole farming community.

Millions listened to them over the New South Wales Broadcasting network on Christmas morning at breakfast time. The choir also sang at some fifteen country halls. They made a lot of money. Their whole community was enriched and Christ's name had been beautifully honoured.

The Dunoon children's picnic and sports day was due to take place one Saturday. I drove my Austin pickup on to the rough country track which would lead down the rocky hillside to the picnic and sports area in the meadow far below. I did not know it just then but the local area policeman, with children in his car, was following close behind me and was startled to see what suddenly happened to me. The rocky track suddenly snapped off the stub axle of my front near wheel. The wheel veered away and my car slithered towards the 100 ft precipice on my left. With presence of mind I grabbed the hand-brake. The vehicle stopped with the other front wheel just over the edge of the precipice. The car was towed away for repairs. After a week or so it was ready for the road once more.

One evening soon after this I had to make two parochial visits. After the first visit it was dark as I set off to visit the schoolmaster and his wife who lived about three miles away. I drove the car down the long steep hill with no other traffic whatsoever on the road. The car was travelling at a good sprightly speed of perhaps sixty mph. I was nearing the end of the hill with a sharp corner at the bottom and had to brake accordingly. There was no brake there! The brake pedal went straight to the floorboards; the vehicle increased in speed. I was on the sharp corner. The pickup would not take the corner. Over she went, at high speed, and then over and over and down and down and over and over and down and down, perhaps twenty or thirty times, before coming to a halt, upside down and with the engine still running. I switched off the engine. Both doors were bashed in and could not be moved. The large rear window had been smashed away and I was able to crawl through this, beneath the truck, over my head before standing on firm ground. Petrol was pouring out of the upside-down petrol tank. I stood away in case it ignited. My vehicle had become a twisted wreck through hitting rocks and boulders as it crashed down the mountain side. I felt myself, my whole body – face, chest, back, legs, head – and could not find anything wrong! Even my glasses were intact. I had not experienced a moment's anxiety throughout the crash! It was a miracle and I offered a prayer of thanks to God, with not even a scratch nor bruise. But, to use again the words of my introduction; *I was flat on my back.*

But where was I? It was a black, moonless night, I had come downwards and so I started to climb upwards, but it was a long way. Eventually I found myself on the road I had left. I walked back to my rectory, and telephoned the vehicle breakdown centre. They arrived at 11 p.m. with all the necessary equipment and searchlights. It took them all the cables they had to reach the vehicle away down there. As the wrecked car was being dragged up, the foreman, standing beside me, said, 'What happened to the driver?' When I told him I was the driver he could not believe it. He could not believe that the driver of this vehicle could be alive. The car was a tangled wreck and was towed away – a complete write-off. The next morning I continued with my parish work as usual.

I had been ministering for the Parish of Dunoon for about one year when it was suddenly announced that my Bishop Clements, the Bishop of Grafton, had been elected Bishop of Canberra, Goulburn, the Federal Capital of Australia – a distinguished preferment.

Soon I was surprised to receive the bishop's request that I should leave Dunoon, accompany him, and become rector of Adaminaby in the Snowy Mountains. This meant sadness for the parish of Dunoon for there were signs of excellent parish progress. I packed my vehicle once more with all my earthly belongings for a new life and ministry.

CHAPTER 19
THE SNOWY
MOUNTAINS OF
AUSTRALIA

People who have not been there can have no idea how vast is Australia and how long some journeys can be. For example, the distance from east to west in Australia is just about the same distance as from London to the China border! This was to be another long journey of about 1000 miles. Of course I enjoyed it and of course once more I was excited about the new ministry and life about to unfold. The last twenty miles or so found the car burdened with its load as it began to climb 3500 ft into the Snowy Mountains region. And of course I was thrilled to arrive at last outside the Adaminaby rectory. But then I found problems!

The parish churchwardens, believing there would be a long interval before the appointment of their new rector, had let the bungalow to Mr and Mrs Sonnenberg, their two daughters and their large Alsatian dog, Rex! Oh dear! We had to work out a solution and come to terms with this situation. Yes, the family would have to be residents for another three months or so. Somehow they found one available small bedroom for me but most of my packages would have to be stored in the shed or in the Church vestry for the time being. Yes, Mrs Sonnenberg would be pleased to supply my meals for the three months. But oh! that Alsatian! I was frightened and the Alsatian knew it. The Sonnenbergs assured me that he would be friendly, and would I sit next to him on the couch? I was terrified as the Alsatian snarled from time to time. Very few things in life ever frighten me but an Alsatian is one. However, hour by hour and day by day, this animal began to accept me and finally I was as one of the family. I lost all fear, and could approach him and pet him freely.

I tried to take stock of this quite extraordinary parish. It was in the most mountainous region of Australia. It contained some of the largest man-made lakes in the world; there were masses of sheep farms, and large virgin forests; and all over the mountains were engineering works. A few yards from the rectory was Adaminaby Church; for reasons I shall soon give, this was a kind of wonder church and the central tourist attraction. All these facets were going to take time to understand and assimilate.

The Snowy Mountains Hydro Electric Authority was at work all over the region and beyond, implementing a scheme envisaged at the turn of the century but commenced only after the Second World War.

The object was to redirect three Snowy Mountain rivers so that, instead of emptying their precious waters into the sea on the eastern coast, these waters would flow through tunnels in the mountains, making electricity en route, before flowing into western areas of hitherto arid country, and creating more than 3000 new fertile fruit farms.

Income from the generation of bulk electricity alone would pay for the whole of the project in approximately twenty years. Ever after there would be, for the government, huge annual returns of income and profit tax from the 3500 wealthy farms. Food supplies and employment would have been significantly increased.

From revenues received from the sale of generated electricity the Snowy Scheme was to meet all costs including the payment of interest on borrowed capital, repayment of capital and all operational, constructional and maintenance costs.

It was to have an installed capacity output of 2½ million kilowatts. The annual value of energy produced was to be over 5000 million kilowatt hours each year and would be worth approximately £270 000 000 (by 1990s prices). Irrigation of farms was to benefit by 2 000 000 acre feet of water. This would increase the value of primary production by some £325 000 000 (again by 1990s prices), providing much food for the nation and creating considerable employment.

Flora and fauna stood high in the provisions of the Scheme. There were to be animal and bird reserves, parks and gardens, and miles of roads through some of the finest mountain scenery in Australia.

The area had become recognised as the 'playground' of Australia, attracting great numbers of tourists. Much of the profits from this enterprise would enhance the National budget.

The scheme was a very large one, embracing nearly 3000 square miles of mountainous country. It involved the construction of nine major and many smaller dams, approximately one hundred miles of tunnels and ten power stations, some of these over 1000 ft beneath the ground surface. There were to be over eighty miles of aqueducts high up in the mountain ranges to catch the mountain streams which would otherwise miss the reservoirs and tunnels.

The Snowy Scheme involved many specialists in geology, surveying, hydrology, town design, all branches of engineering, rock boring, soil conservation and general science. The Scheme was to be a country within a country.

It was wonderful to contemplate that all this newly created wealth, power, riches and growth was to come merely from the harnessing of two mountain rivers and the mountain snow which hitherto had run to waste. What a lesson! What else remains to be harnessed for the good of mankind?

It was the prevailing storms over the Snowy Mountains which were the essence of this Snowy Scheme. The storms created the rivers which made the scheme possible.

O ye showers and dew, bless ye the Lord.
O ye dews and frosts, bless ye the Lord.
O ye frost and cold, bless ye the Lord.
O ye ice and snow, bless ye the Lord.
O ye lightnings and clouds, bless ye the Lord.
O ye mountains and hills, bless ye the Lord.
O ye Snowy Mountains, bless ye the Lord.
O ye children of men, bless ye the Lord.
Praise Him and magnify him for ever.

The whole of the affected region was to be under the control of a commissioner who would hold significant powers similar to those of a prime minister. World specialists would be employed in order to carry out this great and costly scheme. Some 250 existing sheep farms would be lost under the reservoirs together with villages and hamlets. Notably the town of Adaminaby and its church would be sacrificed in this way. The Authority agreed that the church should be dismantled, stone by stone (every stone being marked beforehand) and rebuilt six miles away on a new site at one end of the new town of Adaminaby. So this newly-erected and yet old church building was just a few yards away from my rectory. Tourists in their cars came daily to see it. Adaminaby is an Aborigine word meaning 'Camping Place'. It was here that great numbers of gold prospectors assembled and camped during the gold rush last century. The gold was discovered some fifty miles away, up in the mountains, around a place known as Kiandra. The old church up there was at an altitude higher than any other church in Australia.

So my ministry would be to sheep farmers and their families, engineers and their families and the families living in and around the new town of Adaminaby. The latter included forestry workers, as there was a large sawmill at the outer end of the town.

At last the Sonnenberg family left and I found it a real joy and relief to use the provisions of the rectory and work from my office.

In addition to giving church services at Adaminaby it was necessary to do so regularly for the engineers and their families living up in the mountains at Cabramara. This was the highest town in Australia, some seventy miles away. Their population required a three-teacher school. On the other side of Adaminaby, on the plain some thirty miles away was another centre. This served sheep farmers and their families.

At my first parochial church council meeting I found the members to be jolly tough, rugged Australians, who called a spade a spade. There was no nonsense with them. I liked them for their candour. Perhaps they made me somewhat tough, too, which is hardly acceptable to our dignified and genteel English parishes, as I found out some years later! One churchwarden was the owner and manager of the large sawmill and a forestry expert. He knew all about trout fishing in the area and guided me to the best places.

I taught Scripture and Christian Knowledge almost daily in the schools and loved it. I think the children did, too.

Lake Eucumbene was the largest of the man-made lakes which the Snowy Mountains Hydro Electric Authority had created.

The lake could be dangerous for boating. Its expanse was vast and a boat could be at least half a mile from the nearest shore when a mountain storm or gale suddenly arose, creating six foot waves or more; boats could be awash in no time. Lives were frequently lost in this way. From time to time I found myself in storm conditions which called for patient and careful boatmanship. Once my outboard engine petered out in a storm, refusing to restart; facing the gale and waves, it took me a long time to row back to the harbour. Often, however, the weather and water conditions were heavenly so that no one could be more rewarded for a day's holiday.

Some time later, Bishop Clements came to the parish for a few days' visit, and was very pleased to be taken for a boat cruise on the lake. He was not so much interested in the fishing as relaxing while the boat slowly glided along through the colour-strewn waters. The bishop was so eased in spirit that he begged me not to speak, for quite a long time!

Parish finances were hard pressed for solvency. It was agreed that we would embark on a Christian Stewardship course and, although this helped a great deal, it was not sufficient. The parish then attempted to raise money by embarking on a firewood project. In the whole of this area, including the City of Cooma, some twenty miles away, firewood was the main fuel for all domestic purposes. So the parish enlisted the help of men used to this industry; sheep farmers readily gave us forests (this helped to make more grazing land for them); we bought a large and suitable truck, fitted with cage sides and began to supply loads of firewood to Cooma township. Sometimes I went into the forests. During those years I must have cut down many hundreds of trees, of which there were at least fifty different varieties. Some of them were excellent for firewood and some no use at all. We knew the differences and prepared the loads accordingly. Lunch in the sunny forest was quite delightful, with kangaroos hopping here and there. In common with all Australians we had to be watchful and careful too. At any time poisonous snakes could emerge and, just as bad, though not so easily seen, the Black Widow or Trap Door spider whose venom is the deadliest known on earth. For anyone bitten, death takes place within two minutes and there is no known cure. The trees we cut down for firewood were all eucalyptus of many varieties. Their local name was ash or gum tree. The box tree was best of all.

The first winter season came. And what an experience this was for me, here in so-called sunny Australia! The temperatures fell to minus 50°F at times, and sometimes it was so cold that petrol froze in the motor tanks. Then the snow came! In places it was 40 ft deep and cut off the major electricity supplies by reaching up to the sagging overhead high-tension cables. In such conditions it was grim to journey to Cabramara, as I had to. So thick was the snow that the only way for the engineers to clear the road was to forsake their snowploughs and *machine blow* the snow from the road over to each side. Thus for about fifty miles my car, with chains on the tyres, proceeded between two ten-ft high walls of snow. On my first such arrival at Cabramara I could not find any route around the town. The whole township was levelled with deep snow. How was I to find the school? At last I saw skis sticking up in the snow. I approached. It was the school, half buried. I walked down a flight of steps which had been dug in the snow, to find the children in the warm classrooms.

The incident I now mention I found almost unbelievable. One Saturday evening, there was a knock on my rectory door. There outside was the Cabramara schoolteacher with his wife and baby. Could they come in for an hour out of the cold snow whilst their car windscreen wipers were repaired at the garage? In the warmth of my house they told me how, on coming down the mountain road, the snow was falling so thickly that the windscreen wipers refused to work. They were on their way to Sydney to be in time to meet the wife's mother coming from Wimbledon, England.

I heard the mother's side of the story some time later. On the plane the flight captain asked mother where she was hoping to go to in Australia and she told him to Cabramara. The flight captain told her he had just had a weather report saying that Cabramara was snowed up. She thought he was joking. Was she not on her way to sunny Australia?

Her daughter and her husband duly collected mother at Sydney Airport, placed her in the car, brought her the 300 miles to the Snowy Mountains, took her up to Cabramara between the 10 ft high snow walls and at last managed to get her into their bungalow. The snow surrounding the house was so deep that mother never got outside that house for weeks on end.

For some years, I travelled hundreds of miles on my church and school journeys with snow chains on my car wheels. It was, and is, these melting winter snows which provide the precious water which has made possible the irrigation of the 3500 new farms in the interior of that part of the world. Snowy Mountains is indeed the right title.

Sometimes, even during summer, I have flown in a plane around Mt Kosciusko (the highest mountain in Australia) to see people skiing. They claim to have the longest skiing season in the world. It is the cold winds from the Antarctic clashing with the hot winds from the tropics which produce the violent storms and especially the snow. This is Australia's great playground gain, heavenly in the summer and very sporty in the winter.

I had been at Adaminaby for about a year when the bishop informed me that the Parish of Berridale, next to mine, was becoming vacant and for the time being was to be put into my charge. Would I now do the best I could for both parishes? My two parishes consisted of about 150 miles square, or 22 500 square miles, and included at least eighteen centres.

I now spent at least three days per week teaching in the schools. My mileage on such days was 252. I loved those children, up to twelve years of age. I was prepared to teach the children from as little as four years of age. As in Eureka, many came to school on their ponies, riding bareback. Their stockingless and shoeless toes would wiggle under the desks as I taught them. They loved to sketch the matters of the Gospel – angels, fishermen, boats, Jesus.

Every Tuesday morning was given up to teaching in the Central Cooma High School some twenty miles away. Clergy, pastors and teaching nuns from the enlisted denominations came to the school to teach the children of their respective denominations. The children's ages ranged from twelve to nineteen. My goodness, those Australian children could be tough and had to be handled with all possible skill and sometimes firmness! I shall always remember the attitude of the eighteen- to nineteen-year-old men! Sometimes they would throw their teacher out of the window. Their punishments for such actions were severe. It called for my greatest teaching art to control and persuade them.

This large parish included several more large lakes, some very popular for yachting, and several ski establishments with many swiss-like chalets. As mentioned above this was the playground of Australia. Also, away in the far mountains, were more engineering towns with the schools to be attended to.

Some of the sheep station centres had but one church service a month – not in a church, but in the country hall. Many families would travel twenty or thirty miles to come to the Church service. For those good people, so isolated, it was a great opportunity to see other people. They would bring lunches or tea and spend hours together. Also in some of those areas there would be one hundred per cent attendance at the service with not a single man, woman, nor child absent. Such a ministry was well rewarded.

Mrs Nancy King played the harmonium at Maffra sheep farm centre. She was a New Zealander. Mrs King invited me to her beautiful house for lunch one day. I asked her if she had known Dorothy Redgrave, the young lady I had met on New Year's eve in Melbourne in 1955/56. She knew her very well, and had known her father very well as the very successful Vicar and Canon of St Barnabas Parish, Christchurch, New Zealand. Dorothy Redgrave had recently written to her and she had her address.

I wrote to Dorothy, who suggested I should travel to New Zealand for a holiday. Before long I was on a flight to Christchurch. Dorothy met me at the airport and drove me to her very nice retirement house. Her parents had passed away some years previously and Dorothy was now acting as hostess and extra daughter for the Bishop of Christchurch and his wife.

We became engaged! The Bishop of Christchurch and his wife were bowled over and did not know what to say nor think. The Bishop had whipped out his Crockford's Clerical Directory and could hardly believe that I had crowded in so much experience hitherto. However, there was nothing the bishop nor anyone else could now do. Dorothy and I were to get married next month! Dorothy showed me around Christchurch, the cathedral, her late father's fine church, and the sights of illuminated Christchurch at night as seen from the top of the hills around.

Dorothy's father, the late Canon Frederick Burton Redgrave had given up his employment with the South British Assurance Company in order to be trained for and enter the ministry of the New Zealand Church. He had been particularly keen to promote the Mission of the Church so that, in due time, he was appointed General Secretary of the New Zealand Anglican Board of Missions. In this capacity he visited every Church of England parish in New Zealand as well as the mission stations in Melanesia and Polynesia. Later he became Rector of St Barnabas, Christchurch, which, after his ministry of seventeen years, had become perhaps the most vibrant parish in New Zealand. Dorothy's cousin was Sir Michael Redgrave, the actor.

I was invited to tea with the bishop and his wife. They probably thought I looked thin and somewhat worn out. In fact I always looked like that. I think they felt sorry for Dorothy. And they were certainly sorry for themselves because I was going to take away from them their very valuable extra daughter who had been with them for twelve years. And so back to Adaminaby.

Of course, somehow, I had to let the congregation know. During the notices at an Adaminaby Church service I started to make the announcement. In the heat and excitement of the day, and with so much on my mind, Dorothy's name suddenly became a blank and I could not remember her name. They thought this was most odd!

We were married on 23rd February 1963 in lovely but small St Andrew's Mission Church, Redcliffs, Christchurch. The bishop and his wife had wanted a full cathedral wedding with all the adornments and choir but Dorothy and I chose the small Mission Church. Her father had ministered to this Mission Church when he was a theological student.

Dorothy had taken me to a tailor to fit me out with a good suit. She looked perfection in her white dress and hat to match. Marjorie Braae made a charming bridesmaid. Bishop Warren, the Bishop of Christchurch, performed the marriage service. All Dorothy's well-known relations and people of Christchurch came along. Dorothy had planned and organised the wedding reception. There were witty speeches. It was a lovely sunny day and in the end, somehow, we went away in Dorothy's car. We spent the honeymoon in various beauty spots of New Zealand including Nelson. Dorothy knew England and the continent of Europe fairly well for she had been on visits a number of times and had friends and relations in several parts; she had been presented at Court in 1934. Now, poor Dorothy was to return to my tough assignment in Aussie land, and with me a workhorse.

CHAPTER 20
IN TOP GEAR AND
FAREWELL AUSTRALIA

With Dorothy's partnership, my life and ministry now moved into top gear. The rectory was looked after superbly and hospitality now took its normal course and was a great joy. Because my meals were always ready on time whenever I returned from journeys, short or long, the day's routine was always efficient.

Now, on my day off, Dorothy could come too and so we shared idyllic boating and fishing days on lake Eucumbene. Sometimes Dorothy even came into the Australian bush where the men were cutting down the forests to make loads of firewood for sale for church funds. We had our new corgi dog, Suki, with us and she was always a great joy and centre of attraction. Lunch in the Australian bush was delightful too.

Dorothy had been used to corgi dogs and was very fond of them so we bought a corgi puppy from Canberra and called her 'Suki'. She was a great companion, full of fun and a splendid guard dog. One night at 11.30 she was determined to be let out of the house. We followed her out to see her chase off a thief. Dorothy had also acquired a thin, long-legged black cat. I thought her very ungainly but Dorothy loved her. And, strangely enough, so did Suki. In the house they played great games with each other. The cat's favourite game was to scramble underneath the settee and challenge Suki to nose her out. Sometimes Suki succeeded and then celebrated her victory by taking the cat by the scruff of the neck and dragging her around the drawing room. The cat loved it all. When we walked into Adaminaby township with Suki, the black cat was always there, too, walking behind Suki in her ungainly manner.

When Suki was about eighteen months old she was supposed to be mated with a pedigree dog, and for this we paid a rather expensive fee. In due time, just before I was leaving for an early Sunday morning service, Suki gave birth to one puppy. It was as black as the ace of spades, a very good blending of corgi and sheep dog. The rector's wife of the next parish of Berridale, which by this time had reverted to its own parish status with its own rector, was delighted to have the puppy as a present and she made a very lovable, clever and attractive pet.

Dorothy was in her element in training the parish children for Nativity plays which were much admired in Adaminaby Church. After one such play the children were in their final posture of prayer and adoration of Mary and the Holy Child. They were, of course, kneeling down in a circle. Suki, who had been present in the play as one of the animals, went round and gave each child a kiss.

Early in 1965 Sir Winston Churchill died and the whole western world mourned his passing greatly. Australia was among the nations which expressed their feelings very much. The Revd Frank Hart, Rector of Cooma, the large township next to my parish, invited me to preach at the forthcoming memorial service to be held in his church. I knew what type of congregation would be present. This was because Cooma was the headquarters of the Snowy Mountains Hydro Electric Authority. All manner of chosen experts were in this township. They were very thoughtful types of people and rightly had a high regard for the late Sir Winston. The Church was full to capacity.

I had greatly admired Sir Winston's great leadership and was delighted to present reasons for his worthy praise under God. I spoke of his humble choice of an Englishman's grave in mother earth instead of an exalted place, say, in the basement of St Paul's Cathedral in company with Wellington and Nelson. I mentioned his Christian training at Harrow, his unique experience in martial affairs, his unsurpassed brilliance in repartee. In this respect I reminded the congregation of the time when, after a dinner, Sir Winston was descending in a lift in which also was Lady . . . who remarked, 'Winston, you are drunk, very drunk'. Sir Winston Churchill replied, 'Lady . . . you are ugly, very ugly; tomorrow I'll be sober'. I mentioned also some of his many books which I had read years before: *The Battle of the Malakand Field Force, My Great Contemporaries, Thoughts and Adventures.* I briefly reminded my hearers of his priceless leadership and speeches during the war, which kept alive the determination and hopes of Britain and the free world. I took a great delight in presenting our thanks to God for this very great man and I think members of the congregation were delighted with the service.

I know it was the Spirit of God now telling me that I must bring my wandering ministry to a reasonable end and return to England with Dorothy. I had so far spent twenty-three years ministering in many parts of the world, constantly travelling over great distances, with no rest because of the pressures of this kind of ministry. I knew I now needed to retreat in order to read, think, consolidate and assess the theological thoughts resulting from my experiences so far.

My enquiry to the church appointments secretary at No. 10 Downing Street, confirmed that I was still fully entitled to a Crown Living in England. I was invited to seek an appointment with the secretary when I returned.

I made my views known to my Bishop of Canberra, Goulburn, who would do everything for me, he said, if I would remain in his diocese. But the Spirit wanted me to return to an English parish and I quietly made my decision. Travelling plans were worked out. Of course we wanted to take Suki and not many shipping lines were able to provide for this. But one was – and so we were given a place on SS *Fairstar*.

During ten years of Australian life I had become aware of the annual terrors of bush fires. During the last two weeks of my time in Australia I was to witness and feel one.

One day I went up to the mountain school of Cabramara to teach the children. On the way out of the town I looked away across the huge valley to my left and then, ever such a long way off, I saw smoke of what must have been a forest fire. The spot was many miles away from any human establishment. I knew that for bush fires the fire-fighting authorities would sometimes fly over a stricken area and drop water bombs. I thought they could do so in this case and therefore on arrival at my rectory I telephoned all possible sources to relate what I had seen. Nothing was done, or if it was it was ineffective. That fire spread and spread, through the mountain forests, day and night and gradually came nearer to our Adaminaby area. When the fire was ten miles away I went with a sheep farmer friend right up to the fire area. It was a mighty inferno taking the giant gum trees into its flaming, devouring, roaring and devastating wake. We took our impressions back to our town of Adaminaby. By this time all believed the fire was encroaching and roaring towards the town. Teams of men were organised to prepare to defend the town where most of the houses were constructed of wood. By the Sunday morning (it happened to be our last Sunday) the fire was on the outskirts of the town. Every resident was instructed to pack an emergency bag only of essential belongings. There was no time or possibility to do otherwise. We held our morning service in Church when we prayed for God's intervention without which total destruction of the town seemed certain.

At 2 p.m. the wind direction suddenly changed to blow directly into the fire and away from the town. We were saved. And how relieved we all were – and how we gave thanks to God at Evensong that Sunday evening.

Almost annually, gigantic areas of Australian forests are destroyed in this way. And not all the fires are accidental. The punishment for guilty offenders is considerable, and rightly so.

In a busy ministry, as all Christian ministers know, there is little time to ponder or reminisce or to be sentimental. At last, after Easter 1965, it was time for us to leave. The Rector of Cooma, Fred Hart, had decided to travel with us to Sydney Harbour and indeed, to drive a vehicle containing some of our shipping baggage.

At the quayside a throng of people crowded on board SS *Fairstar*, farewelling their friends. They were there for hours and so was the Revd Fred Hart and several other parishioners. It was not easy for the shipping officers to persuade the great crowd of visitors to leave the ship. But at last it happened, *Fairstar* loosed her moorings and I was leaving Australia after ten years' service in that great Commonwealth country with a great future. It had been a wonderful and enriching experience and I was sorry to be leaving so many friends and parishioners.

Some time later, as we were passing the famous rock point outside Sydney Harbour, there, so near, and standing on the rocks and waving frantically was the Revd Fred Hart and his wife. It was most wonderful of them to wish us God speed and bon voyage in this way as we moved out of sight.

For my wife and me the voyage was bliss. I felt this was some reward for Dorothy for having taken me on, and she was revelling in every moment. Suki was encaged on the topmost deck and we were permitted to visit her twice each day. She was overjoyed to see us each time and if she could have talked would have asked just what was going on for her to be enclosed for all these weeks in the very hot cage.

We sailed past Java and Sumatra and so to the Port of Singapore. We passed close to Penang island. Little did I then know that, before long, I would be living in a parish which had sent out one of her parishioners to Penang. By his actions and influence, this parishioner, Francis Light, caused Penang to become one of the first colonies of the British Empire.

· The *Fairstar* then followed the traditional shipping lanes to Ceylon, the Arabian Sea and so to Suez. We went ashore to see the wonders of the Pyramids, and visited the museums of Cairo where we saw the treasures of Tutankhamen. The rest of the voyage was normal and uneventful, enabling us to disembark at Southampton on May 12th 1965.

I had come home to minister in the heart of the Church of England establishment. In some ways I was frightened at the prospect but then my inner confidence came from knowing that God's Holy Spirit was my own and He had plans for me regardless of anything that the Church or world might do. I was at least confident that I had tried to obey God's call to go into all the world to preach the Gospel. The Lord's rewards had already been most wonderful in so many ways in all my life of ministry. Now I must get on with this new assignment and be thankful.

The interview with the church appointments secretary at No. 10 Downing Street was pleasant and fruitful. I was given the names and descriptions of the vacant Crown Livings and invited to make my choice. I chose the parishes of Dallinghoo and Pettistree in Suffolk. They were small parishes. I reasoned that what I now required was an immediate and reasonable parochial base where I could consolidate my life, serve the parish well, and in due time take on a larger parish. Little did I know then what was to lie ahead! God had His plans for me! At least, I think so now, on looking back.

Suki was in quarantine for six months. Later we were able to arrange for her to be transferred to Norfolk, this being the nearest place of quarantine to our parish and home in Suffolk. We visited her once a week. Her reactions to our visits were remarkable and almost heartbreaking. We took her mutton chops and she excitedly relished them, chewed them, and swallowed them up in no time. But when we attempted to open the gate and leave her she tried to get between us and the gate. If she had been able to talk she would have asked us for what wrongdoing was she being punished by this form of separation? When at last the happy day came for us to take her away with us, her joy and ecstasy knew no bounds. She sat in the front seat of the car with Dorothy, staring through the car windows at normal life once more and not missing a thing – the horses, cows, fields, houses. And every so often she would throw back her head and give Dorothy a kiss. And when we did bring her into Dallinghoo Rectory Suki was horrified to find our new dog Teddy there. It took her a few days of nature's struggle with Teddy to assert her authority. She was our original charge and Teddy must take a back seat, as it were!

Dorothy and I spent a few weeks flitting around the UK visiting friends and relations. My eldest brother Arthur was seriously ill and I found this very distressing. For a few months we lived in my sister's summer caravan in North Wales. It was summertime and we quite enjoyed this temporary lifestyle. Our new corgi puppy dog named Teddy spent much of each day trying to master the wills of the very large Welsh sheep and at last he succeeded in droving them in any way he wished.

At last the Rt Revd Bishop Morris of the Diocese of St Edmundsbury and Ipswich granted me an interview regarding my future. The bishop was very weak after suffering a serious heart attack. Nevertheless, he was kind, gracious and considerate. He said he could induct me on September 2nd and, meanwhile, as soon as the Dallinghoo Rectory was vacated, we could move in several months before the induction day. Until the induction, he said, I could not take any services in the parish of Dallinghoo nor Pettistree but I could take interregnum or any other services in surrounding parishes. I had already visited Colonel Peter Maxwell, churchwarden of Pettistree. In due time the churchwardens of the two parishes had confirmed acceptance of my appointment.

So, with much joy, Dorothy and I moved into the Dallinghoo Rectory at the beginning of July, 1965. This was the start of our new home life in the heart of the Church of England where we were now being offered the comforts and security of the long tradition of the Establishment. This was a splendid rectory, built in 1938. The fine old rectory was still, of course, beside Dallinghoo Church and was then occupied by a Mr and Mrs Thomasson.

On the first new morning of our residence the postman placed one fairly bulky letter through the letter box in the front door. Little did **I know that the contents of this letter would determine my routine for the next twenty years or more!** It was the diocesan architect's latest quinquennial report on Dallinghoo Church. At the end of the statutory and detailed observations of the condition of the church the architect gave a severe warning. It was to the effect that, by his report, given five years previously, he had warned of the serious need of urgent repairs. 'Nothing has been done', he wrote, 'and something must now be done urgently or the church could be in ruins!' I realised that I had an immediate and large problem on my hands and that after my induction on the 2nd September I would have to take strong and quick action in some way. St Mary's Church had been built soon after William the Conqueror had become King of England in the eleventh century. Could we now save it from threatened extinction?

It did not take more than a few weeks for me to observe a number of realities of my new environment. Although the garden had been left to deteriorate it offered a splendid opportunity to turn it into something very good. I would enjoy this. There was a superb view, from the south side of the house and across the agricultural fields of the Suffolk countryside, with not a house in view. The well-built house was superb, with five bedrooms and plenty of space for everything, especially since there were only the two of us.

I was nonplussed by the smallness of these English parishes. It seemed such a small motor car journey of only a minute or two to be in someone else's parish. I happened to have a pictorial framed map of the churches in Suffolk. There were more than five hundred. In my Australian parish of about the same area there were two churches! In England every square yard seemed to count for something for someone. Being so used to vast areas and spaces, I found all this new compactness of everything difficult to assimilate. In this sense my freedom felt squeezed in.

Prior to the induction I was busy with transforming the garden and designing and making a fairly large terrace on the south and sunny side of the house. It transformed the site and made it very beautiful. I bought and planted about twenty pyramid-type fruit trees – apples, plums, pears, and peaches. I would need good grass cutters and it was when I was buying them from the farm stores in Woodbridge that I received some news which came as a shock, howbeit a pleasant one. The salesman dealing with me, and having heard from me that I had once been a chaplain in India, told me that his own vicar had been an army officer in India and that his name was Colonel Garland! I could hardly believe it could be my friendly Colonel Garland who had been commanding officer of the Parachinar Area. On returning to my rectory I looked up the telephone number and within seconds was speaking to this very same Colonel and now Revd Harry Garland. How amazing and pleasant and wonderful! I lost no time in visiting the Revd Colonel to talk about those traumatic North-

West Frontier days in the British India of the past! He had been especially kind in those days, even the saviour of those two missionaries, Mr and Mrs Nicholson. Since Harry Garland and I were now in the same deanery we saw each other often.

. The rural deans planned for me to take services here and there, especially where a parish vacancy had occurred. One of these churches was at a village some ten miles away named Sibton where one of the churchwardens was Arthur Hamilton O.B.E. One Sunday he and his wife invited me to lunch and there we discovered that we had both served in India. He had finished his service as Inspector General of Forestry, India, Burma and Ceylon which meant he was no mean expert in forestry. He had been director in charge of those endless forests in that subcontinent.

As he listened to the need for Dallinghoo Church to have major restoration he said he knew of an Essex parish which had successfully grown Christmas trees to make money to pay for the restoration costs. He asked why I could not utilise the Dallinghoo glebelands to do the same thing? He also offered to guide me should I decide to embark on such a project. The seed he sowed in my mind continued to grow during the next few weeks but until after the induction day I could do nothing at all.

Mrs Thomasson, who lived in the old Dallinghoo rectory, came to see me. She was the parish secretary, she said, and told me of the parish condition as she saw it. I said that, after my induction, we would hold a parochial church council meeting. She asked me what that meant for she had never known one to have occurred in the parish! She only remembered the annual general meeting each year! I began to wonder what kind of a parish this was. Before long I was to find out more strange things which should have been put right.

My induction duly took place in Pettistree Church on September 2nd 1965. The Church was well-filled; the bishop and archdeacon and clergy in attendance were all so good and pleasant. My first official ministry of an English parish had commenced.

I examined the service registers at Dallinghoo to find that the average attendance at Holy Communion per Sunday had been three or four. I was further astonished to hear one church member tell me that the villagers in general were of the opinion that Holy Communion services were somehow related to deaths of parishioners! I began to wonder deeply about the insight of Church of England villagers.

Apparent neglect was widespread. Moss was growing on some of the church windowsills. There had been no heating in the church for some years except that provided by very ugly oil stoves, mounted on the tops of the pews, in various parts of the Church. The parish magazine was printed in London and by the time it was distributed the news was very much behind the times. The large churchyard was covered with long grass and was crying out for cutting. It was even a fire hazard, I thought. I held the first parochial church council meetings for the two parishes to find more and more problems facing my ministry. The situation was challenging and I fully realised that it was now my business to work well to promote and improve good parish feelings and results. Above all I wanted the parishioners to feel that Christ loved them. I would try to do just this in His Name.

The first confirmation classes and studies, and then the confirmation service itself, were most encouraging. Nineteen young people, mostly young fellows, attended the course and were then confirmed. One of them, Philip Reynolds, was particularly interesting. He possessed a revolutionary type of mind, even at thirteen years of age. If I remember rightly, he was the secretary of the young fascist movement at his Framlingham Modern School. Philip had not been in the habit of attending any place of worship and as far as I can remember had never attended Sunday School.

He absorbed every word of the talks I gave in the rectory. After the halfway stage he could do no other than enthusiastically claim his love for and allegiance to Christ and His glorious Gospel. From that time Philip never looked back. The confirmation service was held at Pettistree Church. Other candidates from the surrounding parishes joined with ours, making a total of forty-nine boys and girls. This small country parish had never seen anything like this. All who witnessed the beautiful service were uplifted and encouraged. So was I.

These young people were then encouraged to conduct their own evening prayer service in the large Dallinghoo Church Vestry every Sunday afternoon. I was always present but did not interfere. In next to no time those young people could effectively present this service even at their young ages of fifteen and sixteen. After the service the group came across to the rectory for Sunday tea and afterwards to play croquet although the dogs rather spoilt games sometimes by playing too, for they did not keep the rules.

Philip Reynolds went on first for teacher training, then teaching, then to Lincoln Theological College, and ordination in Wakefield

Cathedral; he became a curate at Barnsley and, in due time, rector of parishes nestling on the Yorkshire side of the Pennines.

Andrew Smith became perhaps the youngest Church Army Captain ever. He has served in many avenues of Church Army service, spent ten years as Missioner and Mission adviser to the Diocese of Blackburn, and is now on the management staff of the Church Army.

No parish rector could have enjoyed such courteous, willing and loyal servers as I was privileged to have in Philip and Andrew.

But there were parish problems galore and this was typically Church of England. Most parishioners had strong views, one way or another, and many parishioners aired their views in strong terms. At times some of the members seemed to be thinking they were members of an opposition party, as in the House of Commons. They considered it right and proper to oppose other people's views, or mine, in no uncertain terms. There were all kinds of temperaments to be dealt with. Some people were delightful and charming. Others could be very difficult. Somehow we tried to build up the Church atmosphere and perhaps progress was being made. At this stage I looked in vain for warm, loving and spiritual parish commitment. There was a long way to go. Quite often and unknown to anyone, I had in my mind the wonders of the ministry of T. L. Osborn. I had in Chile prayed that the Spirit who blessed him would bless the Church of England. That now meant myself as well.

CHAPTER 21
DALLINGHOO CHURCH RESTORATION

The Dallinghoo Church restoration must now be faced with a sense of urgency. First I went to see the diocesan secretary at the Diocesan Office, Ipswich. He was General Manners Smith, and still very much the General. He informed me that no funds or grants were available for Dallinghoo Church restoration. He took another pinch of snuff then curtly told me to tell the Dallinghoo people that they must find the means to meet the restoration costs, otherwise this would be the end of the Dallinghoo Church and Parish. The General then showed me the way to the door!

I brought the matter before the parochial church council, wrote about it in the parish magazine, and drew attention to it in the Sunday services. I kept on asking for ideas for raising the vast sum of money required for the restoration. There was not a single response.

Should I now go the bishop to inform him that the Dallinghoo Parish is beyond redemption? It would not be easy to go to this very kind and very sick bishop with such distressing information. It appeared that, due to many years of clerical neglect, the Dallinghoo parishioners could hardly be to blame for the state of church and parish. Indeed there had been only three parochial church council meetings during the past twelve years. I prayed about the matter and talked with my wife. I then made a decision. I would commence a Christmas tree growing project to raise funds to save Dallinghoo Church.

Like many country parishes, Dallinghoo possessed glebelands, as has been mentioned. By ecclesiastical law of long standing these lands were under the complete control of the incumbent for him to raise money for himself or for any other purpose. By this Church law and tradition it would be quite normal for me to embark on a Christmas tree project.

I made this decision known to the next PCC meeting. I did, however, point out very clearly that I was sad to have to give my attention to this venture and that, as a consequence, my pastoral image would be adversely affected. Yet, the Church must be saved and saved quickly before it was too late. I also said that I now required an assistant worker for this scheme and that he would be paid due wages. In due time Mr Tony Richardson, churchwarden and a dairy farmer, came to me privately and asked for the job.

The Dallinghoo PCC adopted the scheme which was then registered in the name of St Mary, Dallinghoo. They opened a Christmas Tree Project bank account and accepted my offer to finance the scheme on condition that, if the scheme became a success, I would be reimbursed.

My friend, Arthur Hamilton, now gave me introductions to nurserymen who would supply the plantings and he also offered advice on all kinds of related matters. Contractors were employed to erect rabbit wire fencing around some eighteen acres of land. A tractor, a commercial van and other agricultural implements were bought. I helped design and then purchased a dual-tow tree-planting machine. Land was ploughed, rotavated and prepared. Thousands of Norway Spruce plantings were bought and tree-planting commenced. We soon found that our machine planted at the rate of 10 000 trees per day. After a few days' planting it was quite thrilling to see scores of rows of beautiful green trees in the smooth soil with not a weed to be seen. The project was well and truly under way. I had taken action. Jesus was a man of action. Nothing good is achieved without someone taking action. I am appalled when any situation suffers because no one has been prepared to act. This had happened for years concerning the restoration of Dallinghoo Church. I was, at least, trying my best to save the situation. Would I be in time? So far the project had cost a fortune. My assistant was paid full weekly wages and was provided with a car and travelling costs.

So now I was an horticultural worker, working daily in the plantations and then, every so often and as required, returning to the rectory to change into my clerical clothes for a service, clerical meeting or conference.

The exercise on the plantation was considerable and sometimes entailed carrying a knapsack sprayer, weighing 50 lb when full of liquid, and walking long distances up and down the rows, some of which were up to 500 yards in length. My mind was always keenly alert, thinking of God, His ways of working, His Gospel of Christ and how my ministerial experiences fitted in. This kind of life kept me as fit as could be and I hardly ever felt tired or fatigued. At the end of each day Dorothy had a sumptuous good supper ready, I slept like a top every night and the parish outlook was promising.

By this time Philip Reynolds and Andrew Smith, my two devoted servers, spent their holidays on the plantations helping with the weed control and in any other way they could. Every so often we would rest from work and talk theology. Philip's mind was insatiable for more and more information on things spiritual. He had, of course, long ago made up his mind to enter the ministry.

An official notice from the North Sea Gas Board informed me that their new pipeline would cross a section of one of my Christmas tree plantations and in addition to destroying ten thousand trees I would not be allowed to plant Christmas trees ever after on that section. This was a setback. Legal assessors went to work and at last compensation terms were agreed at something a little less than £1000. Had I understood then the true value of Christmas trees the compensation should have been at least ten times that amount.

As the months and first few years of the project went by, many other aspects of parochial and diocesan life were very much in operation.

By the year 1971 we had some 220 000 Christmas trees growing well, with not a faulty tree on the plantation. All being well, 90 000 trees would be ready for sale next year, worth approximately £200 000. This would be more than sufficient to pay for the restoration costs. I and those closely connected with the scheme were very satisfied and greatly encouraged.

Once again the diocesan architect urgently communicated with me. Your Dallinghoo Church tower, he said, is in imminent danger of collapsing. It must be restored forthwith with no delay or it will be too late. There was no money. I consulted the archdeaon who advised taking out a bank loan. The bank sent their inspector to examine my Christmas tree project. After he had spent many hours assessing the value of the project he willingly authorised his Woodbridge branch to provide the loan.

The builders set to work and carefully demolished the tower, stone-by-stone and beam-by-beam. The great tie beams of this Norman Church had virtually no ends left for they had rotted away during the centuries. These remnants were placed in the churchyard for all to see and wonder at. The builders and the architect declared that it was a miracle how the massive four-feet-thick walls had not collapsed long ago. In due time the tower was magnificently rebuilt. In this way the 1000 year old Norman Church had been saved from destruction. The Christmas tree project had saved it.

Bildeston Church, about fifteen miles away, was suffering a similar tower problem at about this time. Bildeston Church officials had left the matter too long, with tragic results. The warnings had been before the parish for forty years when ominous cracks appeared in the structure and were even photographed. Now, in 1971, builders came to repair the tower. They got only as far as erecting the scaffolding when, suddenly, the whole of the tower crashed down, much of it on to and across and into the main nave of the church – and great and drastic was the wreckage. It was a mercy that no workman was injured or killed. I happened to be travelling past this church the day after the tragedy to see this terrible sight. I did not think Bildeston Church would have a tower in the future. But Dallinghoo St Mary's was saved in the nick of time. It seemed that the Lord had sent me to Dallinghoo to save this Church. I praise the Lord for using me in this way.

At this time the value of English money was approximately halved. The causes were two-fold. The 1973 Israeli-Arab war caused petrol and oil prices to rocket, and they have never recovered. Also, decimalisation of English money took place. There were now 100 pennies to the pound instead of 240. The cost of everything virtually doubled. In particular, workers' wages rose by leaps and bounds. So I found myself running out of money to pay for the ongoing project. I was forced, therefore, to apply to the bank for a loan for the project's working expenses and they obliged. Fortunately, this was a bank other than the one which had made the initial Church loan. But both banks were persuaded that, within twelve months, the Christmas tree project sales would yield the necessary funds for repayments. Meanwhile the two overdrafts began to rise steadily!

I now decided to carry out a chemical weed control, not so much because of the nuisance of the weeds themselves, but because the weeds would gobble up the costly fertiliser about to be applied to the trees.

I therefore communicated with a major agriculture company which sent out their head representative to advise. He examined the plantations, praised them highly, and recommended what he said would be the ideal chemical. He went away with a very costly order.

In due time the drums of chemical arrived and with them instructions for use. During the month of March 1972, we applied the chemical in the form of spray. During the midst of the spraying the representative came, saw the spray being applied, checked everything and confirmed that we were complying correctly with the instructions in every respect. Soon we were delighted to see the grasses and weeds dying off, shrivelling up and disappearing.

During the following month of June it was the passing postman, of all people, who asked us what was wrong with our Christmas trees? Even as he travelled along the road beside the plantation he could see the trees had turned brown. We examined the trees and were indeed very concerned to see that the smaller trees had turned brown. As the days passed we noted that more and more and even the larger trees were turning brown. This continued until it was obvious that we had a major tragedy before us. All the trees were dying rapidly. Once again, to use the word of my Introduction, *I was flat on my back*.

I sounded the alarm. Being a member of the National Farmers' Union, I informed my area secretary. The agricultural company which had supplied the chemical was also asked to come and investigate. I informed the nurseryman who had sold me a quarter of a million trees. All could see that a major tragedy had occurred. It began to look like a total loss.

The National Farmers' Union arranged for a solicitor to handle the case. In turn, a London barrister was appointed by the NFU. In due time, after careful study of all the facts, his opinion was that this was a case of misrepresentation, breach of contract and breach of warranty. I certainly knew, without a shadow of doubt, that I was innocent of any cause of this mammoth tragedy. I now hoped for a quick legal settlement, for my financial affairs were now critical. The Dallinghoo Church needed to have its further repairs completed and everything paid for.

Soon after the barrister had supplied his counsel's opinion in my favour the head of the Legal Department, NFU, London, sent me a letter stating, to my intense surprise, that they could no longer support my case! I went to see them in London and was totally unsatisfied with their explanations.

From now on I upheld legal responsibility on my own. For month after month no legal action was taken. However, I had appointed two consultants to work on my side. The first was Peter Garthwaite who had served all his life with the Forestry Commission, becoming one of their governors, and in retirement had been elected President of the Royal Forestry Association for the United Kingdom. My second consultant was Neil Charlton who, prior to retirement, had been a senior financial loss assessor for ICI. From time to time these two consultants visited my plantations, studied every detail of the case and drew up their damage claims.

Time was passing, weeks to months and months to years, and still no action. Parishioners and all who knew about the case considered it was the end, and tragic for me and for the parish. Two banks were pressing for the return of the loans. I kept faith.

In 1976, four years after the application of the chemical, some of the trees had recovered to some extent and we were able to salvage and sell some 25 000 second class trees to the London markets. The remaining 200 000 trees were uprooted and destroyed by fire. The profit from the 25 000 trees helped considerably to reduce the bank overdrafts and that was a great relief.

Then at last, after an eight-year wait, notice was given for the high court case to be held in London in June 1980.

In May another blow struck. My wife went into a coma and after several weeks of medical investigation a clot on the brain was diagnosed. An urgent operation was to take place at the National Hospital, London, in June. My court case was put back to October. My two wonderful corgi dogs died. The rectory was empty. My wife was at death's door. Once again, *I was flat on my back*. I walked about the lifeless rectory praising the Lord for all the wonderful life of my wife and also of my dogs and went to sleep trusting and praising God. Whenever trouble comes it is always good to praise the Lord, not for the troubles, but because He never changes.

The day after Dorothy's eight-hour operation I visited her in the National Hospital. She was sitting up in bed and would not stop talking! I left her to see the doctors for a while. When I returned she told me all that she had read in my *Church Times*. In four days Dorothy went for a walk around Queen's Square. In ten days she was at home running the rectory. I promised the doctors that I would never allow Dorothy to work so hard again. The surgeon's reply was: 'Let your wife do whatever she wants in any way at any time. She has a very good strong body, and she is now healed.'

The High Court case was held in London from October 13th to October 23rd 1980, under Lord Justice Gibson. I found the case intensely interesting from every point of view and I never had a moment's anxiety about the outcome because I knew our cause was based on absolute truth. At the commencement of the case I was called to witness for three consecutive days as well as later. My other two witnesses were of course Mr Peter Garthwaite and Mr Neil Charlton. Our barrister was Richard Havery QC, of Gray's Inn. Witnesses for the defence were: Mr Patrick Clare (manager of the Woodlands Estates, Norfolk), Major-General Leonard Howard Jones, Mr John Grenville St George-Syms QC, Mr Alan Hardy Jones, manager of Yattendon Estate (largest Christmas tree Growers in the UK) and Dr Roger John Whiteoak (soil chemist).

Judgment was declared in our favour including costs. Inwardly I was deeply joyful and vindicated. Immediately after judgment the newspapers and media seized on the outcome so that the whole nation was able to read of this saga. Telephone messages and other communications arrived, offering congratulations and asking for advice with other agricultural problem cases.

However, it was quite some time before any compensation monies were received. As the weeks passed by I felt far from satisfied with certain elements of the case. The judgment had been complicated and drawn out and was given on three different days over a period of two months. When completed it amounted to some 1000 pages. My consultants and I were extremely disappointed over the comparatively small value of the compensation. I could not let the matter drop. I knew that more ought to happen.

I now informed my solicitor and barrister of my dissatisfaction and that I wanted to appeal. They would not hear of it, saying that I would lose all. As the weeks and months went by I persisted in my request. I was given permission to ask my parochial church council for a verdict and this meeting became the most vital and serious of the whole saga. For three hours I pleaded with the PCC to trust my judgment and in the end they reluctantly gave me their unanimous 'Yes'. By this decision I was the happiest person possible and the next morning, to the astonishment of my solicitor, I telephoned the 'Yes' verdict and the appeal was lodged just before the time limit ran out!

More months went by before the appeal. By this time my barrister appeared to have been converted to my way of thinking and in the appeal case I thought he was magnificent. The appeal was before Lord Stephenson (President), Lord Kerr and Sir David Cairns. My barrister, Richard Harvey QC appealed that the learned Judge of the High Court, in his judgment, had been wrong on five major counts. Our appeal was upheld on all issues. The damages awarded were now doubled and again we were awarded costs.

Great was the rejoicing by so many concerns and peoples for our great victory. The newspapers and media spread the details of the case and congratulations came in from every point of the compass. Some parish members, who saw the results on television, wept with joy for my sake and the future good of the parish of Dallinghoo. A member of the European Parliament was particularly interested in the case. The company which had to pay the damages was suffering adverse publicity and financial trouble. A member of the London Imperial College of Science and Technology seized on the case and begged for full details for their permanent records. As from that time it appeared that government legislation was greatly tightened up on the use of pesticides, etc. There was to be greater protection for agricultural and horticultural companies and workers.

My inner joy and satisfaction knew no bounds and I accordingly praised my God Who, all the way through the saga, had garrisoned my heart.

It still took quite a long time for the award monies to come in. As they did, the monies were invested and from the income we began to pay off our many liabilities. Later, further restoration was magnificently carried out on St Mary's Church. There was sufficient money also for the reimbursement of my capital outlay. And all this from the interest alone. The saga had ended in victory and glory, for me, the parish and for the Glory of the God. Against all odds the 1000-year-old place of worship had been saved, and more.

CHAPTER 22
VIBRANT PARISH
ACTIVITIES

The Christmas tree saga took up to fifteen years of my Dallinghoo/ Pettistree ministry. During that time other episodes of ministry were, of course, taking place and running parallel.

One was printing. This arose in a very small way as the result of trying to provide for a simple but good parish magazine. For a long time it had been quite clear to me that a parish magazine was of the utmost importance. Preaching might leave much to be desired and sermons are soon forgotten by the hearers. But a good and acceptable magazine could be before members of a household for day after day throughout the month. If it appealed to them the magazine articles could be read and assimilated over and over again. Therefore I began to spend much time and money on equipment to produce this good magazine. It was a case of little-by-little and step-by-step.

From plain typewriter and Gestetner efforts I (timidly at first) embarked upon offset printing. The second-hand offset machine was of the smallest and simplest kind. It turned out clearly printed magazines. The advertisements in particular looked good and attractive so that more advertisers were pleased to place their notices in the magazine and this brought in extra money to meet the costs. Still my typing left much to be desired even though from time to time I bought several better typewriters. One day a printer friend told me about the new kinds of phototypesetters and on my request he explained them further and I obtained literature and specifications concerning these new mysteries.

The time came at last; I could not resist any longer, and bought a new Whittaker phototypesetter. It certainly upgraded the quality of the magazines and I felt quite proud of the productions. I think the parishioners did too. Then I introduced another improvement: professionally produced pictorial covers. But making parish magazines like this always meant considerable monthly work. Fortunately the spare rooms in the rectory were adequate. My wife loved to help me as we used the large rectory dining table for the monthly collating, stapling and finishing.

A parishioner, having seen this kind of printing, begged me to print some work for him. When he found that his cost was about a half of the commercial cost he was, of course, delighted. The small profit I made was put into the printing fund. This request was followed by one or two others, then more and then others. On a steadily increasing scale this continued. Then clergy made a note and ordered. Then the archdeacon made a note and ordered. He was so amazed and delighted that his order continued to increase relentlessly.

My Whittaker phototypesetter was not good enough for my printing demands. I bought an expensive, phototypesetter. It took me six months to fathom its mysteries but when I did it worked like magic. Without moving from my typing chair, and by merely pressing tabs, I could command any one of up to about 300 different sizes and types of print.

I also bought the latest and most efficient printing machines. Printing orders increased and if I had so desired it would have been so easy to commence work as a full time printer! I did not wish to, of course, and was not allowed to earn one penny for myself and again had no desire to do so. All the work was produced at approximately one half of commercial prices. Sometimes the number of copies required ran into many thousands. The range of customers increased almost daily in the diocese, and they included the bishop, the diocesan office and clergy in general.

I kept a specimen copy of each printing order and these are now preserved in four large albums. I costed the value of printing done in this way over a period of five years. It came to approximately £45 000! This printing, together with other parish duties, allowed me no spare time at all! Finally, when my time of retirement arrived in 1986, the bishop asked if I could stay in the diocese, be provided with a spacious rectory, serve one or two small parishes and continue as diocesan printer?! I could not, of course. I was tired out!

My arrival for parish responsibility in the Church of England in 1965 seemed to coincide with another very outstanding matter. This was the almost total overhaul and readjustment of distribution of parochial clergy. The distribution of clergy had been more or less unchanged for hundreds of years. This would now be coming to an end. Circumstances forced the issue and the upheaval was inaugurated by the Sheffield Report.

This report noted, for example, that there could be a single parish priest in a parish of, say 20 000 people or more – a state of affairs which could be repeated all over England. By contrast, there were many quiet country parishes of, say, 150, or 200 people where the parish priest was living in perfect quietness and ease and peace. Obviously this greatly unfair balance could not be permitted any longer. By agreement of all bishops, changes were commenced. All relative clergy and parish strengths were analysed and the redistributions of clergy became an order.

As part of this procedure I was instructed to take into my charge two further parishes, Bredfield and Boulge. The increased parochial responsibility was a very considerable challenge and caused dismay both to clergy and parishioners.

The old order of ministry changed at a stroke and even more radical changes were on the way, but most people knew they had to come to terms with the changes. In some cases we heard of a single country clergyman now being responsible for up to ten parishes! It now meant that the average country incumbent found himself hurrying from one church to another on Sundays in order to supply at least something like a service for those who wished to worship. These changes were certainly going to take the great pressure off many overworked clergy. We were told of one priest whose parish was so large that in one year he had conducted 500 burials and about the same number of marriages.

As I have indicated, Boulge was one of my new charges. It was a beautiful and very old estate Church, that is to say for centuries it had been the spiritual provision for the Lord of the manor of Boulge Hall and his large retinue. Because Boulge Hall had now ceased to exist the Church was largely unattended and would normally have been declared redundant had it not been for the arrival and attention of Miss Atkinson and Miss Short. Both had been, in turn, headmistress of the Ipswich Girls' School, which, under them, had become renowned.

Now, in their retirement to this area, they saw their opportunity to care for and nurture the wellbeing of this Boulge Church and they did it superbly. They specialised in arranging carol services, harvest festivals, Christmas, Easter and special festivals, with music or otherwise. These occasions were so well arranged and became so famous and blessed that people flocked to the church in large numbers. I certainly encouraged them by putting into the services as much as possible of clerical warmth and love.

Boulge Church was also renowned as the place of worship (and then burial) of Edward Fitzgerald, translator of *Omar Khayyam*. In some way or another his devotees were often present at the Church.

I found Bredfield community and their relation to the Church to be a problem. This was because the county director of village improvement had retired to Bredfield. There he successfully organised all kinds of village life activities: football, tennis, dramatics, bowls, concerts, the building of a new super village hall, etc. He knew how to organise people. He knew how to extract from them funds for all these activities, but in all these matters, good as they might have been, one thing was lacking and did not seem to matter, namely, the value of worship. The Church attendance was extremely poor. As I went along for the average Sunday morning Church service there were crowds of folk on the playing field or in the new hall but only a small handful of faithful people in Church for worship. The community was bent to get everything possible out of life (and nothing wrong with that up to a point) but there was little inclination to worship. This was certainly happening with Bredfield and Dallinghoo and was spreading to other villages in the vicinity.

From time to time, as figures became available, it was clear that about ninety per cent of English people no longer attended a place of worship.

CHAPTER 23
REFRESHER COURSE

In 1974 my bishop requested me to attend a clergy refresher course at St John's Theological College, Nottingham. The course was to last for one month. It seemed fitting to use this time for my wife to have a holiday and so it was arranged that she would stay with a friend who lived at Canterbury.

On the Monday morning I took my wife to Woodbridge station and put her on the train for London. I then made my way to Nottingham for the refresher course. My goodness, what a change I found in the demeanour of the college students and staff compared with my college days, thirty-four years before. In my college we always had to wear college gowns while the staff wore gowns and mortarboards. It was unthinkable not to be so clothed. But now, here at St John's in 1974, gowns were unknown, a relic of the past. The students might be wearing ties but some had open-necked shirts. Neither did the staff wear any gowns at all. In fact when I attended my first lecture on liturgy and worship the lecturer was wearing an open-necked shirt and had his feet up on the desk. For years now he has been one of our well-known bishops!

Series Three Experimental Service was then only in the design stage with the college testing it out for the first time.

And now, I noted further hopes and answers to the prayers I had made in Chile after witnessing the power of T. L. Osborn. This was particularly so at the morning prayer fellowships during which some six or so students grouped for Christian meditation of love, faith and prayer. What big changes had come and would be coming. The Principal, the Revd Michael Green, was himself so minded. Later, as the whole Church knows, his ministry entered into great fruitfulness, especially as Rector of St Aldates, Oxford.

We were instructed in the modern successful way of parish administration. On exchanging our past clerical histories the lecturer and I discovered, with some amusement, that this lecturer and adviser had been my Lay Reader at St John's, Lewisham Way, a quarter of a century before!

Specialists came to address the college as a whole. One such was the Regius Professor of Modern History, Cambridge, the Revd Owen Chadwick DD. His two-day lecture on *The German Church and the rise of Hitler* was outstandingly brilliant and given without any visible reference to a single note. His memory of names, places and circumstances seemed endless. Hitler had been a keen Roman Catholic churchman, he pointed out, and ordered his followers to fill the churches and make sure that their children were taken also for baptisms. He thus became the so-called saviour of both Church and state. And when he had secured the undoubted allegiance of the German Church, he chose men of his way of thinking to become bishops. When the testing time came, during the pogrom of the Jews, the Church was feeble and without resistance to the national trend. Had the Church been strong enough to put the brake on Hitler, the Second World War might not have taken place. The German Church, being the strong seat of liberalism, had lost its moral, spiritual and Christian fibre. Incidentally, I consider this has now happened to a large extent to the Church of England, as I will later reveal.

On the third day of the refresher course news came to me that my wife had had a falling accident while rushing for a bus near the Royal Academy; and she was now in St Thomas' Hospital. On the Wednesday I travelled down to the capital, arriving in a London traffic jam at 4.30 p.m. I went round and round the traffic lanes for ages, with vehicles hooting me from right, left and centre. It was a nightmare. At last, at 8.30 p.m. I found the hospital ward and there was my wife bandaged up for a broken shoulder and a broken thumb on the other hand. She was almost totally immobile. The bed could no longer be spared and I was permitted to take Dorothy back to Dallinghoo on condition that full medical attention was immediately obtained. I did this and within two days Dorothy was admitted to the Felixstowe Nursing Home to remain there for the next six weeks. I returned to Nottingham for the rest of the refresher course.

Back in the parishes the Church in general was attempting to meet the multiplicity-of-services-per-incumbent problem with the creation of greater numbers of Lay Readers and the creation of a new order: Lay Elder. These two orders were proving to be increasingly helpful. I made full use of a number of both. Retired clergy were also helpful so that with these extra helps we were able to provide services every

Sunday and in each parish at the same time each week. This pleased me and all the parishioners.

The new Alternative Service Book was introduced to the Establishment and caused considerable controversy and in some cases much pain. I considered this book to be over complex and confusing. Worship structure should surely be as simple as possible and this new structure was far from it.

Financial strain was now a characteristic of Church life with diocesan quota increasing quite alarmingly every year, and so people's giving had to be increased also.

One aspect saddened me more than all others. This was a lack of concern for Mission – a lack of vision, or giving, for Mission. With the exception of Pettistree my parishes would not respond to my teaching and pleading. I tried, and will always try, to emphasise that the Missionary concept is the Lord's paramount and basic instruction for the Christian Church. I also consider that the Lord cannot recognise the validity of any parish which does not give this missionary concept first priority. Christ was insistent that His name and Gospel be proclaimed as much as possible in ever-increasing circles at all times throughout the world. It is His proclaimed Name which is at the heart of this matter. I was discouraged by the parishes being quite willing to give to the Red Cross, the British Legion, special disaster appeals, Save the Children Fund, Church restoration and many other causes but reluctant to support the cause of missionaries and the proclamation of Christ's precious Name in all the world. I was defeated and saddened in this. And of course I fully realised, sadly, how much time and energy I had been forced to give for the restoration of Dallinghoo Church. I knew of other parishes which had become outstanding for their missionary sensitivity and giving and tried to mention them as examples. I found little response.

But good things were happening. A Christian from Framlingham wanted me to attend a special Christian meeting in Ipswich where the Revd Trevor Dearing would give the address. He was Rector of Hainault, North East London. His powerful address was quite extraordinary and thrilled and encouraged everyone who heard it. Much against his proud Anglican will and through the insistence of his wife, he attended a Chapel Healing Service which had created a startling name in that area. What he witnessed there was devastating to him, his theology and his clerical pride. Before his eyes he saw evil spirits boldly and dramatically cast out in the Name of Jesus. He saw other people healed. His proud Anglican spirit shrivelled up as he saw the poverty of his own ministry that put him to shame.

Of course he had to follow this matter through with the result that, in due time, he himself was baptized by God and received divine power to cast out devils and heal the sick. His power in this field grew. So did his influence in the whole of that area, and his Church was always packed. The services were pregnant with power, adoration of God, compassion and worship, so much so that the television media came and showed his power and his services to a very wide audience. He was filled with grief and sorrow, realising how his past ministry had been bankrupt, a mere religion of words. In due time Trevor Dearing was acclaimed an authority on exorcism and derangements and was eagerly welcomed by doctors into this kind of healing ministry.

I remembered that time in Chile when, after observing T. L. Osborn's powerful ministry, I had prayed that the Lord would send this Spirit to the Church of England. Here was some of the fulfilment happening before my eyes. This was real, this was the Gospel being worked out, this was Divine power flowing mightily.

I attended similar meetings once a month. They offered spiritual strength and encouragement for those who wanted to believe in Jesus Christ and His Gospel. I shall always be grateful for those meetings of the Full Gospel Businessmen's Fellowship International. A very good supper was enjoyed before each meeting.

Fred Smith gave his story at one of the meetings. A detective sergeant of the Oxford Constabulary, Fred Smith was an agnostic up to the age of thirty-nine. One Saturday his aged mother told him of the elderly white-haired woman who used to walk with a stick and was totally blind. She was known locally as the witch, but she had been remarkably healed, with her sight fully restored. All this had happened at the Mission being held in the town nearby.

This was too much for the detective sergeant who ought to know what was going on in his beat, and so he attended the last meeting in order to stop any nonsense. He was totally overcome and converted to Christ that night and his whole life and demeanour were radically changed. Later, he discovered by apparent accident, that he now possessed great powers to heal and comfort people. On his retirement he became a pastor, commenced a ministry of healing and for the next thirty years was the means, under Jesus Christ, of thousands being healed from almost every form and type of illness. Later, I shall say more of Fred Smith and his healing of Ken Harper in my parish of Dallinghoo. The book, *God's Gift of Healing*, with a foreword by Canon Michael Green, gives the story of his incredible ministry.

Again, I rejoiced to behold the Spirit which blessed T. L. Osborn now blessing and using people in England, and before my eyes. I was further greatly encouraged and strengthened in my faith.

After each of these meetings I found increasing glory in the Church services, the Bible and the prayer book. I know that the members of the congregation felt a new surge of Christian strength too.

Sergius Terasanko was another powerful witness for Jesus Christ and His Gospel. He was perhaps, at the time I heard him, one of the foremost nuclear physicists in the world and a senior director of the British Nuclear Research Establishment for peaceful uses of atomic energy at Abingdon, Oxfordshire. He told us briefly of some of the terrific energy potential of nuclear fusion on which he was working, and which would be utilised in the future for almost unlimited supplies of power for generating electricity.

But he was at the meeting to tell of his entire dedication to the Lordship of Christ. 'The Cross of Jesus,' he said, 'is the only factor which will ultimately save and renew the whole world. A year ago,' he continued, 'my telephone rang at 2 o'clock in the morning and I wondered whoever could be ringing me at that time. The call was from a hospital in the north of France to let me know that my daughter had been involved in a motor car accident. X-ray had revealed a fractured skull behind the right eye and the girl was in a coma: "please come as soon as possible," they said.'

Sergius Terasanko then rang his friend, Fred Smith, the pastor to whom I have referred and told him the story. Fred said he would pray to the Lord for Miss Terasanko's healing, even as they were holding their telephone. After Fred Smith had done so, he said that the Lord had already assured him that the girl was healed. George Terasanko believed him and slept in peace.

Next morning Terasanko went to the hospital in France to collect his daughter. They told him that he must be crazy. Look, they said, at the X-ray they had taken and which showed very clearly the fracture over the right eye. The medical authority went on to say that, because a later X-ray did not show up the fracture and was therefore faulty, they had sent Miss Terasanko to another larger hospital. They did admit that **at 2 a.m.** the daughter had come out of the coma and then enjoyed a full night's natural sleep. And they did admit how unusual it was for her to wake up and ask for a normal breakfast.

Terasanko journeyed to the next hospital where similar conversations took place. They, too, said that their X-ray equipment must have failed because it did not show the fracture which the initial X-ray had revealed. Terasanko then remonstrated with the medical expert as one scientist to another. It took him two days before they admitted that there was no sign of damage to Miss Terasanko. Her father then took her straight back to her Paris university. She is now one of the most brilliant young women in France. This is no less and no more wonderful than some of the healings of Jesus as recorded in the Gospels. It does prove that the power of Jesus is just the same today for those who believe and act accordingly.

For several years I attended those monthly meetings and rejoiced to hear one striking and powerful testimony after another. The speakers were from different walks of life and some of their names come readily to mind. I have mentioned Fred Smith and Sergius Terasanko. Others were Fred Delanius, a one-time senior newspaper correspondent in Italy, who was present at the demise of Pope Paul VI; Michael Fenton-Jones, Chairman of the Guildford Chapter of the Full Gospel Businessmen's Fellowship, International and in business life Managing Director of Commercial Union Properties World-Wide; the Bishop of Pontefract, the Rt Revd Richard Hare; the retired Bishop of Singapore, the Rt Revd Ban it Cheu; and Sir Lionel Luckhoo KCMG, CBE, listed in the *Guiness Book of Records* as the most successful lawyer in the world. He was outstanding for his fearless adoration of Jesus Christ. Sir Lionel travelled to many parts of the world, including England, and was influential in both law and in the proclamation of Jesus Christ. The Rt Hon John Gummer MP was due to speak one Saturday. At the last minute it was announced he could not be present and I was asked to fill in the gap. I did so but my coat tails were pulled for going on too long! There were, over the years, many others and they were all marvellous Christians and exalted Jesus Christ and the Triune God fearlessly.

After each of these meetings I returned to my parish services more thrilled than ever with the glorious words of the prayer book, the Holy Bible and the priceless opportunities given to ministers of the Church. I was never short of sermon material.

There were very good gardeners in the parishes. I suppose there are good gardeners in most country districts. The harvest festivals were always beautifully supplied with vegetables, fruits, flowers, jams and honey.

I cannot remember why or how it started, but we held the first village horticultural show in 1969. It was such a success that we planned to hold another in the following year, when it was difficult to find available space for all the exhibits. The year after that marquees were hired and these were filled to capacity, the crowds of admirers being still larger.

Each year the show expanded. I could not have managed without the expert knowledge and help of Mrs Williams who lived at Strawtop Cottage, Pettistree. Before retirement she was in the nursing profession, having reputedly become the youngest matron ever. She was extremely methodical and helped to give great happiness and joy to the parishioners who attended these shows. After some years we had to stop these shows because they had become too big to be managed! It would have been lovely if we could have said the same concerning church attendance!

One summer in the early 1980s, the bishop summoned all clergy in the diocese to a three-day conference to be held at the East Anglia University. The main speaker was the Revd Eddie Gibbs, who had specialised in parish potential and growth, and his addresses were to be along these lines. I noted with satisfaction that he referred to his ministerial experiences in Chile, where the joyful kind of worship there put him on his way rejoicing, as it had with me and with others I know.

Eddie Gibbs had a great sense of humour and had everyone present rocking with laughter. It was agreed by all that this had been their best conference ever. Things were changing for the better.

Some time later I bought two new paperbacks, *Ten Growing Churches* (edited by Eddie Gibbs) and *Ten Sending Churches*. I found these books very enlightening and exciting.

One chapter in *Ten Growing Churches* referred to the Baptist Church at Isleham in Norfolk. The dedicated minister had found his ministry unrewarding and depressing. In answer to much prayer both he and his wife received a Divine blessing of the Holy Spirit, their minds and hearts were newly opened to the treasures of Christ and they received a special and precious new start. Men and women and young people began to come and were converted to Christ. The Baptist Chapel became too small. The Victorian-type organ and all the cumbersome furniture had to go; a new youth orchestra put new life into the service. Blessings abounded in the Church and throughout the village. Twice each Sunday the chapel was filled to capacity (150 people) and considerable sums of money flowed weekly into Church funds.

I attended a number of these services and found them even more acceptable and vibrant than the book had described. I found the people there to be filled with joy and adoration for God, and the pastor and his wife and family quite delightful. The hopes I had entertained in Chile all those years ago were alive here and now in Isleham and in many parts of the United Kingdom and were spreading rapidly all over the world. Renewal hitherto unknown in the Church since the early days of Christianity was flowing from God and millions of members of His Kingdom were being increasingly blessed throughout the worldwide Christian Church.

CHAPTER 24
PARISH PROGRESS

Francis Light, the son of Colonel Edward Light, was born at Dallinghoo Hall and baptized in Dallinghoo Church in 1748. After his education at Woodbridge school he travelled to the Island of Penang for employment. In those times that sea voyage alone must have been for him quite an event with many dangers. It was a very long way from home.

No doubt he commenced his work in a junior way at first, as a clerk in connection with the Maharajah's plantations. With passing years his influence in the plantations grew significantly. He married a wealthy Portuguese woman. In the year 1784 the Maharajah of the Island had become so impressed with the influence and achievements of Francis Light that he presented Penang to the British Crown. So this was one of Britain's earliest colonies. But just as important to Great Britain was the acquirement of a deep-sea harbour which was adequate for the Royal Navy's Far East fleet. From this base, ships of the Royal Navy were able to go out and harass ships of the French and Dutch navies and any other pirate vessels. This harassment of other ships and protection for British merchantmen must have greatly contributed to the early successes of the British East India Company, leading eventually to British India. So in this way Francis Light was a credit to the parish of Dallinghoo and to Great Britain.

He was made Governor of Penang in 1784. His son Edward was born also in 1784 and when he was old enough to travel his father sent him to motherland Suffolk to be educated at his Woodbridge school. At a very early age Edward joined the Royal Navy as a midshipman, sailed around the world, had many sea adventures and eventually became the first Surveyor General of Australia. He was especially engaged in mapping out the River Murray Darling area. Towards the end of his life he conceived the city of Adelaide and lived to see it built. Representatives of Dallinghoo and Adelaide communicate with each other from time to time, and naturally this has been a great pleasure to me.

During these busy years in Dallinghoo we enjoyed three holidays. I knew that Dorothy at least deserved these breaks for she worked with me nonstop, in top gear all the time.

We enjoyed a fishing holiday on the Blackwater river, Southern Ireland. I had seen the advertisement for the hire of the fishing chalet together with fishing rights. The proprietor was a Mr Bosanquet whose address was in Gwent, South Wales.

We made the long road journey from Suffolk across to Fishguard, South Wales, took a boat from there to Rosslare in Southern Ireland and then, by another road journey, made our way to this chalet, which was ideal. The scenery was superb, the river lively and gushing. The gillie was most knowledgeable and we had good salmon fishing. We toured the south western coast area and one could not have wished for more idyllic views and vistas. Also, I thought, the Gulf Stream flows along this coast and so there will be neither frost nor snow. What an ideal place for retirement, someday, I thought!

Some years later a message from the Provost of St Edmundsbury Cathedral informed that he was organising a holiday party to Yugoslavia and would we care to join his party. We did so. This summer of 1976 was proving to be one of the hottest on record. We travelled by coach to London Airport and from there flew direct to Dubrovnik in Yugoslavia. We then made a coach journey to our holiday resort a few miles to the south. Here were modern multistorey blocks of flats, one of which was to be our home for a fortnight. It was hot! The sea bathing was all that one could wish for and Dorothy was in her element. On several days I walked up the high mountains inland and noted some of their little chapels, now locked up, and I could peep through the barred ironwork. The villagers up there were most curious to see me moving around their environment and probably wondered what I was up to. Strangely enough I heard constant cuckoo notes and realised this must be a favourite haunt for these birds. We spent several days seeing the wonderful and historic Dubrovnik, alas now battered severely by war.

I was tortured nightly by the raucous blaring of pop music which continued until about 4 a.m. each morning. I complained to the management but it made no difference. This blaring of sound was one of the main attractions for modern tourists, who apparently revelled in it.

Our third holiday during these years was to the Outer Hebrides. First of all there was the long car journey from Suffolk to the North West of Scotland. Much of this was completed over the first night, so that we arrived on the banks of Loch Lomond during the early hours of the morning. And then through that majestic and fascinating mountain and loch country and across the Isle of Skye. From the west coast we embarked on the steamer which took us to a port on the east side of South Uist. A car journey then took us to the nearest point to our cottage. But, oh dear, it was such a long walk down to our cottage, which was on the edge of a bay, and it was not easy to carry our stores all that way down. The cottage was so near to the water's edge that it was not difficult to throw a stone from the door of the house into the sea. Because of this proximity, we found the rooms of the cottage very damp, and very cold and clammy at night. Even our two corgi dogs felt the cold and begged to clamber on to our beds to keep warm.

We found the island to be bleak. There were no trees worth speaking of and what few there were were stunted and sadly bent over as the result of the salt-saturated gales. The island's surface was mostly rocky because topsoils could not possibly remain in the face of constant – and, for much of the year, ferocious – gales. However, there was a profusion of wild flowers on the hills where we went for long walks with the dogs.

On one of these rather long walks one day, I noticed that my dog, Teddy, was left far away behind. I went to see what the trouble was to find him utterly exhausted. When I saw the cause I was almost ashamed of myself and should have known better. Teddy, with his short legs, was having to jump over every single clump of heather. He must have jumped over hundreds and he could manage no more. I had to carry him.

I am sure that the waters were rich with all kinds of fish but I had neither the skill nor equipment to catch any but a few trout. However, many of the lochs were shallow and so birds of prey had stripped them rather thoroughly, I thought.

It was good to see, even so far away from the mainland, the splendid provision for HM postal services with freshly painted post boxes and telephone kiosks wherever they were needed. The schools were well built and maintained with no lack of attention to detail.

The folk there maintained a zealous Christian faith and practice. No washing must be seen on a line on Sunday and certainly no fishing.

It was the end of October when we journeyed homewards. The colourful shades of the leaves of the Scottish forests were rich and lovely.

One day I was in my office, thumbing through the diocesan telephone directory, when my eye saw the name, Revd John Perrott. The name seemed somehow familiar and interesting. Could it possibly be the name of someone related to Sir A. G. Perrott, previous Inspector General of Police, North-West Frontier, Province of India, who had been a special friend to me all those years ago?

I telephoned him. 'Are you by any chance related to the late Sir A. G. Perrott?'

Back came the astonishing reply, 'Yes, I'm his son!'

Here, then, a few parishes distant from me, was the boy who, at five years of age, was saved from that car crash by stepping out of the car a few seconds before it happened. I have before me at this moment the Diocese of St Edmondsbury and Ipswich Directory and under the name Perrott I read: **PERROTT J. A. C.** (John) LLB Univ of NZ. Clifton Th College. Deaconed 1964, Priested 1965, The Rectory, Elmswell, Bury St Edmunds IP30 9DY, telephone Elmswell 40512.

After A. G. Perrott's retirement the family lived in New Zealand where John received his upbringing and education, graduating LLB at the university. They then moved to live once more in England and then John felt called to become a minister of the C of E.

I was amazed and thrilled. Soon John Perrott was over at my rectory for lunch. I was able to express my admiration for his father and mother. I showed pictures of them all in their delightful garden in Peshawar and reminded him of that day when, as by a miracle, he had escaped death by just a few seconds. I am persuaded to contact him again once more, for who can ever forget his wonderful father!

Kathleen was sixteen years of age when, at the end of a morning service at Dallinghoo, she handed me a white envelope. It contained her complete first week's wage, for she had just started her first job. I was deeply touched. A few years later, just a few days before her marriage, Kathleen handed me another white envelope with the words, 'Here is my final week's wage. I give it to God in thanksgiving, for He has been so good to me while I have lived here in Dallinghoo.' Such actions and attitudes deeply move a minister's soul. Needless to say Kathleen, now approaching middle age, continues to live a mature family life with her farmer husband, children and church.

The Most Outstanding Day of My Ministry

Once the Christmas tree saga was behind us I was able to concentrate more on the parochial and spiritual aspects of ministry. It seemed good to me to have an annual Sunday given over to a Christian rally, and in 1986 this was to be the last Sunday in June. The Christmas tree case compensation enabled me to choose outstanding guest preachers and teachers and adequately pay their fees and expenses. The Rt Revd Richard Hare, Bishop of Pontefract, and Pastor Fred Smith were chosen for this Sunday.

They took part in three services: morning, afternoon and evening. Christian healing was administered at the evening service. Lunches at the rectory were arranged for some people and there was an open invitation to all parishioners to attend a raspberry and cream tea party on the rectory lawns.

The day dawned bright and sunny and remained so all day. The church was filled with parishioners for the morning service when the bishop preached a rousing and splendid sermon commanding the deepest attention and appreciation from the congregation. Pastor Fred Smith told of his experiences in the healing ministry for the past thirty years. The afternoon service concentrated on hymns, prayer, devotion and scriptural thought. This was followed by the afternoon tea when guests enjoyed the raspberries and cream and other good things. The Evening service was to be the outstanding one of the day, for Christian healing was to be offered.

A man named Ken Harper, twenty-seven years of age, had expressed the desire to come for healing purposes. His life had gone to pieces, body, soul and spirit. He had already had two operations for stomach cancer and was shortly to have another very serious one. He was skin and bone and had despaired of life. That Sunday evening there were so many cars lining the country lane leading to the Church that latecomers had some difficulty in finding their way through. The Church was packed to the doors. A feeling of great excitement and expectancy permeated the service as beautiful hymns were sung, scriptures read, and prayers offered.

The time for healing came. People were invited to join in the queue for the anointing by Bishop Hare. Those who wished then passed before Pastor Fred Smith for his Christian laying on of hands and prayer. I took my place of duty in the chancel.

One by one the people were ministered to by Pastor Smith. Some fell into my arms, unconscious by the power of the Holy Spirit, and I laid them down before me until they regained their consciousness.

I saw Ken Harper take his place before Pastor Smith who, in his usual manner, asked Ken what his trouble was. Then Pastor Fred Smith laid his hands on Ken's head and prayed for the power of Jesus to come to Ken, and cast out of him the power of Satan.

Ken suddenly let out a mighty yell which filled the Church and then fell unconscious into my arms. I laid him down where he remained for some fifteen minutes with a lovely smile on his face. He then returned to normal consciousness and returned to his place in the congregation. He was filled with joy and peace. He knew he was healed. His pains had completely gone. Meanwhile the rest of the congregation were administered to in the same way. It was one of my busiest and most wonderful duties ever. How many were healed or helped or comforted in that service we shall never know. Great was the Christian and holy rejoicing as many returned to the rectory after the service. In the drawing room I sat next to the bishop, reclining in an armchair when he went to sleep, utterly exhausted and utterly happy, and he remained there for a long time.

A mini-seminar was held in the rectory drawing room the next morning. Present were the bishop, Pastor Fred Smith, clergy from round about and other parishioners. We were there to recall the glorious events of the previous day. The Vicar of Wickham Market, the Revd Graham Bell, had a message for us. Ken Harper, full of joy and peace, had telephoned him early in the morning to say that not only was he healed, with all pains gone, but also that the large previously made operation marks across his stomach, had completely disappeared. There was no trace of them.

Some days later Ken Harper appeared before his surgeons and doctors by appointment and in readiness for them to perform the next stomach operation. Ken told them what had happened. They therefore now, more than ever, examined him with the greatest possible medical thoroughness. At the end of this prolonged examination the surgeon told Ken that he had not the slightest trace of illness in his whole body. He was discharged from their presence. He was healed, happy, and above all a new man in Christ Jesus. The media got hold of the story and spared no effort in investigating all the elements of the case. In the end they could do no other but confirm that a wonderful miracle had taken place.

Christian newspapers throughout the Christian reading world printed this story to the great encouragement and joy of multitudes of Christians. A few months after this Sunday, Pastor Fred Smith returned once more to my parish on a Friday afternoon to heal the sick. A man of forty-five years of age who had had a palsied and useless hand for five years was one of those present. Pastor Smith rebuked the evil spirit causing the palsied hand which was immediately healed and remains so to this day. For thirty years Pastor Fred Smith had so ministered the Lord's healing to thousands of people.

The healing stories are miraculous and glorious and otherwise unbelievable. His ministry is recorded in his book, *God's Gift of Healing*.

Six years later, the Vicar of Wickham Market telephoned me concerning the latest report on Ken Harper. He now weighs fourteen and a half stone, is happily married, has a splendid job in the USA and is a lively member of a lively Christian Church.

Ken Harper was **instantly** healed of an otherwise incurable and terminal illness. Here is an example of a priceless function which humanity so desperately needs, for life is precious and death so evil. Thousands have been and are being healed by this miraculous power of God, brought about in the name of Jesus. But the need is for millions to be so healed. The Church of England spends a great amount of time and wealth in daily celebrating the Holy Communion in its cathedrals and many of its churches. But within a stone's throw of those cathedrals and churches people are suffering and destined to die through terminal illnesses. Church and NHS are powerless to help. In this sense the church is some 2000 years behind the times of Jesus Who, according to the Gospels, healed **everyone. It was the Lord's undoubted and undisputed instruction that His disciples should heal the sick.** The absence of so doing is the negation of the Gospel. To the Lord's glory increasing numbers of ministers, of various denominations, are now healing the sick, in the Name of Jesus of Nazareth. What a miraculous power! That last Sunday in June 1986 was the happiest day of my whole ministry.

My years in Suffolk had been packed with activity. Probably for this reason I was startled to find that they seemed to have flown by and now there were circumstances to remind of retirement. I could hardly believe in any such thing, but now I realised that I was well past the stipulated minimum age for retirement and had already reached the age for compulsory retirement – seventy years! I somehow felt that I was only just commencing. I never felt tired nor wearied in the slightest and I also felt that my ministry was not nearly finished. I just wanted to keep on going. But the fact had to be faced.

Even so, the Christmas tree affairs, especially the financial aspects, were still dragging on. More costly restoration work had been done on both Dallinghoo and Pettistree Churches.

Pettistree Bells Ring Out Once More

I was now concerned with the Pettistree Church bells which had not rung since VE Day, some forty-five years before. The bell frame had been declared unsafe. Of course the matter should have been righted as soon as the weakness was revealed, but procrastination had stopped any action.

When I had been awarded damages over the Christmas tree saga I said that some of the award money could be used for the restoration of the Pettistree bells. To my considerable amazement some members of the Pettistree parochial church council were not pleased about my offer. The matter was contended for several meetings, but by the encouraging persuasion of some members it was agreed that my offer of £10 000 should be accepted and the matter of the restoration of the bells be pursued. Albert Webster became the dynamic and very able organiser and treasurer for the scheme. He was strongly supported by Mr Hallet, orthopaedic surgeon, and the Chief Constable of Suffolk, Stuart Whitely QM. Since his arrival in the village the chief constable had supported my ministry strongly and so had his charming wife, Dorothy. In due time the PCC was unanimously behind the bells scheme. Inspections were carried out, plans were made, the bells were dismantled and taken to a bell foundry and everyone became excited. Later a coach party travelled to the bell foundry to learn the mystery of bells and especially to see Pettistree's own bells being worked on in the foundry. Gifts of money came in so well that, before the bells were rehung, all the costs of £29 000 had been fully met.

I had retired two months before the bells were rededicated at a special service. I was very ill at the time in my retirement house and could not attend, but I was fully informed afterwards about the nature of the service. The parish had sent me a copy of the service to be used. It was to commence at 3 o'clock on Sunday, December 12th. At that precise time, I stood in my house, and with the service sheet in my hand went through the service stage by stage. At 5.30 p.m. Mrs Gascoigne rang to tell of the remarkable service which had taken place.

Pettistree Church was packed to the limit, with people even seated on the pulpit steps. Bell-ringing teams, and indeed the heads of the Bell Ringing Association, were all there. People had to move out of the aisle to make way for the bishop and clergy processions. Someone had designed a splendid service. At the time of dedication the bells were chimed and, of course, after the service the bells were rung for an hour or so. It was fitting that this day, sandwiched as it was between days of most inclement December weather, was like a summer's day. After the service the people were able to leisurely muster outside the Church in the crimson glow of the setting sun and then walk up to the Women's Institute for tea. The Christmas Tree Project had done it again! *Laus Deo!*

Shortly before these events I had announced to all concerned my retirement date – the end of September 1986. From now on, in addition to the usual parish programmes of services, funerals, marriages, baptisms, interviews, PCC and clergy meetings, there would be all kinds of preparations for retirement. My printing programmes had to be wound up and the considerable printing equipment sold. More visitations to my new property had to be made to verify the moving-in date and for me to examine the property and make preparations and modifications as required. In Dallinghoo a Trust Deed had to be created and agreed on to control the award for Christmas tree damages money.

The diocese had planned that there should be no future rector of Dallinghoo and Pettistree. This was in accordance with the reduction of country clergy, in keeping with the Sheffield Report. So I was able to communicate with the Vicar of Wickham Market who, after my retirement, would be responsible for Pettistree, and likewise the Vicar of Charsfield, who would become responsible for Dallinghoo. I was able to supply them with parish details, man to man, and this was very helpful. The month of September drew near and my last few weeks were in sight. The end of my long and unusual official ministry for the Church of England would soon end.

Parishioners would fully expect some kind of climax or finale and I planned for this. I decided to have my last Sunday in the form of a Christian rally once more. The Archdeacon of Suffolk, the Venerable Terry Gibson, readily agreed to preach the farewell sermon. Yes, I would arrange for a lunch for all parishioners who would like to come, and for other friends of mine from all over the area – friends who had meant so much to me. Yes, there would be a marquee on the rectory lawn. And, yes, there would be a good lunch provided. The idea quickly settled in my mind and gave me much satisfaction. The day would cost quite a considerable amount but I could now afford this. I would show my love and regard for all, prior to my departure, and my wife Dorothy was at one with me in this plan. After all, love is the greatest commandment for the Christian life. An open invitation was issued to all parishioners via the last parish magazine and some 130 people acknowledged and accepted the invitation. A caterer and his wife were chosen and given the menu to be provided. We now hoped for a fine day for September 12th.

The days leading up to the event were stormy and unsettled but the morning of the twelfth dawned clear, warm and still. It was going to be fine.

Pettistree Church was packed. All my special friends had arrived, some from a long distance away. Included were my cousin and her husband, Sir Jasper and Lady Hollam. Sir Jasper, who had recently retired as Deputy Governor of the Bank of England, read the Second Lesson. Unknown to me, some senior parish folk had trained a children's choir and during the service they sang very suitable pieces superbly. The Archdeacon of Suffolk preached his sermon on the theme of 'Once started, keep going', like a modern air pilot who must be sure to keep the airliner in proper flight from beginning to landing. He suggested that I had tried to do this with the parishes even when things were difficult. I had certainly flitted around the world! At the end of the service the churchwardens took over and made a generous presentation to my wife and me.

It remained a fine, sunny and warm day, so how fortunate we were. After the Church service people made their way to Dallinghoo Rectory where they were duly welcomed and mingled together before lunch was served. The weather was so perfect that the ladies were able to wear their summer silk dresses and instead of sitting in the marquee some groups sat outside in the sunshine enjoying the weather, the view, the company and the lunch. Some of the visitors, including my cousins, afterwards went to view the Dallinghoo Church nearby. They knew how its restoration had been made possible by the Christmas tree saga. It gave me great satisfaction to show them the place where Ken Harper had fallen and risen to find himself healed totally from stomach cancer. Then followed, for some, various tea parties and my very happy last official day at Pettistree had come to an end.

Until the end of September I maintained the Sunday services at Dallinghoo Church. And on the last day of September, while still officially in Office, the Dallinghoo PCC together with newly appointed diocesan trustees, created the Trust Deed for the award monies. Then it was the end of my forty-five years of ministry in the Church of England. During this long ministry I had lost only two Sundays through illness.

CHAPTER 25
RETIREMENT

It was time to pack and prepare for removal to South Wales. But I became ill, and not even my homeopathic medicines put me right. Pain and paralysis were creeping all over my body and after a few days I could do nothing. We cancelled the arrangements for removal for a fortnight. My wife was doing most of the packing. I grew worse. Once more *I was flat on my back* and this time literally. Our removal was cancelled a second time. Then the manager of the removal company came, and when he saw the situation he arranged to do absolutely everything himself.

The huge removal van at last arrived; everything was ready and loaded. The rectory was completely empty and I shut and locked the door of the last of many official residences with a twinge in my soul.

With great difficulty I managed somehow to crawl into my car seat and drive the long distance to our new home in Gwent. It was raining and dull. The huge furniture van arrived. Fortunately I had had the barn rebuilt and it now housed practically all our belongings. Only the barest of necessities were placed in the house. This included two beds placed in the downstairs room. I managed to get into bed and from then on could hardly move a limb.

The doctor and a nurse came. Blood tests were made, medicines taken, but I remained more or less the same for two months. If only Fred Smith could come and see me, I thought! But he could not for he had passed away himself whilst in the midst of a healing campaign during which people were being healed. He himself suddenly died at midnight. Why? Did he take in some illness from someone afflicted? We shall never know. This great man, humble and mighty in healing thousands, had now gone to heaven to receive the glories of Christ and a certain, 'Well done'.

Without Dorothy's help I could neither rise from nor get into bed, nor could I rise from nor sit in a chair. I could neither dress nor undress. Dorothy had to do every little thing for me. With difficulty I ate my meals for I could hardly hold a knife, fork or spoon. Night after night I relaxed in the thoughts of Christ and His ability to heal and help, and refused to worry as a result. His will be done in all things, and I silently praised God for all His wonderful care I had experienced and all the joyful ministry He had given me.

In November 1986, in the midst of my illness, I received a letter from a Mrs Powell, who lived at Llandysul, Dyfed, South Wales, concerning a corgi bitch I had ordered six months earlier. Some time after Suki and Teddy had died in 1980 we had another corgi called Teddy. We had considered how good it would be for this new Teddy to have a girl friend. But, I had said, she must be complete with tail. This had been agreed and Mrs Powell now wrote that we must please collect Vicky. Oh dear, I thought, how can I make this long journey in the midst of this crippling illness? There was no way out but to try.

It was hard enough to get to my car and harder still to somehow sit in my driving seat. I could not even pull out the choke to start her up. My wife, who was with me, had to do all this. My wife also had to do the gear changing for me, at least to begin with. I managed to get the car moving along the roads and knew that once we reached the motorway it would not be too difficult to steer the car because the motorways have no sudden turns. We reached the M4 and travelled via Newport, Cardiff, Swansea and beyond, and from there we travelled along lesser roads. We found the kennels and little Vicky. At last she was placed in her bed in the car and we made the long and difficult return journey. It had been a round trip of about 300 miles. I did not want any more journeys like that until health returned, if it would return. Vicky and Teddy became very good companions from the start. They adore each other and our idea of companionship for Teddy has been thoroughly rewarded.

These two dogs mean so much to us. They have the six acres of dog-proof protection and can run after the rabbits, which should not be there, as much as they like. They walk with me daily around the plantation and in the house they are the most perfect pets and companions. Vicky is my shadow and follows me wherever I go, especially into my office. She is here with me now as I type these words.

With regard to my illness, after another two months, the doctor came and made another diagnosis. With the assistance of further blood tests my illness was shown to be myalgia. New tablets were prescribed and within six hours of taking the first two, pains diminished and I was able to raise myself up from and into a chair for the first time. It was wonderful to do so with little pain. The improvement rapidly continued and was more wonderful. I could now help Dorothy by doing a few light jobs. Still continuing to improve, I could now help bring furniture from the barn and we began to set up house. Then I became able to use a drill to make rawlplug fittings and put up shelves. I could use the wheelbarrow and my car to transfer the needed furniture from barn to house. We were becoming organised.

At last we were sensing our new environment and seeing the countryside around us. Everything was lovely, peaceful, and private. We were thrilled! I started to attend the Church services on Sunday. The Welsh Church Prayer Book was good, I thought. It was so clearly and beautifully printed, and contained all the essential elements for Christian worship and also was much simpler than the complex English Alternative Service Book which I had been using for the past few years.

All around us are narrow country farm roads with major roads some miles away. The countryside is undulating with greater hills and mountains all around us but at a distance, and with great valleys in between. The views from our house are striking and, with the ever-changing cloud effects, very pleasing indeed. Tranquillity and restfulness characterise the area. On average, we do not have more than one visitor per week. All this is in sharp contrast to my previous years of dealing with people, people, people.

I am asked to take services from time to time and doing so keeps alive my spiritual sensitivity. The rural dean requires my help from time to time to take services in any part of a wide area, along mountain valleys and on the plains – anywhere, in fact. So the service requirements are almost weekly, and sometimes twice, and on occasions three times.

However, I find the level of Church or Christian enthusiasm to be tranquil and unmoving, something like the environment. In this area very few people attend Church. They do come very well to the annual harvest service followed by the harvest supper. It could be common sense for some to say 'what more can one expect?' The people here have everything they need in life and that is indeed the trouble. There is little regard at all for the paramount call of Christ for Christians to *go into all the world and preach the Gospel*. And if parishioners cannot, of course, go into all the world they can take note of all the world and how Christ is pleading for his Church to help the downtrodden, war-stricken, disease-ridden and famine-stricken multitudes of mankind. If they would do this the parishes could burst into spiritual and joyful life, but not otherwise. Missionary vision opens up new worlds and new vistas. In this, Christ Himself and His Holy Spirit will descend and give great joy.

The monthly Christian publication entitled *Challenge* is a joy to read and so refreshing. It contains stories of Christ redeeming and blessing people right now. I tell my congregations about these stories and they, too, find them refreshing, vibrant and convincing.

I enjoy also the monthly magazine *Renewal* at present edited by Edward England. I like it because it records the results of the New Testament Gospel in its completeness, including Christ's calling, healing, prophecy and wonders. The magazine is a medium of great joy and triumph for Christ and His Church.

I chose this area to retire because I considered it would be suitable for growing Christmas trees. From the start, even while I was ill, I set the project in motion. I was very fortunate in being introduced to David Whistance, excellent agricultural contractor and a very likeable person. At my invitation David had my lands weed controlled; his team erected rabbit wire posts and fencing around the whole property and, in April 1987, 60 000 trees were planted. The planting took a mere four days. From my previous experience with the Dallinghoo plantations I knew that the hard work would follow ever after, and it has.

The plantation has to be kept free from weeds, the trees protected against birds and aphids and other pests and they have to be supplied with correct but costly fertiliser. In performing these operations for the plantation I cover some twenty-five miles each time and this is repeated about twenty times a year. So the annual walking is around 500 miles. I have therefore walked some 2 500 miles in the last five years. Half of these operations entail carrying a knapsack sprayer which, when full, weighs at least 50 lb. In the spring and summer, it is a twelve-hour day. So, as you can see, I recovered from the myalgia, at least mostly, for the medical authorities say it never fully goes away. By sheer hard work I try to drive it out of my life. But above all I never cease to thank God for His endless mercies, the joys He gives us here, and for keeping my once-undeveloped heart as strong as the heart of a lion. Thank you, Lord!

I came to the West Country chiefly to benefit from greater rainfall compared with East Anglia. There could not have been worse dry weather over the past five years. Because of my illness there was no hope of planting the trees in the coolness of the 1986 autumn although they had been ordered as from September of that year. Winter and spring rains prevented ground preparation (and so planting) until the third week in April. This was rather late, but all would be well, I thought, if we could soon after have a shower or two. We did not have a single drop of rain until 2nd June. It was cruel. I bought long lengths of hosepipe and watered as best I could throughout each day from the light of dawn until darkness fell. Fortunately the water pressure here is very high which was a considerable advantage. The trees were saved from what would otherwise have been certain destruction.

Nineteen eighty-nine saw a further prolonged and severe drought – so much so that, when harvest time came in late November, the young trees were in no condition for sale. So there was no thinning out either and this would be serious later on. However, the weeds managed to grow and had to be treated.

Nineteen ninety saw an even more severe and prolonged drought but by this time the trees were well and truly rooted and stood up to the dryness. The rains came in late September and the trees began to show new life.

In October representatives of a large garden centre came to see me. They begged me to allow them to buy every available tree. From that time they kept in close touch and their workers came to colour-code the trees they would buy. They were supplied with some 12 000 trees which normally should have been paid for ex-plantation. They had reminded me that they were the main garden centre of the area, well known and in excellent standing. Their banking facilities were frozen in mid-December 1990 and six months later the company was wound up, having been declared insolvent. I lost all my expected income. Another company also defaulted in payment, so it was a very disappointing year. Once again I was flat on my back. I had spent a fortune on the project and after five years there were no financial rewards.

In 1991 the rains came quite well. Now the trees bolted and, because they had not been thinned out during the two previous years, they were in danger of smothering themselves. Some 5 000 trees were cut down and burned. But this proved insufficient and so men were engaged to come in with high-powered trimmers to trim 40 000 trees. The trees did not come out of the trim in time for the November/December sales and very few trees were sold. It was my hope that the trees would be good for sales during the 1992 harvest, barring misfortunes.

But the project has done for me what I had planned it to do. It has given me a positive health-giving and wonderful occupation and I am sure that in due time it will yield good financial results. This will ultimately be for the support of Christian Mission work in a desperately needy and sin-sick world. No endeavour could be more healthy or precious for me in my retirement years.

CHAPTER 26
INTERFAITH SERVICES

As stated earlier, I became a life member of the Royal Commonwealth Society as far back as 1948. I am regularly supplied with their literature, information and programmes. Until retirement I had little time to look at such matters and therefore missed noting an annual programme of great significance and importance.

I refer to the Annual Commonwealth Day. Four years ago I read about this in the annual programme of events for the year. To be included in the celebrations was the Commonwealth Day service in Westminster Abbey. At this service leaders of other religions – Hindus, Buddhists, Muslims and Jews – were encouraged to present portions of their respective writings, prayers or songs in a kind of 'let's all get together' idea.

I could hardly believe it. I read it over and over again. The idea worried me. If this service was grossly faulty then Westminster Abbey, of all places, was producing a pattern for all to follow. I remembered the Church rules when I was ordained. At my first service following the ordination I had to read out a declaration that I would never use any other form than the Book of Common Prayer or a service authorised by the bishop. And every newly ordained cleric did the same. And from time to time clergy who dared to share any service with say a Methodist or Presbyterian, were severely reprimanded in spite of the fact that they were sharing with Christians.

But now, in contrast, the nature of this Westminster Abbey service was astonishing! It was to be led by HM the Queen who, in her coronation oaths, had vowed to maintain and uphold her Christian services and Holy Bible entirely.

The unacceptability of this began to rouse me to think further and carefully, and then to take action. In the name of God the Father and His Christ of the Gospels I felt I must protest. But why hadn't other people protested? And who was I to so protest? Something must be done, I decided.

I remembered that some months earlier the Revd Tony Higton had protested about a similar service in Canterbury Cathedral and in doing so had been slighted by the Church authorities.

My sense of indignation caused me to write a very severe letter of protest to the Very Revd the Dean of Westminster Abbey. The dean duly replied and also enclosed a copy of the previous year's Commonwealth Service. Quite clearly the dean was arguing from the human standpoint of being kind and thoughtful and tolerant towards the other faiths. There appeared to be absolutely no thought or consideration for the nature of the Biblically revealed Godhead including the unique Christ as the only Lord with whom we have to do. There appeared to be no consciousness that throughout the Bible God's people were constantly warned *to be intolerant* towards other deities. I was sure that this kind of service was a total affront to sincere Christians but more importantly an affront to God Himself. The service totally cancelled out the ABC of the Christian religion which is, of course, 'Thou shalt have no other gods but me'. In answering the dean's letter I stated that his letter had revealed the matter to be even more serious than I'd thought and showed HM the Queen's intricate and dangerous involvement. Of course I realised what had caused this service to be allowed to take place. It was the outcome of liberal theology which, for a long time, step-by-step and little-by-little has been eroding Biblical Revelation and theology. I realised that the dean, like many other of today's theologians, had lost his sensitivity towards Christ and His pure way of life and unique claims. Christ expects his followers to be totally proud of Him to the exclusion of all other powers or deities. The Church of Christ is spoken of in Scripture as being the same as the perfect marriage bond which should not be interfered with or fractured in any way.

This matter was of great concern to the Revd Tony Higton who worked further on this matter in his own methodical way. As a result Mr Higton was able to present a petition to HM the Queen with some 76 000 signatures of Christians from throughout the Commonwealth. It was presented to the Queen one week before Christmas 1990. Whatever in the world is happening to Christian England, I thought?

Television comments by His Royal Highness the Prince of Wales in April 1991 caught my attention. His Royal Highness was commenting on the nation's poor educational results. Previously the Prince had complained about the poor liturgical quality of the Alternative

Prayer Book, and some time before that he had complained passionately about poor architecture.

I sent a letter to His Royal Highness in April 1991 saying that most people would agree that many matters *are* wrong and that the Prince would have been right to have included the Northern Ireland situation, law and order, the economy, unemployment and the state of the National Health Service. It was obvious to all that the United Kingdom was suffering from a general malaise and the question was, why? I suggested that a part of the answer could be that God is withholding His Divine Blessing, in which case another question arises, why? I suggested that one reason could be that the Royal House, in connivance with the Established Church, has spearheaded interfaith services to create what amounts to a 'Commonwealth type of religion'. Certainly all subjects of the Crown would immediately be up in arms should anyone challenge Her Majesty's sole right to the Crown. Similarly, all sincere Christians are appalled when, in Christian theology, the unique claim of Christ and His Gospel are challenged by interfaith theological merging. This merging of beliefs is now seeping rapidly through Christian cathedrals, Churches and schools and in time the essence of the Christian Faith, as we have known it in the past, will be lost. The unique Lord Christ and His Testament warns that this practice must never be tolerated in the Christian Church.

The outcome cannot be anything but disaster for the Crown and country. 'As Your Royal Highness knows,' I wrote, 'the recent petition signed by 76 000 member Christians of countries of the Commonwealth, has been rejected by the Royal House. I pray that some wonderful turnabout in this respect can be hoped for. If this happens there could be splendid hope for renewal of our country's harmony and progress.'

In the *Church Times*, 29 November 1991, there was an article headlined: **Dr Carey Puts the Case for Tolerance**. This caused me to write to the archbishop as follows:

'Your Grace,

I have read the *Church Times* account of your Morrell address at the University of York. I am particularly and deeply concerned with Your Grace's views relating to interfaith services.

'My Bible studies at Tyndale Hall showed quite outstandingly that the main warning from Jehovah throughout Old Testament history and Jesus in the New Testament was concerning interfaith associations and that **intolerance** of all other deities was to be followed at all costs. "Thou shalt have no other gods but me" was Jehovah's basic demand at all times. This is surely the basis of the Biblical Godhead. The Old Testament story of Queen Jezebel, Elijah and the prophets of Baal is a typical example of the intolerance demanded. Invitation of other deities into theological fellowship in Westminster Abbey and in other cathedrals and places of worship is dangerously close to his story. The Christian Revelation is being trivialised. To have had the Presence of Jesus Christ glorifying our national way of life for so long makes the matter even more serious.

'Intolerance, perhaps, plays a more important role in life than tolerance. Intolerance has to be used in many a twist and turn. When a mother sees her child about to place its fingers into an electric plug she quickly slaps the child's hand away to save the child from being killed. In the same way it is abundantly clear that Jehovah and then, in turn, Jesus Christ, warned of the great dangers of accepting any other deities or powers into any consideration of Godhead sharing. Such is portrayed as inviting great evil and forfeiting Divine Blessing. This is surely the outstanding instruction of both the Old and New Testaments and has been accepted as such by all Christians up to recent times.

'Tolerance is the outstanding excuse and plea by those who wish to promote interfaith services. I find this plea hollow in the extreme for theologians who believe in the Biblical triune Godhead. It is also extremely serious if maintaining absoluteness of the Godhead means life or death to mankind as declared by Jesus.

'I do, of course, accept with all normal people, that Christians are to love everyone as much as possible regardless of creed, nationality or colour. For many years, in lands overseas, I had the closest of relations with Muslims, Buddhists and Hindus. But this must not lead me to interfaith worship'.

I continued:

I do not expect this letter will make any difference to the operations of interfaith practises. The matter seems now to be too far gone. I send it as a duty to my God and His Christ **and shall sadly expect to see further deterioration in Church, State and Crown as the result of this total disobedience to Biblical Revelation.**

'The matter appears to me to be so vital that I shall send copies
of this letter to the undermentioned and I can assure your Grace
that this matter will not be allowed to go away.'

Copies of this letter were sent to: Her Majesty the Queen's Private
Secretary; The Prime Minister; The Rt Hon John Gummer MP; the
Very Revd The Dean of Westminister Abbey; and the Revd Tony
Higton.

Shortly after I had sent this letter there was, in the *Church Times*,
one of the most remarkable insets I have ever seen. It contained a
copy of an Open Letter surrounded by a minutely printed list of
some 2000 names of Church of England and Church of Wales clergy
who had signed their names in support of this Open Letter to the
leadership of the Church of England. The letter is printed in Appendix 4.

Even as I write these words the sad news of 1992 is that, on the
one hand, Scotland is striving to sever its national links with the
UK and Australia clamours for independence from the Crown and
Commonwealth and so to become a republic. I had said in my letters
that God could not bless a nation disobedient to the ancient and
Biblical Revelation of Jesus Christ. The theology of the Godhead must
never, ever, be tampered with by any person or persons on earth.
To do so makes God a toy to be played with and that is blasphemy.

In recent months there have been newspaper headlines such as
the following one in the *Church Times*:

Uneasy Westminster Traditionalists Draw Robust Answer from Dr
Carey

This was another letter of protest, from thirty-four MPs and peers
from the House of Lords, who also asked for 'a clear and unambigu-
ous moral lead' from the Church of England.

Such important people do not easily write a letter such as this.
They are sure, as many others are, that conditions of the present
Church of England are causing basic dissatisfaction and unrest. In
these and other theological matters my mind continues to work
continuously.

I am drawing to the end of my story.

My life seems to have come almost full circle from the time when
I spent such happy days on my father's seven-acre smallholding in

Cheshire. I then enjoyed perfect country freedom and this has moulded parts of my life and way of living. So now, with my wife, we spend happy days on this six-acre smallholding. It seems to be a life of bliss and happiness and perfect freedom. Our two corgi dogs, Teddy and Vicky, are perfect companions and full of fun and loyalty. We would not like to be without them. We have dear friends on the farms around us as well as parishioners in the churches, far and wide. It is our aim, for just as long as we can, to serve and love people and above all to serve our great God and His Christ and Holy Spirit and to promote and support Christian Missions, that is uphold those who try to spread around the glorious Name of Jesus Christ.

For me, so important are the things of God and His Church that I shall append several chapters on these matters. God has been speaking to me from lessons learnt in many parts of the world in unusual circumstances.

So the time will come for me, as to all people, to close my eyes on this world and this life. This life has been for me, in many ways, so amazingly wonderful, thrilling, beautiful, intriguing and exciting. In this respect I think of the words of Jesus: 'I have come that they might have life, and have it more abundantly'. He fulfilled this promise in my life and I am grateful and fully satisfied. On the other hand I have seen, with so many, so much cruelty, suffering, calamity, disease, death and ignorance in the world.

I trust, then, to awaken in the Presence of Christ and His Glory. I shall immediately ask for His mercy for my many, many sins. I shall say, 'Lord, by your grace and by your leading, I tried your way; You bid me "Go into all the World" and I went. Lord, you know the rest'.

Even from a creation point of view, astronomy reveals there will be no shortage of space for the new heavens and the new earth. There are untold billions of worlds. Some of them are likely to be places of sheer perfection from every point of view; and Almighty God will be in the midst of them, with the Son, who made all things; and love will be the central motivating life.

Dorothy will be with me. I know I shall behold my mother and embrace her and my father and brother and sisters. Shall I see parishioners from Upper Burma, India, Great Britain, Chile, Australia? Will those singing families from Australia be there? Perhaps we shall sing again in the glories of heaven! Will Ken Harper be there who fell into my arms as he was healed in Dallinghoo Church? I shall look forward to seeing those I might have wrongfully offended and rejoice in our complete reconciliation.

And what about our corgi dogs, whose affection, loyalty and life entwined into our very souls while we had them? They did no sin and showed no greed and other faults as in humans. Surely they will be resurrected and part of our surprise, joy and delight in heaven?

The resurrection life will reveal joys untold and for eternity; perfection will reign and evil, suffering and death will be unknown. Hallelujah! The Scriptures declare this over and over again. God will keep his word.

In the centre of heaven will be the Lamb of God, Jesus the crucified, the Saviour of mankind and indeed of the whole of creation. His adoration and praises will be for ever and ever.

This, then, has been my story, such as it is. It has been the result of my unworthily and feebly saying 'Yes' when Jesus said to me, some sixty years ago: **Go ye into all the World**.

REFERENCES

Gibbs E. (Ed.) (1984) *Ten Growing Churches*. MARC Europe, London.

Griffiths M. (Ed.) (1985) *Ten Sending Churches*. MARC Europe, London.

Neil C. and Willoughby J. M. (1912) *The Tutorial Prayer Book*. The Harrison Trust, London.

Osborn T. L. (1955) *Java Harvest*.

Smith F. (1986) *God's Gift of Healing*. New Wine Press, Chichester.

Other Christian publications referred to in this book

Challenge, Monthly. Ed. by Donald Banks. Revenue Buildings, Chapel Road, Worthing, West Sussex BN11 1BQ

Church of England Newspaper. Weekly. Ed. by John K. Martin. Fifth floor, 77 Farringdon Road, London EC1M 3JY

Church Times. Weekly. Ed. by John Whale. 33 Upper Street, London N1 6PN

Renewal. Monthly. Ed. by Edward England. Broadway House, The Broadway, Crowborough, East Sussex TN6 1HQ

APPENDIX 1
REFLECTIONS ON
THEOLOGY AND
HEALING

T. L. Osborn

From my observations, the nature and fruitfulness of T. L. Osborn's ministry would be more than sufficient to reinforce the full authenticity of the Gospels of Jesus. By this same fruitfulness any Gospel doubts are completely dissipated.

To have observed his ministry in Chile in 1954 was for me the most profound discovery and blessing of my whole life, and the value has been beyond words. His ministry, then and since, has been for me, and for many millions of people, like a shining beacon of Godly light, confirming the truth of the New Testament and putting to shame and flight false theology, so prevalent in some Churches. My previous theological education had contained a part of that false theology.

The outstanding Gospel truth his ministry revealed was that of the *proclamation* of Jesus Christ with healing and other miracles taking place freely. In other words it was and is the *application* of the Gospel and not the learning of the Gospel which, in his ministry, was all important. In my theological college, both by word of instruction, and in the standard textbooks provided, we were taught and believed that New Testament miracles ended with the Apostles. This was the standard teaching for all being trained in the Church of England in those days. One of our text books for liturgy and worship was *The Tutorial Prayer Book* by Charles Neil MA and J. M. Willoughby. DD. Under the subject of Confirmation, on page 429, are these words:

'The gifts received by laying-on of the Apostles' hands were extra-ordinary gifts (miracles, prophesy) which have long ceased.'

I am sure that lecturers could hardly be held responsible for this erroneous statement, simply because the error had been maintained in standard theological teaching in the Church of England for a very long time.

If the official Church training has been in error for so long on such a vital and fundamental issue as healing the sick then, I ask, in what other teachings has the Church wrongly instructed me and others?

Common sense stands out so clearly and strikingly in T. L. Osborn's ministry for evangelism. (And we note that at the present time the Church of England has also, with all other denominations, embarked upon a decade of evangelism.)

This matter of common sense was to be seen, for example, in the way T. L. Osborn conducted his great meetings, and especially his preaching, by the use of an interpreter. This evangelist came to any country, from his home in the USA, as fresh as a daisy and immediately began to preach with his dynamic and powerful and effective persuasion. In this manner the Gospel of God produced wonderful responses in the shortest possible time. Chile was the seventeenth country to which he had ministered. Today he has ministered to over seventy countries, in each case building an immediate rapport with the people. This because of effective and good interpretation; by this means there were no language barriers at all.

Now contrast this with what has been the standard way of training, sending out, and commissioning evangelists who, at the beginning, have a burning desire to preach God's Good News as quickly as possible. This potential evangelist, of course, receives his average school education. It is likely that it was in his teens that he felt called to be an evangelist; nevertheless, he must wait until a 'reasonable' age before he can be admitted to a training college and at last, after years of training, he is sent overseas to his Mission station. But he is certainly not yet allowed to preach nor teach (and here I speak from actual experience). He must spend more time learning the language. After this he then does not have very long to go before his first furlough is due and he returns home, very often without having seen one single convert. All this preparation has taken many years and has cost a small fortune with no real results. The common sense use of evangelist speaking through an interpreter ought to be of paramount importance and necessity

Missionary societies will rightly argue that they send a missionary to a specific area to identify with the people around and especially to be able to converse with them in their own language and so minister to them. T. L. Osborn would be the first to say how fundamentally true and important this is. Nevertheless, I think there is something more to consider concerning this. The missionary, especially if called by the Lord to be an evangelist, should not be halted in any way in this burning Divinely-inspired desire. Therefore, even though the new recruit must surely learn the local language as soon as possible, *he or she ought to be encouraged to preach the Gospel on arrival at the new Mission station – and to preach it with an interpreter.* There is nearly always someone on a Mission station who can act as interpreter for the new evangelist. 'Quench not the spirit' is supremely important here as a duty to the Lord who has called this missionary to proclaim Christ's glorious Name. To quench the preaching desire could dangerously undermine the inspiration and efficiency of the missionary. As a new recruit in Upper Burma, amongst the Kachins, and present at their Sunday services for several months, I was never given the opportunity to speak one word of the Gospel. It was quite wrong. Missionary societies should watch this matter most carefully, I feel sure.

I remember hearing T. L. Osborn, while preaching words of encouragement to potential evangelists, saying: 'You don't need to go to college; read your Scriptures and rely on the instruction of the Holy Spirit!' To him, and indeed to all average Christians, the Gospel is so transparently clear, profound and simple, in its few fundamentals. It tells of the Victory of the Lord's Cross, his glorious Resurrection, His commissioning of His Church, the promise and fulfilment of the Holy Spirit and the evangelistic successes which naturally followed.

In his youth T. L. Osborn was a member of his father's farm. When he felt the great desire to evangelise, he left the farm and simply began to preach, teach and heal. For him college training was unknown. From the start fruitfulness attended his ministry increasingly as he advanced in the Gospel power from strength to strength. His fruitfulness continues to increase.

For years I have received his monthly missionary report which always reveals staggering Gospel successes. This pictorial monthly report always reproduces his own hand-written messages and declarations. The larger pictures show vast congregations which so often must be in the region of a million people. So vast is the average throng that often it is hardly possible to scan their perimeter. In the smaller pictures are the photographs of men, women or children who have been healed from 'incurable' and often terminal illnesses. The crippled stand straight and walk, the lepers are healed, the deaf are made to hear, the blind can once more see and the great throng of people rejoice and sing praises to Jesus their Saviour and Healer. And recently, in one of his great Missions in Africa, T. L. Osborn shows and gives evidence of hundreds healed from AIDS itself.

This fantastic ministry has been repeated, day after day, for fifty years. Whole communities are accepting Christ and His kingdom. Has anyone influenced so many countries in such powerful ways?

His wife, Daisy, and daughter Donna, have always been closely integrated in his ministries. His wife is always in the midst of organising and speaking and specialises in the women's section of the work. She has also written several books which specialise in helping women to understand themselves in relationship to their wonderful Saviour Jesus Christ and the Holy Spirit. Donna, too, symbolises the role of women and is very influential in promoting their status especially when Jesus becomes their Saviour and Lord.

Donna's life has been unusual and perhaps unique. From childhood she always accompanied her father and mother in their travels and Missions internationally, and as a result she never attended normal schools nor college. Her learning was to see and feel life at all angles every day of her life in many countries and amongst many peoples of the world. Her knowledge, in many ways, would surpass by far that of other girls of her age.

As a result of each Mission the local Churches are multiplied many times over and so the Name of Jesus is praised in every village. This certainly was so in Chile. After Missions like this, practically every village in Chile witnessed, almost nightly, by open air meeting of praise and adoration of the Lord. It was impossible to meet the never-ending requests for Bibles, New Testaments or Gospels. Every month, the T. L. Osborn Headquarters arranges for the dispatch of tons of Christian literature – mostly Bibles and New Testaments – and in many languages.

I consider that T. L. Osborn has no equal in the world today for fruitfulness for Jesus Christ and His way of Life. His results frighten me in some ways because they reveal just what the world has lost through its theological ignorance.

Many doctors are dismayed at the claims of Christians to heal the sick. They consider that healing should be left to the medical profession and that any other course of action is a slight on their profession. But think of just one case, Ken Harper, who, in my Dallinghoo Church, was healed of terminal cancer. Surely professional doctors can rejoice in this case. As everyone knows, there are hundreds of thousands of people with incurable illnesses in Great Britain alone. Illness is on a vast and terrible scale and every possible help should be welcomed. In the world at large much disease is almost impossibly beyond human cure.

Yet T. L. Osborn was led to meet this challenge head on and single handed and his successes have been phenomenal. As I have written elsewhere, if only there could be more T. L. Osborns! Or if only the Church in general, throughout the centuries, had not lost this precious gift which Christ had vouchsafed to be used. May the gift of healing return to His Church a thousandfold and as speedily as possible. Humanity is agonising and desperately trying to fight disease. It is an appalling nightmare.

When I saw him preaching some forty years ago I envied his glossy jet black head of hair (he still seems to have this). He was very good looking, lithe and handsome, and it seems that even now he still is. But of clerical garb there was none! He always wore a good looking man's outfit with smart collar and tie, but even a clerical collar was never seen. He would know absolutely nothing of the ecclesiastical systems of the various denominations. He was free, ignorant of, and independent of the lot. What a fortunate person, surely, when we consider and think of the awful entanglements, ramifications, complexities, red tape, rules and regulations, and the do's and don'ts of the average denomination of Christendom. When I attend the doctor's surgery for medical help I notice the doctor is dressed in an ordinary suit. He does not need to put on special uniform to impress his patients. His patients know that he is a man whose brain is full of healing knowledge and they have confidence in him. Yet so many in the Church, and especially the modern bishops and deans, dress up like silly colourful dolls and most of them have no knowledge or capabilities of healing whatsoever.

T. L. Osborn possessed the powers which matter – the blessings and the great power and favour of Christ. And in this he lacked for nothing at all times. His Christian understanding and preaching were always what we would call Scripture-based, orthodox and very simple. He drove each sentence home to his congregation in a way so forceful that it would be the envy of any British sergeant major.

Always at his command was the most efficient public address system possible.

Application of the Gospel

What I have tried to say about T. L. Osborn (and this should apply to every evangelist) is that it is the *application* of the Gospel which is of paramount importance and priority. He was not so much interested in trying to explain the textual meaning of the Gospel – which he took for granted – as in making the Gospel promises known and felt by his hearers. As he applied the Gospel, God responded with mighty power, especially to heal the sick. It would appear that each success proved a stimulus for greater success next time. So he went on increasing in power.

His main point was to show **the Lord's compassion, love and action**.

I have never seen love and compassion demonstrated as his ministry demonstrates it. Just recently, at a Mission in Africa, he hugged closely to him a young man who was beyond hope, a twisted cripple and beggar from birth. Continuing to hug him T. L. Osborn said to him: 'You have been a crippled beggar all your life so far, but from now on you are going to be a prince of God; in the Name of Jesus I command that Satan releases his grip and leaves you and that from now on you will have the health of Jesus'. That young man was instantly healed, stood erect, laughed with joy, and took on perfect young manhood. This is merely but one case of thousands so healed during the last fifty years.

By contrast, the basis of the Church of England for centuries has been mostly (but with exceptions) that of words, learning and scholarship. It is mostly by his achievement in scholarship that a cleric receives preferment. But what profit is it to God if a scholar, by his great intellect, works on Biblical criticism and in the end is able to prove that the Gospel is true – and then that Gospel is not applied to the everyday needs of the people? What profit has that been to the sin-sick, the diseased in body, the broken hearted, the defeated world of humanity?

'For the preaching of the cross is to them that perish foolishness; but unto us which are saved it is the power of God. For it is written, I will destroy the wisdom of the wise, and will bring to nothing the understanding of the prudent.

'Where is the wise? where is the scribe? where is the disputer of this world? hath not God made foolish the wisdom of this world? For after that in the wisdom of God the world by wisdom knew not God, it pleased God by the foolishness of preaching to save them that believe.

'For the Jews require a sign, and the Greeks seek after wisdom: But we preach Christ crucified, unto the Jews a stumbling block, and unto the Greeks foolishness;

'But unto them which are called, both Jews and Greeks, Christ the power of God, and the wisdom of God. Because the foolishness of God is wiser than men; and the weakness of God is stronger than men.

'For ye see your calling, brethren, how that not many wise men after the flesh, not many mighty, not many noble, are called: But God hath chosen the foolish things of the world to confound the wise; and God hath chosen the weak things of the world to confound the things which are mighty; and base things of the world, and things which are despised, hath God chosen, yea, and things which are not, to bring to nought things that are: That no flesh should glory in His presence.

'But of him are ye in Christ Jesus, who of God is made unto us wisdom, and righteousness, and sanctification, and redemption: That, according as it is written, He that glorieth, let him glory in the Lord.' (1 Cor 1:18–31)

God's blessing and power is poured out principally upon those who, in the first place, leave all to follow the Spirit's leading and who then reveal Christ's compassion to the world so that, in the compassion, they have power not only to offer comfort through words alone, but to heal the sick and the downtrodden.

When a congregation sees in their midst a very sick person suddenly healed by Christ's power then that congregation holds its breath and is ready to praise and adore the Lord, mighty in power, and true to His Gospel promises. Throughout the world today Churches are experiencing this wonderful power increasingly. A new and exciting Christian age has dawned and millions are taking notice.

Some people might wish to receive the attractive T. L. Osborn monthly report which I have mentioned. I know that he would be

delighted to respond to any who make such a request. The address
to write to is:

OSFO INT'L,
Box 10,
Tulsa,
OK 74102 USA

The receipt of this report could give new joy, life and insight to
any person or church. It could be just the news you have been
longing for. I have received it for years and would not be without it
for anything. The Lord's Mission progress should always, I believe,
be the best of the Good News. I never take a service without some
fresh mention of the ever-outreaching results, either to an individual
or a community.

T. L. Osborn is an evangelist to the multitudes. He would be the
first to say that this is only a part of God's Gospel provision for the
nations. Just as important are those who find themselves in one place
for many years serving patiently and faithfully as pastors, teachers,
doctors, nurses. The two forms of ministry are complementary. However, T. L. Osborn's Missions support the latter and in many cases
cause the local endeavour to be mightily strengthened, and often all
within a few weeks. Frequently lonely Missions and missionaries
have been filled with sheer delight to see this blessing happen in
their case.

APPENDIX 2
'EDUCATION SECRETARY WANTS SERMONS ON HELL'

In an article in the *Spectator* on Saturday 18 April 1992 John Patten, the new Education Secretary, says: 'The demotion of God signals loss of belief in the fundamentals – redemption and damnation – and loss of two of the key drives in the way we behave in our daily lives. Dwindling belief in redemption and damnation has led to loss of fear of the eternal consequences of goodness and badness. It has a profound effect on personal morality – especially on criminality . . .'

I am of the opinion that it is only by the grace of Jesus Christ that mankind can distinguish between the motivations of God and the Devil.

By this grace of Jesus Christ the goodness of God has benefited the human race. The opposition of the Devil results in evil.

Deceiver is the main title by which Jesus and other writers of the New Testament describe the character of the Devil or Satan.

Again, the Devil's ability to appear to be like God is *superhuman* and, without the grace of Christ, human beings have no chance whatsoever of escaping this deception. So the deceived think they are following divine impulses when, in reality, they are becoming the servants of Satan.

Because of this deception, much of the world cries out in anguish because of its corruption, sorrow, suffering and death. As the Scriptures say, 'And we know that we are of God, and the whole world lieth in wickedness' (1 John 5:19). In these days it is fashionable, in theology, to declare there is no such person as the Devil. I believe that those who hold such views are in the hollow of the Devil's hand.

In one term or another the Devil is mentioned some eighty-three times in the Bible; seventy times the name Devil or Satan is used. Other names used are Tempter, Beelzebub, Enemy, Evil One, Belial, Adversary, Deceiver, Dragon, Father of Lies, Murderer and Sinner.

According to the Scriptures the Devil belongs to the angelic order of beings. He is by nature one of the sons of Elohim. He has fallen, and by virtue of his personal forcefulness has become the leader of anarchic forces of wickedness. As a free being he has submerged his life in evil and has become altogether and hopelessly evil. As a being of very high intelligence he has gained great power and has exercised a wide sway over other beings. Sometimes, however, and perhaps most frequently, Satan's devices include human agents. Those who are given over to evil and who persuade others to evil are children and servants of Satan. Satan also works through persons and institutions supposed to be on the side of right but really evil. Here the same ever-present and active falseness and deceit are exhibited. When he is called, 'The god of this world' (2 Cor 4:4), it would seem to be intimated that he has the power to clothe himself in apparently Divine attributes. He also makes himself an angel of light by presenting advocates of falsehood in the guise of apostles of truth (2 Cor 11:13–15; 1 John 4:1; 2 Thess 2:9; Rev 12:9; 19:20).

The worldwide and age-long works of Satan are to be traced to one predominant motive: he hates both God and man and does all that in him lies to defeat God's plan of grace and to establish and maintain a kingdom of evil, in the seduction and ruin of mankind.

The balance and sanity of the Bible is nowhere more strikingly exhibited than in its treatment of the work of Satan. Not only is the Bible entirely free from the extravagances of popular Satanology, which is full of absurd stories concerning the appearances, tricks, and transformations of Satan among men, but it exhibits a dependable accuracy and consistency of statement which is most reassuring. Almost nothing is said concerning Satanic agency other than wicked men who mislead other men. The agent of Satan is always a victim. Satan may be said to be implicated in all the disasters and woes of human life, in so far as they are more or less directly contingent upon sin. On the contrary, it is perfectly evident that Satan's power consists principally in his ability to deceive. It is interesting and characteristic that, according to the Bible, Satan is fundamentally a liar and his kingdom is a kingdom founded upon lies and deceit. The doctrine of Satan therefore corresponds in every important particular to the general Biblical emphasis upon truth. 'The truth shall make you free' (John 9:32) – this is the way of deliverance from the power of Satan.

There appear to be endless examples of how mankind has been deceived.

Historians have said that John Wesley was the greatest of all Englishmen. Why then did the Established Church view his ministry with such great and deep suspicion that he was forbidden to minister any more in any Church of England? Why, in spite of his breaking Church laws, did the Church not try to come to terms with this great Christian genius?

Why was the Revd Charles Simeon looked upon with suspicion for so long during his ministry in Cambridge? This suspicion was so intense that his own churchwardens locked him out of his church for ten years. Graduates were encouraged to walk on the other side of the road in order to avoid meeting him. By his ministry he created a spirit of purification in a hitherto corrupt Cambridge. By his influence on graduates who came to his private Bible studies many were ordained for the ministries at home or abroad. It was said of him that his ministry was more influential than that of the Archbishop of Canterbury. He saw the great need and opportunity of looking outwards to regions beyond and was one of the founders of the Church Missionary Society. Why was the Church of his day so blind to the working of God's Holy Spirit through Charles Simeon? It was because the Church in general could not differentiate between darkness and light, between God and the Devil.

Yet, by the time of his death, Cambridge, and indeed much of England saw him as a very enlightened and dedicated man of God. For the provisions of his funeral all Cambridge otherwise closed down for the day. He was honoured by the greatest funeral assembly of personages and people ever known by Cambridge, before or since.

Wilson Carlile is a further extremely interesting example. History tells of his dramatic conversion to Christ and his great love to go out and seek the lost. But he was curate of a fashionable Church at the time of his yearnings to rescue those perishing outside the influence of the national Church. Therefore he went into the streets with his trumpet to call the people to come to him and listen to the Gospel. By this practice he at first brought upon himself the derision of Churchpeople who considered him to be downgrading the dignified image of the Church of England. It did not occur to those people that Prebendary Carlile was obeying implicitly the command of Jesus to bless the outsiders. It did not occur to those complaining people that, by their pride and smug complacency, they were in the hollow of Satan's hand. Satan had appeared to them as God Himself and they considered that Wilson Carlile was devilish. This is but one of endless examples of the deceit of the Devil.

For Christians, the greatest proof of all, that God appears to some to be like the Devil, and the Devil appears to be like God, is seen from the Gospel records.

> 'Then answered the Jews, and said unto him, Say we not well that thou art a Samaritan, and hast a devil?' (John 8:45). 'Then said the Jews unto him, "Now we know that thou hast a devil . . .' " (John 8:52). 'Then took they up stones to cast at him' (John 8:59).

Later Jesus proved, by His defeat over death, who was God and who was the Devil. Jesus always has and always will show the difference, to the benefit of His followers and for the benefit of mankind in general. He is a true and wonderful Saviour.

Consider Adolph Hitler and his rising to power in the 1930s. Most of the people of Germany acclaimed him as their great saviour both of the German state and Church. He was all but worshipped. He ordered his soldiers to make sure their children were baptized and themselves to attend church. He appeared to be like God. Later he led Germany and the world into hell! Satan always does.

How wonderful to have Jesus Christ as the Saviour of the world. And that means salvation from the power of the Devil and death.

APPENDIX 3
THEOLOGY OF THE
CHURCH OF ENGLAND

Dr Gareth Bennet's Preface to the 1987 edition of Crockford's Clerical Directory sent shock waves throughout the Church of England and beyond. The article savagely questioned the competence and leadership of the Church of England.

The Times newspaper dealt with this matter by its whole-page treatment on December 3rd 1987. The page was headed with the words, **'Unprecedented attack on Primate'** and **'Insider's Portrait of a Church Without a Soul'**

Within a few days of the publication of Dr Bennet's Preface a second shock wave announced that he had committed suicide.

Obviously this distinguished theologian had been dealing with weighty theological and church thinking which had proved too much for him to bear any longer.

But this theological shock wave was merely the beginning of greater disturbances which have continued and increased up to the present time, perhaps greater than ever previously known in the Church of England since its beginnings at the time of the Reformation.

Church personality frictions are not new nor surprising. Indeed the Gospels clearly and surprisingly show that amongst the twelve disciples, chosen by Jesus Himself, their number included those who created friction. The case of Judas Iscariot, the traitor, is well known. We read also how the disciples had to be rebuked by Jesus because they were discussing which of them should have superiority. At the trial of Jesus, Peter denied the Lord with an oath and indeed, later, all the disciples forsook Him and fled. In the early Church, Peter and Paul quarrelled vehemently. Galations 2:11 reads, 'But when Peter was come to Antioch, I withstood him to the face, because he was to be blamed.'

So from when Jesus created His Church, friction had to be included as a part of this Church and the Church was to prevail notwithstanding the friction within. This by no means condones friction, which is to be deplored and should be avoided as much as possible at all times.

The Church of England came to birth at a time when the battle for the Bible had deeply engaged the attention of European Church leaders. The Church of England embraced this Bible as the great and sole basis of its existence and teaching; and indeed Archbishop Cranmer, other bishops and many clergy and laity were put to death for the sake of their Scripture-based doctrinal beliefs.

This was clearly stated in its great formulary, The Thirty-Nine Articles. Article number six reads, 'Holy Scripture containeth all things necessary to salvation: so that whatsoever is not read therein, nor may be proved thereby, is not to be required of any man, that it should be believed as an article of the Faith.' For several hundred years Church life in general was nurtured by this fountain and foundation of Holy Scripture and even up to the present time the bulk of the health of the Church feeds on this Biblical base.

As a result, a unique people of England came into being and were known as 'The People of the Book'. And certainly from those people great and exciting developments took place, culminating in Great Britain becoming the controlling power of the greatest Empire in world history. For a very long time the remarkable Catechism was taught in Church every Sunday and later in the Church schools. The Catechism placed a 'moral policeman' in the heart and mind of every child who learnt it. It certainly was so in my own case and I can never cease to give thanks for this priceless enrichment of life.

So far so good; but were the Thirty-Nine Articles fully satisfactory or sufficient? In my view they fell far short of what Scripture and especially the New Testament clearly revealed and expected.

As every average Christian knows, Jesus ministered gloriously for three years, was crucified, triumphantly rose again and with great enthusiasm commissioned his disciples to evangelise the world and proclaim His name; and this to be *under the direction and motivation of His Gift, the Holy spirit.*

The Thirty-Nine Articles deal fairly fully with the Jesus story up to the Resurrection. They fail to mention or give priority to the most important and wonderful things of all: namely, *Christ's Commission, Ascension and the sending of the Gift of the Holy Spirit, by which the*

Church was inaugurated and motivated. It was a Divine Church and not of men.

Notice, for example, the very significant words in Acts 1:4–5, 8–11:

'And (Jesus) being assembled together with them, commanded them that they should not depart from Jerusalem, but wait for the promise of the Father, which, saith he, ye have heard of me. For John truly baptized with water; but ye shall be baptized with the Holy Ghost not many days hence . . . But ye shall receive power, after that the Holy Ghost is come upon you: and ye shall be witnesses unto me both in Jerusalem, and in all Judea, and in Samaria, and unto the uttermost part of the earth. And when he had spoken these things, while they beheld, he was taken up; and a cloud received him out of their sight. And while they looked steadfastly toward heaven as he went up, behold, two men stood by them in white apparel; Which also said, Ye men of Galilee, why stand ye gazing up into heaven? this same Jesus, which is taken up from you into heaven, shall so come in like manner as ye have seen him go into heaven'

The disciples might easily, and with apparent good reason, have said to Jesus on this occasion, 'Master, we have been with You for three years, have listened to Your discourses, witnessed Your miracles, witnessed Your Resurrection, have slept and eaten with You. Therefore we are fully convinced that You are the Christ, the Son of God. We now need no further persuasion; we are now ready to go forth in Your Name and proclaim Your kingdom.'

Fortunately, they did no such thing, but obeyed the order of Jesus, waited for and in due time received the promised gift of the Holy Spirit. They were, from that time onwards, motivated and maintained by God the Holy Spirit and the Christian faith became indeed a Divine way of Life. It was not the religion of men. If those Apostles, so close to Jesus, were insufficient despite their knowledge of him, how much more do members of the age-long Christian Church need to depend upon the Holy Spirit! This new Divine way of life produced splendid results and will continue to do so until this same Jesus shall return in glory and triumph to create His Kingdom on earth, perhaps very soon.

The Articles of the Church of England mention nothing of these culminating and all-important glories and declarations of Jesus Christ.

I find it impossible to understand why the Articles did not include statements which could have been as follows

Of the Commission of Jesus Christ
Holy Scripture doth clearly set forth the Lord's Charge and Commission to His Apostles. They were to create an ever-expanding ministry seeking to proclaim to all the world the Name of Jesus Christ as Lord, thereby creating the pattern for the Church of all time.

Of the Promise of the Holy Spirit
The Second Chapter of The Acts of the Apostles doth clearly set out how the promised gift of the Holy Spirit descended and filled the Apostles, and all who were assembled with them and thus inspired Peter and the others to preach the Good News of Jesus Christ. Therefore the Church, being originated and motivated by this Holy Spirit, is of Divine origin. The Church, at all times, should pray for and be directed and inspired by the same Holy Spirit.

The inclusion of such Articles could have steered the Church of England on a very different course from that which she followed in history.

Most clergy know, only too well, how difficult it is to persuade parishes to be outward-looking in ministry. The Church, by general nature, was inward-looking. When at last servants of the Church such as the Wesleys, Charles Simeon and Prebendary Carlile strove for such a missionary endeavour they did so against the apathy and often the solid opposition of the Church in general. This terrible apathy is so prevalent in great numbers of Churches today.

Great are the parochial and ministerial rewards for those, in these days, who put missionary news and endeavour in the vanguard of their parish life. I seek to follow this wholesome rule in every Church service I take. I try to do so with brevity, artistry and dramatic truth. There are untold instances these days of glorious Gospel News in all parts of the world. This is what the Church has a right to hear so that she may rejoice in Christ's continuing triumphs. Many Churches following this kind of ministry report much blessing, life, love and excitement. Such Churches become ALIVE.

By ignoring the Holy Spirit Divine Gift elements the Church of

England left itself open to self-centredness, self-importance and an unbalanced, unhealthy and far-too-severe emphasis on sin.

How often do we hear our bishops or clergy say to their congregations, 'Brethren, do not look on us but look unto the Holy Spirit of God to give the lead we and the world are looking for'. True, bishops and clergy mostly hope that they are following the Holy Spirit's lead, but the congregations should be told so – especially when clerics are addressing millions on the media. The world is waiting to hear this!

In 1973 the saintly Pope Paul VI was dying. Amongst those called to the Pope's chamber on this occasion was the leading newspaper correspondent in Italy named Fred Delanius. Some time later, at a meeting in Ipswich Town Hall, (one of the meetings to which I referred in Chapter 23), Delanius told us what happened on that occasion in that room. Pope Paul opened his eyes to find the blinds drawn. He asked for the blinds to be drawn aside to allow God's daylight to brighten up the room. He then called one of his Cardinals to open the Bible and read the whole of Chapter Two of the Acts of the Apostles which tells, of course, about the outpouring of the Gift of the Holy Spirit and the birth of the Christian Church. The Cardinal read the Chapter, closed the Bible and put it down. Pope Paul said to him: 'Take up the Bible and read through the same chapter again'. The Cardinal did so. Pope Paul then prayed in tongues and in due time died in peace. In his last moments the Pope had supreme regard for the most vital news the world has ever known – Hallelujah!

These vital omissions in Anglican Articles left the way open for deterioration which has come upon the Church of England now, leading to:

The Bubble Theology of The Church of England

Instead of the theological emphasis being based on Scripture, and so on the guidance and motivation of the Holy Spirit, the Church's theology became more and more moulded by the wisdom of scholars of the Church: men. These men and leaders became gradually and increasingly more powerful, more and more feared and increasingly self-sufficient. At the 1988 Lambeth Conference bishops, reporting their findings (especially through the media) told the millions of people what they, bishops – men of the Church – had decided to do. It was indeed the Church of men seeking to act. What the millions needed to know (and what God wants!) is that the Church is a Divinely originated and motivated Body and the leaders in the Church are always seeking His guidance. The media failed to transmit any such proclamation. If only archbishops, bishops and clergy would tell their congregations, from time to time, 'Do not look unto us, look unto Him, look unto the Holy Spirit' then, surely, there would be much healthier prospects for Divine progress.

Certainly, and for a considerable number of years, the scholars accepted the final authority of the Scriptures and were quite happy to accept that Christian theology was 'The Queen of the Sciences'. This meant that they accepted that in the New Testament they had a faultless historical record of what actually took place in the life of Jesus and his Apostles and in the early Church, as recorded in Holy Writ.

In time, as scholars delved deeper into this Christian theology, some became rather daring and, to the consternation of the Church in general, instructed that the New Testament records are less than perfectly infallible. Once this 'wedge' was placed in position, the door of questioning and criticism opened ever more widely until, at last, many years ago now, modern criticism declared that the New Testament can only be understood by the interpretation and elucidation of the scholars and professors of the Church. Going further, many liberal theologians now believe that what we have in the New Testament, as well as the Old, are the views of what later writers suggested had happened to Jesus. Of course, they make out, the miraculous elements of the life of Jesus and the Apostles never happened at all.

Today, all theological students of the Church of England, being prepared for the sacred ministry, are moulded in thought, not by the example, ministry and the life of Jesus, but by the reasonings and thinking of the so called 'Scholars of the Church'. So in this way and especially for theological students, it is no longer true to say 'There is one mediator between God and man, the man Christ Jesus'. As a result, the strength of Christ, our Lord, has departed very largely from the Church of England in general. No wonder it is on the decline and no wonder other churches such as the Pentecostals and the Assemblies of God, are increasing in numbers and influence. It cannot be otherwise.

So now, therefore, the Church of England theology is a **Bubble**

Theology which is a theology in the hands of and controlled by men, with no direct roots in factual Gospel history at all. It is a floating theology, like a bubble. And just as a bubble needs colour to make it even more impressive, so the scholars and leaders of the modern Church add colour in any way they can in order to impress and win confidence unto themselves. This modern colouring is very much seen in the flamboyant and colourful copes, mitres and robes being added increasingly by clerics of the modern Church.

On the Everyman Programme on BBC 1 on Sunday 9th February 1992 the Bishop of London showed his episcopal outfit to children. As he himself said, on that programme, 'I feel a fool when I put these things on'. Exactly! The modern flamboyant, gaudy, clerical dress makes men look like silly dolls. They actually cheapen their status in the Church and put themselves light years apart from people like the Prime Minister and top businessmen who arrive at a Summit Conference dressed in ordinary suits. These things never used to be until the last few decades. I am sure that Christ will have none of it.

Everyman to Himself – A free-for-all Theology

Because of the process, described above, every cleric can now choose what he believes or does not believe and he is rarely questioned. On Easter Day evening 1992 a BBC programme showed clerics who openly declared their pride in renouncing the authentic and orthodox elements of the life of Jesus. On the same programme the Bishop of Durham stated that it was right and proper that any cleric or any Christian should believe whatever he or she liked. Indeed, the bishop has stated in public and in print that he disbelieves the Incarnation and the Bodily Resurrection of Jesus. Neither would he believe in any other miraculous operations in the life of Jesus or of the early Church. For the Christmas season 1991, a Church of England rector wrote an article for the *Church Times*, openly joking at the thought of the Incarnation of Jesus. He would enjoy the idea at Christmas, he wrote, just as children enjoy Santa Claus. Recently a Provost of Birmingham Cathedral wrote a letter to the *Church Times* advocating interfaith worship and declaring that the Jews, Muslims, Hindus and Buddhists are far better examples of divinity than Christians themselves. The Provost knows in what manner I wrote to him!

Mental Reservation

By the unwritten, but widely accepted, thinking known as *mental reservation*, clerics of the Church of England are encouraged repeatedly to *say* the office of the Church without believing the face value of the dogmas they read. Thus their congregations are in no wise disturbed by their cleric's unrevealed denial of the glorious and fundamental doctrines of Christ. I can think of no evil greater than this. It is deceit in Divine matters and can do no other than bring God's condemnation on the Church which condones this deceit. The judgement of the Lord must have been working for a long time concerning this and will continue, I feel sure. Is the present Church of England an apostate Church?

APPENDIX 4
THE 1991 OPEN LETTER TO THE LEADERSHIP OF THE CHURCH OF ENGLAND

'Believing that Jesus Christ the Incarnate Son of God, is both God and man, the unique revelation of God, the only Saviour and hope of mankind – we, the undersigned members of the Church of England, are concerned that his Gospel shall be clearly presented in this Decade of Evangelism.

'We desire to love and respect people of other faiths. We acknowledge and respect their rights and freedoms. We wholeheartedly support co-operation in appropriate community, social, moral and political issues between Christians and those of other faiths wherever this is possible. Nevertheless, we believe it to be our Lord's command that his Gospel be clearly proclaimed, openly and sensitively, to all people (including those of other faiths) with the intention that they should come to faith in him for salvation.

'In this we affirm no more and no less than the Apostolic and Anglican tradition. Article XVIII says: "Scripture doth set out unto us only the Name of Jesus Christ, whereby men must be saved."

'In consequence we are deeply concerned about gatherings for interfaith worship and prayer involving Christian people. These include The Interfaith Commonwealth Day Observance in Westminster Abbey and other such events in some of the Cathedrals and Churches of England, whether they refer to Jesus Christ or whether such references are minimal or excluded.

'We believe these events, however motivated, conflict with the Christian duty to proclaim the Gospel. They imply that salvation is offered by God not only through Jesus Christ but by other means, and thus deny his uniqueness and finality as the only Saviour.

'These events are frequently deeply hurtful to those in this country who have come from other religions into the Christian faith, and also to Christian minorities in other lands, both of whom have frequently experienced persecution from the other faiths, and especially where such faiths are unwilling to tolerate conversions or the existence of minority Christian communities.

'We, therefore, appeal to the leadership of the Church of England to oppose and, where possible, prevent such gatherings for interfaith worship and prayer in the Church of England and to seek to discourage them elsewhere. We also call upon Christian people to pray that this will be done.

'Our objections to interfaith worship are theological, spiritual and, indeed constitutional. Recognising that the Christian faith belongs to all races and nations, we deplore objections to such worship arising from racism or nationalism.

'To avoid all misunderstanding, we wish to make it clear that we seek the good of all, of whatever faith, and obedience to our Lord Jesus Christ obliges us to proclaim him as uniquely Lord and Saviour for all.'

POSTSCRIPT

By the time this book has been published the serious and grievous matter of interfaith worship will have been debated in the General Synod of the Church of England and watched by the whole Christian nation with profound interest. True theology is of great importance, first to the Lord Jesus Christ, Head of the Church, who is the Lord of all our thinking; and secondly to His Body the Church. If true, this Law of God can wonderfully guide into all truth from the things of earth to things in heaven, from darkness to light from slavery to freedom, from sorrow to great joy, from sickness to wholeness, from death to eternal life.

In the Church of England there are probably more Spirit-filled clergy and people than ever before in history. During the past few decades the knowledge of the fullness of the glorious Gospel has broken forth as never before and multitudes of people are being filled with abounding and lively faith.

Stories of the spreading of the Gospel throughout the world are endless and breathtaking. Within this Body, the Church, miracles and wonders are taking place. The Lord is with us. He is in the midst, helping us to overcome and rejoice. His glorious Kingdom is being fulfilled and before long He will see of the travail of His soul and be satisfied and glorified. Hallelujah! The glory of the Lord is perfectly expressed in the Holy Communion service or the Prayer Books by the following ascription.

> For thou
> Only art Holy;
> Thou only art the Lord;
> Thou only, O Christ, with the Holy Spirit,
> Art Most High in the glory of God the Father.

Surely Almighty God is waiting, as always, to bless the world. For this, man's free will and the obedience of Christ's Body, the Church, are essential. Will this renewal take place? Humanity is at the cross-roads!

INDEX